··The Way of the Earth··

Native America and the Environment

BY JOHN BIERHORST

In the Trail of the Wind
American Indian Poems and Ritual Orations

Four Masterworks of American Indian Literature
Quetzalcoatl, The Ritual of Condolence, Cuceb, The Night Chant

The Red Swan *Myths and Tales of the American Indians*

Black Rainbow *Legends of the Incas and Myths of Ancient Peru*

A Cry from the Earth *Music of the North American Indians*

The Sacred Path
Spells, Prayers, and Power Songs of the American Indians

The Hungry Woman *Myths and Legends of the Aztecs*

The Mythology of North America

Cantares Mexicanos *Songs of the Aztecs*

A Nahuatl-English Dictionary and Concordance
to the Cantares Mexicanos

The Mythology of South America

The Mythology of Mexico and Central America

History and Mythology of the Aztecs
The Codex Chimalpopoca

Codex Chimalpopoca *The Text in Nahuatl with a
Glossary and Grammatical Notes*

The Way of the Earth *Native America and the Environment*

Heron Spirit,
print by Carl Ray, Cree, ca. 1972.
John Anson Warner collection.

The Way of the

EARTh

NATIVE AMERICA AND
THE ENVIRONMENT

·· John Bierhorst ··

WILLIAM MORROW AND COMPANY, INC.

New York

Library of Congress Cataloging-in-Publication Data

Bierhorst, John.
The way of the earth:
native America and the environment / John Bierhorst.
p. cm.
Includes bibliographical references and index.
ISBN 0-688-11560-8
1. Indians—Philosophy.   2. Human ecology—America.
3. Indians—Religion and mythology   4. Indians—Legends.
[1. Indians—Philosophy.   2. Human ecology.   3. Ecology.
4. Indians—Legends.]   I. Title.
E59.P45B54 1994
179'.1'08997—dc20   93-28971   CIP AC

Sources for quotations on pp. 18, 52, 124, 201–2, 219, and 219–20 are as follows, respectively: Karl W. Luckert, *A Navajo Bringing Home Ceremony,* copyright © the Museum of Northern Arizona Press, 1978, courtesy of the Museum of Northern Arizona Press; James Rementer, Letter to John Bierhorst, May 11, 1990 (Giant Squirrel Story as told by Nora Thompson Dean); David Guss, *To Weave and Sing: Art, Symbol, and Narrative in the South American Rainforest,* copyright © 1989 David Guss, courtesy of the University of California Press; Christopher Vecsey and Robert W. Venables, eds., *American Indian Environments,* Syracuse University Press, 1980; Gerardo Reichel-Dolmatoff, *Amazonian Cosmos: The Sexual and Religious Symbolism of the Tukano Indians,* University of Chicago Press, copyright © 1971 by The University of Chicago; *American Anthropologist,* vol. 93, no. 3, Sept. 1991, by permission of the American Anthropological Association.

For further acknowledgments, see Notes on Sources in the back of this book.

Sources for pictures on pp. 39, 99, 115, 170, 205, and 214 are Blodgett, Kroeber 1905, Reichel-Dolmatoff 1978, Cronquist et al., Danter, and Houston, respectively. For full authors' names, titles, and publication data, see References in the back of this book. The drawing on p. 115 is copyrighted by The Regents of the University of California and is reproduced with their permission. The drawing on p. 170 is copyrighted by The New York Botanical Garden and is reproduced with its permission. All other credits are given in the captions that accompany the illustrations. Every effort has been made to contact copyright owners. Where older material has been reproduced, or if the present whereabouts of artists or collectors could not be determined, credit has been given to the fullest extent possible.

··PREFACE··

At the outset, the modest claim can be made that Native America contributes to an understanding of the relationship between humans and the rest of nature. A simple formula for environmental protection cannot be promised. No single idea, no set of rules, has yet been discovered that can prevent human society from overburdening the web of life that supports it. Yet the situation is not hopeless.

The underlying question, perhaps, is whether humans can consciously safeguard the environment or whether protection must come from instinctive customs and deeply held beliefs that preserve nature in spite of our will to use it up. A little of both, the plainly expressed and the deeply subtle, are essential to the Native American approaches—which center on unifying themes that can be recognized without denying the fascinating variety of the cultures that have expressed them. The book in hand is dedicated to the premise that these themes and their related practices are not merely fascinating but worthy of close attention.

For help in starting this project, and for conversations that provided encouragement along the way, I thank two friends, Bob Steuding and Don Bahr—one a poet, the other an anthropologist. For help with research I am particularly grateful to Rosalie Burgher, Haig Meshejian, and Robert Simmons. Numerous individuals and institutions have been generous in providing specific information or granting permission to use sources within their keeping. I thank them all, especially Patrick Breslin, Mac Chapin, David Guss, Tony Hunt, Jim Rementer, Dan Savard, Pablo Wright, and, again, Don Bahr.

J.B.

West Shokan, New York

··C O N T E N T S··

· · Illustrations · ·

ALWAYS LEARN, NEVER TEACH.

—Aymara maxim

THE WAY OF THE EARTH

NATIVE AMERICA AND THE ENVIRONMENT

Introduction

It is no compliment to the dead to notice the vacant stare of a corpse and remark—as a Zuni might once have done—that its eyes are "not closed but counting the stars." The scornful undertone comes to the surface in a saying attributed to the ancients of Peru: "Whoever claims to be counting stars, when he can't even count the knots of a quipu [or string book], deserves to be laughed at." Among the nineteenth-century Lakota of the North American Plains, such foolishness was forbidden from an early age. "Children were told not to count the stars," recalls a Lakota who had been brought up as a warrior in the 1870s. "Though I never heard of a reason being given," he continues, "I suppose the impossibility of counting them made of it a foolish pastime."

Human understanding, evidently, has its limits; and what little knowledge there is becomes even more precious when combined with well-studied modesty. Indeed, the more one knows, the more circumspect one becomes. "Well, I still don't know it. I am still learning," suggests a twentieth-century Lakota elder, whose knowledge is in fact much sought, not only by Lakota but by English-speaking outsiders.

Even when recounting one's own exploits, it is better to hold back. Thus a Winnebago father, in former days, could advise his son, "Tell a little less. The old men say it is wise."

In the face of reticence and humility it may seem unlikely that Native American knowledge, increasingly scarce in any event, can survive to the next generation. Making the link more fragile, young people are inclined to turn a deaf ear; and elders are aware of their indifference. Toward the end of one of the great nine-day ceremonials of the Navajo, a Finishing Song includes the gently accusatory phrases "the young man doubts it," "the young woman doubts it." With less patience, an elder among the Munsee handles irreverent young people by threatening them: "If you don't listen to what I have to say, I'll take all the knowledge I have in my head and put it high up in a basswood tree and put the bark over it."

Even where children are cooperative, chances are missed. Although there are exceptions, modern schools do not generally teach American languages or the ways of thought that are expressed in these languages. Many would no doubt agree with the Wintun woman who lamented, "Our children arouse compassion, speaking as they do in a strange tongue." Yet language alone is not enough. In eastern Panama, Kuna young people who attend school during the day are reported to be acquiring the Kuna names of rare plants but not the ability to identify them, with the result that species in need of protection are becoming rarer.

Nonetheless, there are methods for stemming the loss of traditional lore, some more subtle than others. After their forced removal to Oklahoma, Shawnee parents instructed their children at home at night, because after dark "the birds who will take away your memory have roosted." From a Toba community in Argentina it is reported that a father on his deathbed made sound recordings of *ngatagako'* (traditional speeches of instruction) in order to guide his family in the future.

Well versed in parental teachings, a middle-aged native Californian remembers his father saying, "If you believe, then you will get old," and observes of himself: "Surely I got old already because I believe the talk of my own father." But the teachings are operative strictly within a framework of humility. As Navajo parents used to remind their children: "Don't act smart; you'll never live in old-age-home."

Accordingly, any approach to Native American knowledge should proceed with caution. The problems and potential pitfalls are not inconsiderable. To begin with, there are innumerable gaps in the record, making it easy to conjecture that important ideas reported from heavily documented cultures are missing from those that are less well known.

On the other hand, what is known is voluminous. But since the information is widely scattered and in many cases unpublished, the sources are difficult to view as a whole.

Finally, rather than allowing native voices to speak for themselves, there is a persistent temptation to interpret. If such a temptation can be resisted, and if one can accept that one's own command of even the available material is incomplete, then it may be possible to offer a glimpse of native thought without fear of "counting the stars." At least, this book will not attempt to survey the whole subject. It will keep to a narrow course, concentrating on knowledge that pertains to the relationship between humans and other parts of nature. To be sure, this is only one branch of Indian knowledge.

But it is a branch that reaches out to the world.

Up from the unthinkable

Ever since the Americas came into contact with what is now known as the Old World, there has been a disparity between native ideas and the ideas of the newcomers—especially with regard to balancing people and land. At first, where the land was thickly populated, as in Mexico and Peru, Europeans seized upon the native practice of "payment," which they called "sacrifice," and demanded a campaign to abolish it. On the other hand, in places like Virginia and New England, where the land was found to be lightly populated, Europeans abominated its presumed underuse, demanding a campaign of increased settlement; and this, as in the former case, became a justification for conquest.

Both campaigns—against the numerous and against the few—were carried out in the name of Christianity. In the words of the sixteenth-century historian Francisco López de Gómara, the first chronicler of the conquest of Mexico, the result was "great" because, among other benefits, the native people "cast down their infinite number of idols, believing in Our Lord God, [and] abandoned the sacrifice of humans."

A more widely read author of the same period, Father Joseph de Acosta, imagined that in both Peru and Mexico, by the time of the Conquest, the "burdensome and intolerable yoke of Satan's law with its sacrifices and rituals" had made the people so "weary" that "the law of Christ" seemed "just, gentle, clean, good, and equable."

Gómara and Acosta were only two of the many colonial reporters who wrote negatively of the payments to nature spirits (to the earth and the sun in particular), lamenting the "thousands" who had been sacrificed and mentioning with approval the "millions" baptized after the Conquest.

In eastern North America, by contrast, native settlement appeared sparse and the concept of payment, though not absent, went largely unreported. But God's will, it seemed, was equally opposed to the prevailing arrangement with nature. The eighteenth-century militarist and politician Benjamin Lincoln expressed the objection in plain words: "To people fully this earth was in the original plan of the benevolent Deity. I am confident that sooner or later there will be a full accomplishment of the original system; and that no men will be suffered to live by hunting on lands capable of improvement."

Thomas Jefferson himself, in a message to Congress dated January 18, 1803, explained that in order to "provide an extension of territory which the rapid increase of our numbers will call for, [we must] encourage [the Indians] to abandon hunting. . . . The extensive forests necessary in the hunting life will then become useless, and they will see advantage in exchanging them for the means of improving their farms and of increasing their domestic comforts."

As late as 1855, a writer from western New York could hopefully (if inaccurately) recommend that prejudice against the Iroquois be set aside at last because "the Indians on all these lands are tillers of the soil, and you may ride miles in every direction, and see their fruitful fields and comfortable dwellings, indicating an industrious people, a Christian people."

But along the way to the twentieth century, non-Indian Americans began losing their confidence in the boundlessness of a land that waited only to be worked. They became willing to hear the voices of Henry David Thoreau, who prescribed the "tonic" of wilderness, and of the naturalist John Muir, who, like earlier spokesmen, invoked God's plan, but now in defense of nonhuman species.

From the vantage point of the present, such attitudes seem to lie within the range of "American" values, while those of a Gómara or a Benjamin Lincoln have become quaint. The change, over the years, has been sufficiently great that a respected thinker like the Mexican poet and essayist Octavio Paz can approach even the concept of "payment."

According to Paz, "the concept is one of terror—in order to create, the earth must devour." This, he observes, "is the exact opposite of our modern conception, which sees nature as an enormous reservoir of energy and resources that the human race can dominate and exploit with impunity. In this way we have destroyed our natural environment and endangered the very survival of our species."

But Paz touches an issue that has not yet reached the general debate. Environmentalists in the late twentieth century are still grappling with the more elementary, much tamer, question foreshadowed by Thoreau and Muir: whether there are values, even rights, belonging to nature apart from humanity.

This basic question was addressed in a now famous essay of 1949 by the naturalist Aldo Leopold, who argued for a "land ethic" derived from European and—once again, biblical—traditions. A concept of the rights of others implied by political democracy and the Golden Rule, Leopold advised, could simply be extended to the environment. Moreover, since humans and the natural world were interdependent, it was a necessity to make this "extension."

In the late 1960s, as the environmental movement gained momentum, many in America as well as abroad began to feel that the American Indian had been the true pioneer in the field of environmental ethics. Respect for nature, including the personification of creatures and forces, strikes virtually every non-Indian as the salient feature of Indian thought. An awareness of this very kind—among non-Indians—had caught hold in the 1920s and 1930s, but it had faded by the early sixties. By 1970 it had again taken hold. Since then, oddly, the idea has been so easily popularized, often in a shallow way, that it has encountered both wide acceptance and wide resistance.

Two contemporary scholars who have sifted the evidence are the historian Calvin Martin and the philosopher J. Baird Callicott. Both investigators are interested in the Algonkian cultures of eastern North America, yet both are willing to consider other Indian cultures as well, in search of a general principle.

In Martin's view, the Native American does have an authentic respect for nature, but this is not an "ethic." Rather, it is a contractual arrangement based on a wary esteem for nonhuman "persons" in nature. Although the arrangement is immensely attractive, Martin concedes, it could never be absorbed into Judeo-Christian tradition, which makes room not for "persons" but only for a single God. Thus Martin believes that the "native ideology of land-use will not be acceptable to, and is incapable of adoption by, Western man, at least as long as he remains a Christian."

Callicott, equally mindful of Christianity, concludes that even if certain elements in the environment are feared, many others are loved. The native system therefore incorporates an ethical regard for nature very much in keeping with biblical teachings on divine punishment and neighborly love.

Callicott asks, "Can a traditional American Indian land wisdom help to guide the United States and other modern nations out of the present environmental malaise?" His answer: "I think it certainly can."

Throughout such discussions, there is an underlying assumption that modern humanity, even if determined to break with the past, remains mired in the old patterns that gave rise to industrialism and its ills. The notion that Native America may offer some relief has progressed only from the unthinkable to the debatable. But it has progressed that far.

Questions

The manner in which knowledge is passed from parent to child, or from teacher to student, varies according to the culture. Yet there are hemisphere-wide patterns that may be

An Aged Tutor and Young Students,
casein by Harrison Begay, Navajo, 1966 or earlier.
The Philbrook Museum of Art, Tulsa, Oklahoma.

noted. Among the most persistent is the set speech of instruction, which typically opens with a formula such as "My little daughter, pay attention" (Argentina), "Let me teach you, boys, and you listen" (California), or "My children, you must listen to my words if you wish to see many good days and evenings" (New York).

By and·large, however, these formal speeches pertain to obedience and personal conduct. The practical aspects of livelihood, including healing and the arts of war, are taught in the field or through apprenticeship; the esoteric aspects, through ritual. Philosophy, or what is sometimes called worldview, is handed down in myths.

Note that instruction in the conservation of natural resources does not figure in this short list.

In Native America, as no doubt in cultures the world over, there is no real will to conserve. Prayers are not offered for smaller harvests or fewer children. In fact, knowledge of all kinds is directed primarily toward human increase, not decrease. And yet the element of reduction, like a tolling bell, makes itself heard through vast stretches of traditional lore.

Stated in the broadest way possible, the pertinent themes (so far as the preservation of the environment is concerned) seem bland enough. Young people growing up in a traditional Native American society learn to think in terms of personality. They develop a sense of kinship. They come to recognize the need for restraint. They learn to accept death, and they acquire techniques of renewal.

Closer examination, however, shows that hard choices must be made. In the area of personality and kinship, for instance, we encounter the as-if-human species, including the ubiquitous animal masters, who invite exploitation, yet punish it. Here also are the animal-human and even plant-human marriages that are both loving and dangerous; and, on a grander scale, the sun as an untrustworthy overlord who must be both courted and shunned.

In the area of restraint, there are difficult choices as well. Here we find not only lofty ideas but workaday techniques, such as the imposition of game laws and the fallowing of gardens.

The distinction that may be made between the two realms—ideas and techniques—corresponds roughly to the modern tension between two schools of environmentalism, the so-called deep ecology, with its emphasis on changing the way people think, and the less inflammatory land stewardship, which encourages practices such as crop rotation and recycling. In many cases the distinction is observed in Native American cultures, too; and yet it is typically blurred. The choice, philosophically speaking, is between an absolute ideal and a working compromise.

The problem of whether to actually cheat on the established rules, much pondered in certain myths, presents yet another hard choice that humans must make.

It would seem, then, that native ideas relating to land use cannot offer easy solutions for the outside world, since the solutions are not easy even for insiders. Yet if the ideas, underneath, have a gritty realism, they may be perceived as inspirational for that reason alone.

Those who would suspend disbelief may ask, nevertheless, whether Indian thought is legitimately Indian insofar as it applies to the land. This is a question that is sometimes heard, evidently because much of the data comes from the same period that saw the rise of modern environmentalism (but also, of course, modern anthropology). Moreover, native land claims have benefited from a changed political climate in which native land wisdom, as a religious value, is taken seriously by courts and legislatures—and may therefore be cultivated merely as a legal expedient.

The suspicion that the American Indian has recently been converted to land consciousness is put aside, I think, by the weight of evidence offered in this book, most of it well shielded from environmentalism. As a single example that at first glance invites distrust, consider a comment by the sober-minded anthropologist Robert Heizer, who has written: "In the Inca Empire was what might be termed a Department of Conservation which regulated the use of natural resources." Heizer does not give details or references. Yet these are not difficult to find.

The early chronicler Garcilaso de la Vega, himself an Inca, has left a description of the communal hunts of his ancestors and how they were timed, how the game was tallied, how breeding pairs were released, and how off-season hunting was only "by express permission of the authorities." An even earlier source, the lawyer and government official Juan Polo de Ondegardo, reports in the mid-1500s that "a regular account was kept of all the hunts, a thing which it would be difficult for me to believe if I had not seen it"; furthermore, "the Inca [that is, the emperor] made similar regulations with regard to the forests." Addressing his words to the king of Spain, Polo advises that the system be continued, "for to frame new rules would be an infinite labor." (Need it be said, the advice was not followed.)

One further question that may be raised at this juncture is whether there is a telling difference between agricultural societies, such as the Inca, and those that have relied on hunting and gathering, such as the Lakota. This is fair to ask, since it has often been postulated that the history of land abuse begins not with industrialism but with the rise of agriculture. If in truth it does, then the Inca, the Aztec, and perhaps the Hopi, to mention a few, could be conveniently banished from the study of land wisdom.

Without denying the differences between the two kinds of culture, it can be pointed out that they overlap, sometimes more than has been realized. Recent studies in the supposedly primeval rain forests of Amazonia have suggested that certain areas are actually plantations, managed by people classed as "gatherers." On the other hand, old records demonstrate that hunting and the gathering of plants played a role in the lives, if not the survival, of even the Aztecs. Obviously, as shown above, the Inca fall into this category, too.

To offer a more specific example, the concept of the animal master, classically associated with small, hunting societies, is found also in Aztec lore. More specific still is the idea of an animal master in the guise of a white deer. Known to Algonkian hunters of eastern North America (as well as other groups from Colombia to the Arctic), the master as white deer was also known to Aztec hunters.

Conversely, the idea that human flesh is required by supernatural powers is classically associated with the Aztecs; but the concept, if not the practice, is also found in smaller cultures from Canada to Brazil. Moreover, in many of these cases (as with the Aztec), it is specifically the sun that makes the demand.

It is not unfair, then, to recognize unity as well as diversity in the various native approaches to the natural environment and its proper use.

Proverbs and parables

Wisdom is condensed—and often concealed—in two well-known, perhaps universal, ways of communicating knowledge: the proverb and the parable. Well suited to the sage's preoccupation with self-effacement and humility, the element of concealment is to be found in the Tzotzil Maya word for proverb, *k'ehel k'op*, which means "indirect (or obscure) speech," and in the Aztec word for parable, *machiyotlatolli*, meaning "sign-like (or symbolic) speech."

It is appropriate to say a few words about these two kinds of speech, since they form a part of this book as chapter epigraphs and as special texts within each chapter. As suggested above, proverbs and parables may well be of worldwide distribution. Yet outsiders, including folklorists, have been slow to recognize them as features of Native American lore. So far as proverbs are concerned, one simple reason is that field-workers have not thought to ask for them.

Two recent and notable exceptions are the anthropologist Gary Gossen, working among the Tzotzil, and the folklorist John Holmes McDowell, who has studied the Sibundoy of Colombia. Both workers have made collections of proverbs, placing these securely in a cultural context.

Less careful but still useful are the scantily annotated lists of proverbs published by Frank Cushing for the Zuni and Carl Lumholtz for the Cora of Mexico. Native authors who have set down proverb lists out of their own memory include

Francis La Flesche (Omaha), Luther Standing Bear (Lakota), and Eleuterio Poot Yah (Yucatec Maya).

Proverbial expressions may also be gleaned from studying the literature. Sometimes these turns of speech can cross language barriers. A case in point is the Delaware admonition "Don't listen to the singing of the birds which fly by" (i.e., don't believe idle gossip). This has also been recorded as "Though you may hear birds singing on this side and that side, you must not take notice." Interestingly, the expression was once known as well from the Algonkians of the old Illinois territory, who could say, "We have been fools and have listened to evil reports and the whistling of bad birds," and even from the old-time Iroquois (linguistically unrelated to the Algonkians), who could dismiss a rumor as "but the singing of ugly birds."

Another example of the cross-cultural expression is the widespread warrior's proverb "Nothing lasts forever" (in a Lakota form), of which two variants (from the Aztec and the Kiowa) are given as epigraphs to chapter eight.

Although native equivalents for the word "proverb" have been discovered in a few cases, the terminology is mostly unreported. Nevertheless, a few distinctions can be noted, if only for the sake of writing clear English. Thus, first, from an outsider's point of view, "proverb" itself may be saved for the terse, pithy expression of a general truth; second, in its looser form it may be called a "saying," which applies to any habitual expression; and third, the proverb may become a "maxim" (or even a "commandment"), serving as a rule of conduct. Examples of all three of these presumed types will be found in the chapter openings below.

Even less well studied as a Native American speech form is

the so-called parable, which can be defined as a narrative, preferably short, with an inner meaning. In European scholarship, the parable has been a subject of study for literary critics, not folklorists or anthropologists; and evidently since the critics seldom venture into oral literature, Native American parables have been overlooked.

An exception must be made for the team of Nora and Richard Dauenhauer, two linguists who have identified the literary forms of the Tlingit of southeast Alaska. Owing to the Dauenhauers we know that the Tlingit parable exists and that it has a native name: *at kookeidí*.

An example of the *at kookeidí* is the little story used by the Tlingit orator Thomas Young, in which a sea lion is saved from being washed away by a ptarmigan who fills the sea lion's body with rocks. At the end, the orator explains to his audience that the story is really about the power of wisdom to help younger people resist tides of change. "This is how you will be," he says, "with your grandparents sitting in the back; their speeches will be as if they are putting rocks inside you."

Even if not known by a particular name, parables of the Tlingit variety are a recurring feature in Native American literature.

In addition, many native myths that are neither short nor neatly explained are parable-like in that they, too, have inner meanings or potential inner meanings. Using a well-known myth as a parable, a chief of the Panamanian Kuna in 1983 persuaded other native leaders to accept outside help in a local conservation effort. The story he told was of the culture hero Tat Ipe, who tamed the dangerous spirits of the ancient world by borrowing secrets from the spirits themselves. "In this same tradition," the chief concluded, "we Kuna are learning the secrets of the foreigners so that we can arm ourselves to protect [our nation]."

Though myth in general may contain the raw material of parable, it usually lies dormant, waiting to be exploited. As observed in one instance by an Arikara narrator, after telling the story of his people's emergence, "This will give an idea to all how the Arikara originated under the earth. Yet it seems a mystery to us, and it is for us to solve."

Among European literary scholars, parables that are at least partially solved are said to be "mixed." In the Tlingit and Kuna stories summarized above, the "mixed" or explanatory part comes at the end and has been given as a direct quote: "This is how you will be . . ." and "we Kuna are learning. . . ." From here on out, in the following chapters, wherever the text is given as a "mixed" parable by the native speaker, the explanatory portion will be printed in italic. This is merely an editorial device, added in the hope of making a decidedly subtle kind of reading a little less formidable. Note that several of the parables are pure, not mixed.

One of the problems in translating native parables, or native instructional texts in general, is that what comes out in English tends to sound either much too difficult or much too simple. Some of the parables in this book are likely to call forth one or the other of these reactions. I hope, however, that the context in which they are given will help show that the hard ones are not impossible, and that the too-easy ones are more meaningful than might at first be apparent.

It should be kept in mind that the stories are more than

mere curiosities. They are meant to be valued highly. In the words of the Navajo ritualist Claus Chee Sonny, stories and other instructional lore are the same as goods, or possessions; and these are "difficult to obtain." In order to obtain them, "you have to make yourself strong, you have to think strong."

After a session in 1977 with the ethnographer Karl Luckert, Claus Chee Sonny commented that the stories he had just recorded would allow the "teaching and the thinking" to be "revitalized and renewed." "As things which were planted on earth grow," he explained, "so these stories, they will grow again. Young people desire many things, and as they listen for them they find them. Their heads are like radio. They hear many messages and songs, and their minds gather them up. And that is how I want you [my audience of the future] to receive these stories—in your minds. And then try them."

PART ONE

PERSONALITY

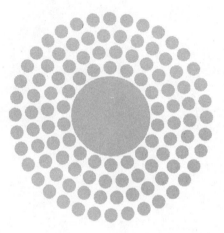

Inner Forms

A deer, although toothless,
may accomplish something.
—*Tsimshian proverb*

If animals and other parts of nature are spoken to in prayers,
and if in folktales they do the talking themselves, it would
appear that for the native cultures that produced such prayers
and tales all nature consists of persons. Yet as a bald generalization the statement has no native authority. Nor is it subtle
enough to pass for a genuine native pronouncement. Furthermore, a contradiction is left hanging: Can nonhumans be
persons?

In a celebrated essay devoted to this question, the late
anthropologist A. Irving Hallowell decided, in effect, that the
answer could be both yes and no. Using information gathered
in the 1930s from the Ojibwa of the Lake Winnipeg region,
Hallowell concluded that animals, plants, and objects were

indeed persons—except that here, "person" is not the same as "human." Rather, it is a larger, more inclusive category. "From the standpoint of the [Ojibwa]," wrote Hallowell, "the concept of person is not, in fact, synonymous with human being but transcends it."

An earlier student of the Ojibwa, the more plainspoken Diamond Jenness, had expressed the same idea in simpler terms. "Rocks, trees, and animals," he had written, "had attributes and powers" different from those of the human being, although the human was "one of them."

Such an observation seems clear enough. Yet it does not explain *how* a human can be one of "them." In fact, the basic concept has an important further dimension: not only are we "different from" yet "one of" them, we (and they) are different from our own selves. As Hallowell observed, again somewhat mystically, "Outward appearance is only an incidental attribute of being."

Similarly, for the Yekuana of Venezuela, creatures and objects—in the words of the anthropologist David Guss—are "much like humans," yet they "conceal their true identity." Essentially they are spirit beings, even though to humans they may appear as fish or game. For the Yekuana, as understood by Guss, "illusion masks another more powerful reality."

Attempting to shed light on the idea for a very wide audience, the Lakota writer Luther Standing Bear, in one of his book-length essays on the lore and history of his people, suggested that the linking of human and nonhuman nature is a means of acquiring knowledge. As he states it, speaking for the old-time Lakota, "Everything was possessed of personality, only differing from us in form. Knowledge was inherent in all things. The world was a library."

It may be conceded that Standing Bear's "knowledge," like Guss's "reality," pertains less to nature itself than to an attitude on the part of the native beholder. What one seeks to grasp is the "person," "knowledge," or "reality" that lies within. It is this unseen core that unites species, forging a bond between humans and animals or even between humans and plants.

Souls and hidden bodies

Though other terms may be used, translators often choose the convenient word "soul" to mean the part that constitutes the inner essence. But further explanation is usually necessary.

In the case of the Tlingit of southeast Alaska, animal souls are called *qwani*, "inhabitants of," because they are believed to live inside the animal's fleshly body. Since the same word is used for the inhabitants of a house or a village, the alternate translation "people" is permissible. One speaks of *xat qwani*, "fish people."

As for the creature's visible body, this is always a separate quantity. For example, a Tlingit may say that the body of the killer whale is the canoe for the killer whale *qwani*. The more widespread idea, however, is that the body is merely a disguise, perhaps a cloak or a mask.

A myth from the Inuit of western Alaska explains how the raven, using a mask, can be both man and bird: "It raised one of its wings, pushed up its beak, like a mask, to the top of its head, and changed at once into a man." Later, "he drew down the mask over his face, changing again into a bird, and flew far up into the sky." In English translation, the shift from "it" to "he" helps to convey the double idea.

Unusual lore from the Machiguenga of Peru reveals that in the eyes of animals, humans themselves are concealed forms. The vulture, it is said, sees a human on earth as a tapir. When someone dies, the vulture sends his "dog," which we see as a wasp, to get him a piece of our meat. Evidently, for the vulture, the tapir flesh conceals our human selves that exist within. On the other hand, the vulture, who to us seems merely a bird, would appear in human form if we lived in the sky world. In short, the body, according to the Machiguenga, is only the clothing, or *imanchake*, of the inner being, or *iseire*.

But not all inner forms are immediately human. For the Naskapi of Labrador, the soul of a tree resides in its "heart," which is the sap. Among the Tarahumara of northern Mexico, souls of most plants and animals are said to have the same form as their outer selves; thus the soul of a tree would be a smaller tree within. Humans themselves typically have a non-human soul, variously described as an "in-standing wind" (Navajo), a bird residing in the nape of the neck (Kwakiutl), an interior "flower body" (Yaqui), a macaw (Bororo), or a rock crystal (Huichol).

The same may be said of sky, earth, and mountains in Navajo lore. These, as well as the four directions and certain star groups, have inner forms shaped like humans; yet the inner forms, being human, have "in-standing wind" as *their* inner form.

A still-closer look reveals that the essential core may possess personality nonetheless. With regard to Navajo wind, it is well known that this element is envisaged as a person, or

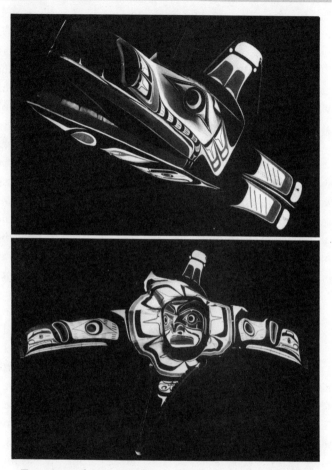

Two views of a raven mask carved and painted by Tony Hunt,
Kwakiutl, 1971 or earlier. Closed, the mask represents the raven (top);
open, it represents the human face of the moon. Courtesy of the
artist and the Royal British Columbia Museum, Victoria.

group of persons. Wind People, we are told, were present at the Creation. It was they who entered the newly created, lifeless bodies, enabling them to stand up.

As noted above, the soul of a tree in Naskapi belief is its "heart," or sap. But this soul is the equivalent of the life embodied in human beings, and the Naskapi word for soul, whether of tree or of human, is "great man." And so the soul, at bottom, has personality after all.

Such lore as this contains two productive ideas: that the soul and the body are distinct (as between flesh and wind, for instance); and that the soul (as wind, to take one example) is shared, or, to put it another way, that the human soul reaches out into nature. The first of these ideas sets the stage for the universal belief in immortality; the second accords with the more restricted concept known as tonalism. Each in its way promotes a careful regard for nonhuman elements in nature.

Immortality

Sometimes called "spirit," "self," "life," "double," or "shadow," it is the soul, or human form, that continues after death. As expressed in Navajo belief, a plant or an animal returns to its human form after the "earth surface people" (i.e., ordinary humans) have made use of it. In Iroquois lore, plants and animals "die in their bodies" but their "lives" go on—or, as one text has it, they go "straight on without stopping."

Souls, evidently, have a way of finding their own destiny. Nevertheless, it may be necessary to make sure that the process is completed. When an Inuit hunter brings in a bear, the severed head should be laid on the windowsill with the back of the head facing the outside. This is done so that the animal's soul will not have too much difficulty in "getting home." Presumably for the same reason, Tlingit say that the bear must be placed with its head "against the sun."

Influenced by a similar belief, the Shuar of eastern Ecuador avoid eating brains, since to do so would be to eat the "life" of the animal. Evidently the "life" is irreplaceable, because the taboo is observed not for the sake of the individual but, as the Shuar say, to prevent the species from becoming extinct.

In general, heads and bones are the parts that hunters reverence. Bones perhaps receive more attention than heads. The Shuar themselves refrain from cracking bones to suck the marrow; nor may bones of game animals be thrown to the dogs. After butchering, old-time Navajo hunters used to place all heads and bones of the deer under a piñon tree or a cliff rose. Prayers were then offered to the spirit of the deer, using such phrases as "now that you may return to the place from which you came" and "to the home of the dawn you are starting to return."

Merely depositing the bones may be sufficient, especially if they are placed near a plant or on its branches. Often, however, it is necessary to subject the bones to either water or fire.

A text from the Yekuana tells how a peccary hunter in the ancient days threw the picked bones of his kill into a magic pool, which restored them to life. But in a myth of the Thompson of British Columbia, the following advice is given: "When you kill deer, always see to it that the bones are not lost. Throw them into the water. Then the deer will come to life. . . . If it is impossible to throw the bones into water, then burn them." In fact, burning is probably the more common method.

The practical Koyukon of Alaska prescribe the water treatment for the bones of aquatic game, such as beaver and mink, while bones of land animals are to be either stored or burned. More selective, the Popoluca of southern Mexico save just the jawbone of the deer and use fire to smoke it.

Even fish, though they are water creatures, may be restored by fire. Thus a Tlingit fisherman takes care to burn the bones, so that the same individual can be caught year after year. It never actually dies, because, as the explanation goes, "When you get that fish, it's not the real fish. It's just the picture of it."

Tonalism

Although the soul is distinct from the body, the two are connected, and in many cases this connection is a source of risk not only after the body's death, but during its life. Accordingly, Kwakiutl fishermen, when hauling in live salmon, used to club the fish just once, then lay the bodies carefully on the beach, saying, "I do not club you twice, for I do not wish to club to death your souls, so that you may go home to the place where you come from, Supernatural Ones."

A bird might escape death altogether. As mentioned, the Kwakiutl regarded the human soul as a bird residing in the neck. During an illness, when the "bird" was thought to take flight, the shaman would catch it, so to speak, and put it back on the right side of the patient's neck. The particular species said to carry—or to be—the soul was the owl.

Therefore, if an actual owl was seen, a Kwakiutl might speak to it prayerfully: "Welcome, Supernatural One, thank you for coming, trying to come to me that I may see you, Long-Life-Maker. Please do this often, you who are the owner of my soul, for you are not seen when you are inside of me. Now you are good, when you pretend to be a bird, for you come and sit down on my head, Healing-Woman."

Among the Kwakiutl, the result of such lore was that owls were protected, since it was thought that a member of the tribe would die if an owl were killed.

But spiritual connection with an animal is seldom a direct route to species preservation. Its more immediate, more self-ish, aim is merely to heal a disease or a wound. The manner in which medicinal power is thought to proceed from this kind of partnership is shown in a myth from the Pawnee, where a wounded warrior is described as having been healed by bears. When the healing is complete, the man is approached by a bear elder who makes the man a doctor, saying, "Now you are well, and I shall take you back to your home, and after this I want you to imitate us. This shall be a part of your greatness. I shall look after you. I shall give to you a part of myself. If I am killed, you shall be killed. If I grow old, you shall be old."

The partnership between the bear and the Pawnee, or between the owl and the Kwakiutl, is such that each shares the fate of the other—a type of interaction that is most preva-lent in the lore of the southern half of Mexico. Typically, for the cultures of this region, each person acquires a partner spirit at birth, which has its embodiment in an animal. From then on, if either suffers an injury or falls ill, so will the other at precisely the same moment. Among the Zapotec, for instance, a child might acquire a sandpiper if it flew overhead as the child was born. Subsequently, if that particular sandpiper was killed, the one "born sandpiper"—that is, the human child—would die.

In Spanish such beliefs are referred to as *tonalismo*, or in English, "tonalism," from the Nahuatl word *tonalli*, meaning "fate." The animal itself is called a *tona*, though it may also be known by the Spanish word *suerte*, "luck."

The Chatino of Oaxaca State recognize plant tonas as well as animal tonas. As part of the ritual for a newborn, the father may plant a tree, which he continues to care for. If the tree proves robust, the child will be, too. If the tree dies, so will the child.

In some parts of the region the idea is elaborately developed, as among the Totonac of Veracruz State, where each human is said to have twelve companion animals. Elsewhere, as with the Popoluca, there may be only a vague awareness of tonalism. A member of the Popoluca community who became so sick that he was unable to earn money tells of thinking back to the time when he had killed a jaguar in the mountains, now realizing—too late—that he had found and killed his *suerte*.

The animal master

It will be noticed that the souls of nonhuman creatures are sometimes said to have "come" from a certain "place." Evidently, when we see them in plant or animal form, they are

away. When we have harvested them and they have given up
their earthly bodies, they "return home."

Often this "home" is imagined as a village or a corral. For
the Tzotzil of Mexico the spirits of animal tonas live together
in a corral within a distant mountain. Likewise, for the Bella
Coola of British Columbia the spirits of game animals congre-
gate as humans and hold dances inside mountains. Referring
to the isolated rocky hills that rise out of the forests, a Desana
of northwest Amazonia speaks of the "house of the hills"
where the animals "live like people."

Often it is water that separates the human from the nonhuman. According to the Kwakiutl, fish people live in a "rich
country" on the other side of the ocean; while Ojibwa imagine animal people in wigwam villages under deep clear lakes.
In Pawnee lore, animals hold council in riverbanks or deep
within river islands.

PARABLE / The owls that talked

There were once a father owl and a mother owl with their children,
and the children were big enough to go hunting already. Some of
the bigger ones were out hunting marmot, while the younger ones
remained at home. Then the old father and the mother owl said:

"Children, look out and see if your big brothers are coming
home with a marmot."

The children went out and looked, and sure enough, they came
back in and said:

"Here come our brothers, each dragging a marmot."

Then the old owl said to his wife:

"Where's the dog's harness?"

"It's lying there beside the passage," answered his wife. "But one of the breast straps is missing. I was going to mend it yesterday, but I forgot."

Then the old owl raised his voice and cried:

"What were you so busy with yesterday to make you so forgetful?"

And here ends this story, which shows that owls talk, live, and quarrel among themselves just like human beings.

—Told by Inugpasugjuk, Inuit
(Northwest Territories)

In their own world the animal people live as humans would. In Venezuela they keep "gardens." In eastern Canada they make camp and build "fires."

In addition, they may have the same social organization as humans do. As noted for the Pawnee, they hold council. Among the Cherokee, animals have their own tribal governments. Although animals, not plants, are usually the subject of this kind of lore, the Iroquois used to say that all trees, shrubs, and herbs were divided into families, having fathers, mothers, brothers, and sisters. Since Iroquois society itself is matrilineal, presumably such brothers and sisters took their clan names from their mothers.

By contrast, the Tucano of Amazonia trace ancestry through the male line. Therefore fish and other animals, according to Tucano belief, are organized into patrilineal clans, each headed by a "senior," or "oldest brother." It is this head of the family who protects the animal group and retaliates if one of his charges is killed.

Even where animal society has not been clearly envisioned in terms of clan or tribal government, the idea of the animal master who guards the lives of his "people" is likely to be present. In the lore of the Kariña of Venezuela the master of each species is thought to possess shamanic power, which protects the members of his "tribe" just as ordinary shamans protect humans. In some cultures the master of the species is embodied in an unusually powerful or sacred specimen, often an albino.

From Amazonia, Central America, and eastern Canada come reports of fish, tapir, peccary, and bear masters said to be white. Deer in particular have white specimens as their leaders. For the Ojibwa the white deer is "chief" of its species; in Aztec lore it was the "king"; while among the Guajiro of Colombia the white deer is "uncle." Similarly, for the Inuit of Baffin Island in northeastern Canada the caribou master is a female spirit whose name, Pukinna, means "white parts of deerskin."

In the lore of the Cahuilla of southern California, however, the white deer is master not only of its own species but of other hooved animals as well. Group masters such as the Cahuilla white deer, and even general animal masters, are widely reported. Plant masters are less common. One example is the "spirit" of the ceiba tree, said by the Shipibo of Peru

Owl with Catch of Rabbits, felt-pen drawing by Agnes Nanogak,
Inuit, 1972. Holman Eskimo Cooperative,
Holman, Northwest Territories, Canada.

to be the chief of all the trees in the forest.

It is well to keep in mind that the master is not the ceiba or the deer itself but the soul that inhabits a particular body. Since souls are essentially human, the masters often appear in human form.

In a myth of the Canelos Quechua of Ecuador the soul who protects fish inhabits the body of an armadillo; but the fisherman sees only a "man" who stands upstream trying to hold back the fish. Enraged, the fisherman wrestles the "man" to the ground and, as he kills him, watches him disappear in his hands. The next day he returns with his kinsmen to find an armadillo lying dead on the spot where the "man" had been.

This is not to suggest that the Canelos routinely antagonize the protective spirits. In another, similar, myth we learn that a tapir hunter was once stopped in his tracks by an animal master who appeared as "a white, beautifully dressed man." The "man" warned the hunter that in the future tapir meat would be poisonous unless certain rituals were observed. Thereafter, although the instructions were clear enough, the hunter was afraid to eat the flesh—which explains why the Canelos, in one community at least, avoid eating tapir meat completely.

The sense of danger revealed in the Canelos myths is typical of the native response in general. But the outright enmity, even avoidance, is unusual. More frequently the attitude is one of appeasement; and in many cases the underlying fear is replaced by a sense of duty, even courtesy.

The Iroquois, to give an example, tell of a man who visited the village of the buffalo and was escorted back to his earthly home by two buffalo women. Approaching the human village, the "women" requested that hunters come out and shoot them in order to speed their return journey. As it was requested, so it was done, enabling the "women," in spirit form, to hasten back to the home of the buffalo.

The story illustrates the general truth that creatures are willing to give their bodies, provided their spiritual needs are respected. The rituals of the heads and the bones, described above, are one of the commonest means of fulfilling this obligation, thereby gratifying the masters. This is why the Popoluca smoke the jawbones of the deer—to "please" the masters. As the Huichol say, the deer bones "are given to Tatewarí [the guardian of the deer], and in this manner, Tatewarí, with his power, revives the deer and a new one is born." The basic assumption, in case after case, is that the creature is willing.

If the Shuar hunter, so it is reported, perceives that an animal is not willing—if it exhibits shyness—the hunter quietly announces that he is giving up the chase, using the word-sentence *pampartí*, "Let it increase!"

The innocence of so simple an expression contrasts with the complexity of the native lore that lies behind it. This perhaps is why the skeptical outsider can dismiss the theory of natural persons as shallow, and why, at the same time, those who patiently explain it appear overprofound.

If the gap in understanding is to be closed, the lore of concealed and apparent forms, the nuances of immortality, and the concept of nonhuman societies and masters all need to be carefully considered. Yet these features of native thought are only the first steps toward a full appreciation of personality theory—and personality itself forms merely the threshold of the relationship between humanity and the rest of nature.

· · 2 · ·

Former Lives

Even a dog has
a father.
—*Maya proverb*

Safe from the harsh light of everyday reality, the hidden forms of animals assume their human shapes and go about their housekeeping in a distant location, apart from ordinary humans. They have their leaders, or masters, their rules of conduct, and their social relationships. But this is only the situation as it exists today. There is a historical, or mythological, background that deserves to be taken into account.

Virtually every native mythology speaks of a distant time— the ancient days—when the present separation between humans and other species did not exist. "People and animals lived on earth," explains an Inuit narrator, "but there was no difference between them; a person could become an animal, and an animal could become a human being." Phrasing a

Friendly Spirits, pencil drawing by Mark Uqayuittuq,
Inuit, 1972. Sanavik Cooperative, Baker Lake,
Northwest Territories, Canada.

slight refinement of the same idea, a Hopi storyteller states, "Thus it used to be: they would be in the form of people in the daytime, and at night be clothed as animals."

Such ways of thinking lead easily to the notion that humans and animals, since they were once interchangeable, have ancestors in common. If they do, all creatures must be blood relatives. So hasty a conclusion, however, would be widely denied. Through their former lives the creatures do indeed reveal information about their personalities, but a blood link with humans is not necessarily implied.

A famous exception is the report from the Yuchi of southeastern North America made by the anthropologist Frank Speck in the early years of the twentieth century. Speck found that each Yuchi clan carried the name of an animal regarded as the clan ancestor. As for actual, present-day animals, these had the same beginnings as the clan animals. Therefore, humans and other creatures were blood relatives, since, as Speck put it, "they trace their descent from the same sources."

Other exceptions could be cited as well. The Chipewyan of Canada, for instance, formerly held the dog in high esteem and would never take a dog's life, because the Chipewyan themselves, so it was said, were descended from this animal.

But reports such as these are often tempered by denials or at least called into question by real-life practices. Even the Yuchi, according to Speck, exploited their clan animals, excusing themselves by having nonrelatives do the killing. As a case in point, Bear Clan members could use bear products, provided Deer Clan members were the hunters; and vice versa.

Like the Yuchi, the Winnebago had clan animals that some

(though not all) clan members claimed as ancestors. Those who hunted did so on the theory that the ancestor had not been the actual animal but a *spirit* animal who alternated between human and animal form. Therefore a man of the Deer or Buffalo Clan could kill deer or buffalo, secure in the knowledge that he was not killing his relative. Notice that for these particular Winnebago the doctrine of inner forms, whereby the creature exists inwardly as a person, applies only to the ancient time, not the present.

Acceptance and denial of animal ancestors, within a single culture, has also been reported from Guyana and from northwest Amazonia. In the latter region, among certain groups, "to suggest that any animal is an ancestor would be the direst of insults"—as one investigator has written—implying, as is true, that the idea is accepted by other segments of the population. Half a continent away, among the Guyana groups, many people used to claim that their ancestors were plants or animals, as the case might be, while others said the clan designations were merely "names."

Similarly, in the words of a North American Osage, "We do not believe that our ancestors were really animals, birds, and so forth, as told in the traditions. These things are only symbols."

For the Kogi of northern Colombia, the anthropologist Gerardo Reichel-Dolmatoff has explained: "The Kogi call themselves Jaguar People and claim to be the 'Sons of the Jaguar,' not so much in the sense of genealogical descent as in that of a spiritual participation in certain supernatural qualities they believe to be embodied in the beast." Here, clearly enough, the emphasis is on personality, not on kinship.

Rather than insist, simplistically, that animals were our ancestors and are therefore our cousins of today, it is more instructive to note the far-flung network of belief which holds that animals once were human and are to be reckoned with in this light; and that humans once were animals and may still have animal-like qualities, for better or for worse. Thus there are two lines of thought, deriving on one hand from a belief in ancient "animals" (who were really people); and on the other from the idea of ancient "humans" (who were really animals).

When animals were people

As we learn from numerous traditions, the nonhuman creatures of today existed as people prior to an event in the deep past, which brought the ancient days to a close. Often the change comes with an earthquake, a flood, or some other crisis.

In the mythology of the Camaracoto of Venezuela, the tremor that ended the myth age shook the whole world for three days, during which time "everyone" became stones or birds or animals. In a tradition of the Seminole of Florida the turning point comes not with a world quake but with a world flood; and the animals' inability to speak dates from that event. For the Tojolabal of Guatemala the early people were driven to seek refuge in caves during the flood; when they emerged, they had become animals according to their personal characteristics (those who had been crafty, for example, became rabbits).

In unusual myths from Tierra del Fuego, animals of today

are shown to have originally been women. The change, so it was said, came about during the Men's Revolt, the great turning point in world history. Formerly society had been ruled by women, who had tricked their husbands into believing in female power. Discovering that it was only a ruse, the men rose up against their oppressors; and as the women fled, they changed their forms. Those who went into the water, for instance, became waterfowl and sea creatures.

In many cases, as with the Seminole, the crucial difference is that animals of today no longer have the gift of human language. For the Navajo both animals and plants ceased to be "speakers" at the time of the Emergence, when all creatures came out of the earth. In a typical myth of the Nahua of central Mexico, this loss of speech occurred with the change-over from darkness to light: the sun rose for the first time, and "from that day on, the animals could no longer talk."

Such events took place long ago. But they are not forgotten. As Navajo observe, the nonhuman creatures of today breathe, walk, and give their calls. Therefore we know that even if the animals are no longer "speakers," they "also have souls."

One result is that there may be communication between humans and other species, which, even if nonhuman, have a humanlike past.

Making the point perfectly plain, a member of the Jicaque tribe of central Honduras reports that one day while passing the mouth of a cave, he heard a voice ask a threatening question: "Why do the deer hide?" Fearing that he was being challenged by the deer master, he answered respectfully, saying that he would refrain from killing deer and take a squirrel instead. The conversation was possible because the deer master, now a deer himself, was human (and therefore a speaker) during the ancient days. According to Jicaque theory, animals were left with the power to understand—and to have their thoughts read by—present-day people. Thus the hearing of the question was true communication, in the form of mind reading.

As explained by a member of the North American Blackfeet: "At one time animals and men were able to understand each other. We can still talk to the animals, just as we do to people, but they now seldom reply, except in dreams. We are then obedient to them and do whatever they tell us."

If former membership in the human species gives animals the right to be heard, it may also give them the right to be left alone. In the words of a modern Alaskan Koyukon: "We have respect for the animals. We don't keep them in cages or torture them, because we know the background of animals from the Distant Time. We know that the animal has a spirit—it used to be human—and we know all the things it did. It's not just an animal; it's lots more than that."

When people were animals

An alternate way of looking at the ancient time is to imagine an age of animals who either were replaced by humans or were themselves changed into human form.

Replacement is the method described in the Popol Vuh, the well-known sacred book of the Quiché Maya of Guatemala. Here we learn that the first earthlings were birds and animals created by the gods. But when the gods commanded them, "Talk, speak out," the creatures "just chattered, they just howled." Consequently they were destroyed, to be replaced by humans.

Replacement is also a feature of the mythologies of California, Oregon, and the Great Basin. Here, however, the animal nation is highly competent. It is the animals who arrange the physical world and establish future customs, because, as they sometimes say, "the people are coming" and everything must be made ready. One of the animals, Coyote, himself creates the future race of humans.

Traditional histories in which the first animals are not replaced but actually changed are much rarer. An example comes from the Yokuts of central California, where it was once said that the eagle sent all the animals in different directions to become people. As remarked by Alfred Kroeber, a distinguished collector of the myths of the Yokuts and of numerous other North American groups, in cases of shape-shifting it is usually the "first people" who turn into animals, not vice versa.

Yet various folk beliefs imply a change from animals to humans even where this cannot be validated by mythology. Of the Incas it has been reported in the early sources that on feast days the people came out "according to their tribes and lineages"; those who "claimed to descend" from the puma— or "lion," as the old chroniclers put it—wore the skin of that animal. Still others came "with the great wings of the bird called condor, which they considered to be their original ancestor." But myths of the Inca period, whether from the Incas themselves or from the peoples they conquered, do not record a time when animals changed into humans.

In other cases the mythology itself is ambiguous. That is, it can be taken either of two ways—as in the case of the Kwakiutl and the Bella Coola, two tribes of British Columbia. Explaining why a tribesman was blessed with hunting power, a nineteenth-century Kwakiutl could say it was because "a great killer whale was the ancestor" of the man's family group; therefore the famous hunter "came really from the great killer whale." In fact, certain Kwakiutl myths do allow that "ancestors" arrived on earth in the form of animals. Yet the "ancestors" do not give birth to their descendants. Rather, the "ancestors" create the future people from wood or some other material.

A similarly provocative belief, reported from the Bella Coola, states that when people die, their spirits travel back on the paths of their ancestors from generation to generation until they reach the spot where the first ones came to earth; there the spirits put on the bird or animal "cloaks" that were used in the ancient days, and float up to the sky in nonhuman form.

The related mythology, however, shows that the Bella Coola ancestors were originally human and just wore the "cloaks" during an interlude before the present era began. Here, once again, is lore that affirms personality while both affirming and denying kinship.

Often it is merely a manner of speaking to say that the first beings were "human" or "animal." A closer look reveals that they could be neither or both—though it is safe to say that they possessed at least a minimum of personality.

One set of consequences that derives from this kind of ambiguity has been described by Richard Slobodin, a longtime student of the Kutchin of northeastern Alaska. For the Kutchin the caribou is the principal food animal. Yet it seems that in the ancient time, human and caribou lived together. Not until hunting was established did humans become a separate people. Today, as a vestige of the old relationship, every caribou has a bit of the human heart inside it, and every human has a bit of caribou heart.

Therefore, in Slobodin's words, "Humans will always have partial knowledge of what caribou are thinking and feeling, but equally, caribou will have the same knowledge of humans. This is why caribou hunting is at times very easy, at other times very difficult."

Evolution

In traditions where humans are preceded by animals, the changeover is not always immediate. If it is gradual, the process itself shows that humans do indeed derive from other species—happily or unhappily—again calling attention to humanity's mixed feelings about animal ancestry.

One kind of myth describes a process in which a single human lives among the creatures, mates with one or more of them, and has offspring who are, or who become, permanently human. Evidently the transition can take place within a single family.

In a story from the Bororo of southern Brazil, the original couple produced a son "who had a face and feet like those of a deer; the second child was a daughter with a human face but with fur all over her body; then they had a son whose hands, feet, and head were like our hands, feet, and heads, but who had patches of short fur." And so on, until finally the sixth child is born completely human.

A different kind of myth, involving emergence from the underworld, has the first humans still encumbered by animal characteristics as they crawl into the light. In Zuni lore these early beings had tails and webbed fingers. Called "moss people," they were covered with slime.

According to the Brazilian Tupari, "They were ugly to look upon; they had long canine teeth like wild boars, and between their fingers and toes the flesh was webbed like a duck's." In a myth of the neighboring Paressí, the first man to emerge had a tail, also a membrane between his arms and legs. A Guayakí text, from the same region, notes that the emerging ancestors' "armpits smelled bad; their skin was bitter. . . . Like armadillos the people's first ancestors scratched their way out with their nails."

Keeping such lore in mind, native people have not missed the opportunity to draw a parallel with modern ideas on the origin of species. In a commentary delivered in the late 1920s, the Navajo elder known to outsiders as Sandoval observed succinctly, "The Navajo people have always believed in evolution"—implying, as can hardly be disputed, that Europeans are newcomers to the theory.

Nearly a generation earlier, the Santee physician and author Ohiyesa, known to the world as Charles Eastman, had published an evolutionary myth of the Santee, noting that among his tribesmen the story "was often quoted in support of our close friendship with the animal people.

"I have sometimes wondered," Eastman continues (using the Edwardian English his readers expected to hear), "why the scientific doctrine of man's descent has not in the same way apparently increased the white man's respect for these our humbler kin."

The transformer

Although the development of humans from animals may progress by evolutionary stages, the shift from animals to humans is almost always abrupt. Often it seems to occur spontaneously. Yet in many cases it is the work of a deity or hero.

In a matter-of-fact story from the Yavapai of Arizona, the narrator states quite simply, "It was the desire of the first people that they remain human, but Coyote insisted that they become animals and live in the wilds." And so it occurred.

A more complex myth of the Aztecs explains how a man of the ancient time transformed himself by leaping into a bonfire, becoming the sun; then, after rising for the first time in the east, the new sun transformed everyone else into animals.

If a reason for the transformation is given, it is usually that the early humans have failed in some way. As Sandoval makes clear, for the Navajo, "Up to this time all beings were people and could remove their coat forms at will; but because of wrongdoing they were made to keep their coats; and they were made to keep to their kind and to live among themselves in different parts of the earth."

In the Aztec story the people are transformed into "good" animals, except for one man who fails to make the proper prayer offerings. As punishment, the sun turns him into the nighthawk, perpetually condemned to grasp at shadows.

Lore of the Pomo of California includes a story of the transformer Coyote, who became exasperated at the ancient people because they did "not seem to care to do the proper things and try to be somebody." Each was changed and given a short lecture, as in the case of the deer, who was told, "You shall always live in the mountains; you shall be afraid and will be shot for meat; your name shall be Deer."

In the North American Northwest and in eastern Bolivia, the role of the transformer is particularly well developed. Mythologies from these areas are marked by mysterious parables, strung together one after another, on the theme of transforming predatory humans into the game animals of today. As is evident from the words of a Bolivian narrator, the early beings got what they deserved: "The ancients were very bad people. They killed and ate each other. Duhvít [the transformer] changed them because this killing and eating, of each other, did not please him."

Telltale signs serve as reminders of the transformer's good work. In a parable of the Kaska of British Columbia it is revealed that the tongues of sheep are black because sheep formerly ate humans. In a similar text from the Lushootseed of Washington, the deer's hooves are the spearpoints it once hoped to use in killing the transformer himself. Since the "sheep" and the "deer" were originally in human form, their underlying offense is what often comes through in translation as "man-eating," or cannibalism.

In some instances, however, the ancient offenders were animals to begin with, even if larger or more warlike. The act of transformation merely makes them more manageable. In myths told by the Beaver Indians of British Columbia and Alberta, the hero Swan reduces the size of the giant animals that used to seize and eat human children. These monsters were animals, no doubt. Yet they talked and lived like people.

PARABLE / The transformer and the deer

Moon [the transformer] came upon Deer making spearpoints of bone and singing, "This is what I am making to kill the transformer."

While he was yet singing, Deer looked up and saw the transformer standing there before him. "What are you doing?" Moon asked him.

"Making a weapon to kill the transformer," said Deer.

"What is it? Let me see it," said Moon.

Deer gave it to Moon. Moon placed the spearpoint upon the wrist of Deer and turned him into a deer, saying, "You shall be something good to eat."

—Told by Snuqualmi Charlie,
Lushootseed (Washington)

In weaker concentrations, such lore is found in other regions, especially in the eastern half of North America. A story from the Santee of Minnesota tells how a hero "transformed" the offenders—not physically but mentally—forcing them to give up their warlike ways and permit humans to exploit them for hides and meat. Although hunting today is not always easy, the animals are expected to abide by this "treaty" to which they agreed in the ancient days.

A myth on the same general theme used to be told in the 1960s and 1970s by the Delaware traditionalist Nora Thompson Dean. Although Delaware mythology does not recognize a transformer in the full sense of the term, the "Creator" sometimes plays this role. According to Dean, the Creator once caught a squirrel in the act of eating a human. (This was in the ancient days, when squirrels were larger than they are now.) The giant squirrel had already consumed everything but the victim's hand. The Creator said to him, "Now, truly you have done a very terrible deed. You have killed my child. Now, from this time on, it is you who will be little and your children and your great-grandchildren will be eaten, and the shameful thing you did will always be seen [by a mark] under your forearm."

To this day the uneaten hand can be found under the squirrel's front leg, where the squirrel had tried to hide it from the Creator. On one occasion, after telling the story to a visitor, Dean added, "I've dressed many squirrels, and there's a little hand right here, and we were told not to *ever* eat that, so I always cut it out."

"You mean a little piece of meat?"

"Um hm, little piece of meat, looks like a human hand—with five fingers."

In this case, evidently, the former life of the squirrel argues neither for mercy nor for preservation. It is the life of humans, rather, that cries out for protection.

A backward glance over the other transformer myths that have been sketched above will show that human preservation is in fact the common thread—except, of course, for the Aztec story, where the moral is exactly reversed. The Aztec transformer changes the ancient people into animals not as punishment but as a reward for their prayer offerings; and as we know from the various texts of this story that have been preserved, the "offerings" are their own bodies. To state the matter concisely, in the North American and Bolivian myths the consumption of humans is abolished; in the Aztec myth it is instituted.

The total picture provides other contradictions as well. For instance, it is easy to see that in many traditions the former lives of humans and nonhumans are intertwined, suggesting a basis for mutual respect, even affection. Yet the distance humans have traveled—along the evolutionary scale—tends to separate them from the ugliness, slime, odor, and hairiness of nonhuman creatures.

In all its wealth, passing back and forth across language barriers, the lore of former lives offers a flexible rationale for taking from nature or for giving back to nature, as the culture may require.

· · *3* · ·

The Organic
Alternative

Everything is alive; there is
nothing dead in the world.
—Cora saying

Hidden souls in the animal world and ancient personalities long since transformed help put nonhuman creatures on an equal footing with humans, conceptually speaking. Competition for resources is not eliminated in such a scheme; rather, it remains just that: a competition between human and nonhuman partners, not always friendly, in which each side gives as well as takes.

Unrelated to the concept of souls, a quite different kind of equality is suggested by the transferral of flesh from one form to another. Usually plants, not animals, are involved in this process—which can hardly be called imaginary, since it rests on humble facts of nutrition and chemistry. Yet the associated ideas, if realistic enough in their underpinnings, have a decidedly unreal quality.

Plant material, in other words, becomes human flesh, and vice versa.

Rare indeed are the passages from native lore in which animals play this typically botanical role. They do occasionally, however, as in an old story from the Ottawa, where it is said that after the Creation, when the various animals had been established in their feeding places, they began to die; whereupon the Creator "caused the birth of men from their corpses, as also from those of the fishes which were found along the shores of the rivers."

Note that this is not the same as animal "people" changing into humans. Rather, it is a kind of growth, in which humans rise up from an organic substance.

In reverse, the process works just as well, again connecting humans more often with plants than with animals. Here, though, the idea of an animal connection is not quite so rare. In a simple myth of the Chinantec of central Mexico, a little girl pushes an old woman into the water as the two of them are crossing a bridge and says, "You will be the mother of all the wild animals"; immediately the deer, the rabbit, and other species begin climbing onto the riverbank. Similarly, in a story from eastern Mexico, a wife provides fish directly from the flesh of her body; and in British Columbia the fish-producing wife has only to dip her toes into the stream and at once the salmon are jumping in the water.

But, as mentioned, when living things issue from humans, they are more likely to be plants or plant products, not animals. The variety and ingenuity of such lore can be seen from the following examples, drawn from North, South, and Central America.

Flesh into crops

The idea of a young boy—a corn boy—whose body is either identical with or turns into food plants figures prominently in the lore of cultures reaching from the Great Lakes to Mexico and southward into Brazil. A Winnebago text refers to this child as the "little boy with yellow hair."

Well known in central Mexico, the corn boy is called Homshuk by the Popoluca, Thipaak by the Huastec Maya, and Cintectli by the Nahua. In a myth of the Popoluca, Homshuk is born as a tiny child with hair soft and yellow like corn silk. "I am the one who is going to give food," he announces. "I am he who sprouts at the knees. I am he who flowers."

Homshuk himself, however, is usually invisible, as is the Thipaak of the Huastec. But Huastec farmers say that if they hear a boy's laugh in the cornfield, it is a sign there will be a good harvest. The sound of a crying boy means that the harvest will be lost.

Sightings of the corn boy, elusive as he may be, have been reported even in recent times. In a much discussed incident of 1977, covered by the local press, a young Nahua man claimed to have seen the seated figure of Cintectli near the town of Tampamolón in the state of San Luis Potosí. After his disappearance a corn plant appeared on the spot.

But even if he is not seen, the child's presence is felt. Writing in the 1990s, an ethnographer of the Popoluca states emphatically that Homshuk is "still alive in the minds" of the people.

Farther north, among the Hopi, the corn boy is called Moing'iima. Every summer he becomes heavy, so it used to be said, when his body fills up with corn, watermelon, and other fruits and vegetables; "they grow in his body," according to one native source. But after the harvest he becomes thin again.

A similar figure is known from Brazil, where an old myth of the Tupinamba tells how the culture hero, Maira-monan, saved his people from starving. Changing himself into a little boy, he incited the other children to beat him, and with each blow grain and vegetables dropped from his body.

In other, somewhat different, lore the crop producer is a mature woman—as in Guyana, where she draws manioc flour directly from her flesh. Likewise, the bean mother of Central America shakes white beans from her head (for men to eat), black beans from her hips (for women to eat).

In the southeastern United States, crop mothers are important figures in Cherokee, Creek, and Natchez lore. In the mythology of the Cherokee the woman's name is given as Selu. Both a corn and a bean woman, Selu stands in the middle of the room with a basket in front of her on the floor. Leaning forward, she rubs her stomach, and the basket is half-full of corn. Then, when she rubs under her armpits, the basket is full to the top with beans. The Natchez mother simply shakes herself, and in Creek myth she does the same; or, according to a variant tradition, she scrapes her thighs.

Narcotic plants, also, may spring from human flesh. In the lore of northwest Amazonia, such plants are said to grow from the fingers of women in the pangs of childbirth; and in an important myth from the same region it is told that the female Creator made tobacco from her own body.

Tobacco and other crops can arise from human wastes and secretions—from feces (Amazonia) or semen (North America). In a myth from southern Mexico it is related that fava beans were originally Our Father's fingernails; as he walked over the earth, he cut his nails and the trimmings turned into favas.

In rare instances the idea of turning flesh into food finds a place in ritual. Remembering a technique used by shamans to ensure the acorn crop, a Cahuilla woman in southern California describes the performance as follows: "When the witch man made acorn trees in his palm, he got hot coals in his hands and he held it there and it came like a weed grown in the ground. It grew that high [about two inches]—this would make food come." The reference, presumably, is to a blister on the shaman's hand, perceived as a symbolic oak or acorn.

If, figuratively speaking, plants and humans share a common substance, the process of change, or outgrowth, should also work in reverse, as indeed it appears to do in various myths and rituals. The Guatemalan sacred book, Popol Vuh, offers a well-known example: the gods are said to have ground yellow corn and white corn, working the mixture with water, using "yellow corn, white corn alone for the flesh, food alone for the human legs and arms." In this way they modeled the body of "our first mother-father."

A Navajo myth describes the ritual somewhat differently and in greater detail: the gods arrived carrying two sacred buckskins and two ears of corn, one yellow, one white. They "laid one buckskin on the ground with its head to the west;

on this they placed the two ears of corn, with their tips to the east, and over the corn they spread the other buckskin [and allowed] wind to enter. [When] the upper buckskin was lifted, the ears of corn had disappeared; a man and a woman lay there in their stead. The white ear of corn had been changed into a man, the yellow ear into a woman. . . . The pair thus created were First Man and First Woman."

But the idea of equivalence between human flesh and plant flesh is not limited to crops. It extends beyond the garden to a more general category of plant matter represented by seeds, woods, and grasses—implying generative power, durability, and rejuvenation.

From seeds and trees

In the ancient days, according to a myth from the Upper Xingu region of Brazil, a prehuman "grandfather" went into the forest and cut five lengths of *weigufi*, a hardwood. After carving and decorating these, he "placed them in seclusion in order that they would grow. Some time later, he took a cotton belt and beat them until they cried out; he then knew they were alive." In a variant of the story, he cut six logs, put them in a tightly closed hut, and covered them with fragrant *enemeóp* leaves; then "he began the incantation to turn the logs into people. He began by saying this: 'I want you to turn into people.' And the logs actually turned into people."

In the mythology of California the same kind of ritual is said to have occurred, though not with logs but with slender wands, or sticks. As told in a Yuki tradition, the sticks with knobs on the ends were destined to be men, while the smooth ones became women.

In a version reported from the Pomo, another of the California groups, the act is accomplished by the deity Madumda. "By the side of a river he dug a hole," it is said. "Then he went off, and breaking some willow wands he brought them back and planted them around the hole. It was evening. To one of the sticks he tied a string. He passed the other end through his ear-hole and made it fast. Then he lay down with his back to the fire. He went to sleep; and while he slept, the string jerked his ear. He sat up quickly. He looked toward where he had planted the sticks. . . . It was dawn. He thought he could see people moving about."

Logs and sticks are not the only materials that reshape themselves into human life. Myths of the North American Great Basin specify grasses, seeds, or a combination of the two ingredients, usually incubated in a basketry water bottle. Among the Washo, for instance, it is told that Wolf, who was chief of the animal people, decided that everyone should become an animal and make way for humans. To create the new race of beings, he put cattail fluff, seeds, and grass into a bottle; and after one moon he poured out the tribes.

A variant has it that Coyote and his wife were the planners, again in the ancient days when animals lived the lives of humans. After Coyote's wife had woven a large round water bottle, Coyote filled it half-full of seeds, took one whiff of tobacco smoke, and blew it through the opening. Then he sat down and talked for a while, saying, "Anything I expect to make I never fail in. Whatever I think always goes right with me." In a while the couple heard a buzzing sound. The basket began to move by itself. Then Coyote took hold of it and poured out the people.

PARABLE / How humans continue

[Raven] wanted to create people. He fashioned humanlike shapes out of stone. He blew his breath on the stones and they came alive, but soon they were dead again.

Then he made humanlike shapes out of earth, blew his breath on them, and they came alive. But again they were soon dead.

He carved humans out of wood and made them live by blowing his breath. And also they died.

Then he made humanlike shapes out of grass and blew his breath on them. They came alive and were the ancestors of the human race.

From then on people grew up and died back like grass.

—Anonymous, Tlingit
(Alaska)

In lore from various cultures, instead of reconstituting itself as human flesh the plant material serves as a kind of womb. Logs and tree trunks are the parts most often mentioned.

Myths of tree emergence, either spontaneous or at the instigation of a culture hero, are to be found in northern California (the people issue from an oak tree), New England (an ash tree), Paraguay (a quebracho tree), and eastern Brazil (the tree called *anawira*).

But in an unusual myth from the Inuit of western Alaska

the first man is said to have lain coiled up in the pod of a beach pea. After five days had gone by, he stretched out his feet and burst the pod, standing up as a full-grown human.

Other unusual myths designate growing tips as the source of human life, again from trees. In the lore of the Arawak of Guyana the Creator causes the ceiba tree to grow into the sky, then scatters its twigs on the ground below to make all living things, including humans. In a Munsee story the process occurs automatically: the first tree to grow on earth sends up a sprout from its base, which becomes the first man; then the tree bends over until its top touches the ground, where another sprout shoots up, forming the first woman.

Rare lore from tropical America makes the tree a nurturer in an even more literal sense. That is, the tree not only gives rise to humans but provides breast milk as well. According to a myth of the Piaroa of Venezuela, the ancient world, after it had been destroyed by flood, was repopulated by "a great chicle tree full of suckling children, each one grasping its teat." In Aztec tradition the *chichihualcuahuitl*, or "breast tree," existed permanently in the afterworld, where it suckled all those who had died in infancy. Twentieth-century Tzotzil—in southern Mexico—have retained the concept of the breast tree, thought by some to be covered with human teats by which the deceased children are suckled; or, as some say, the babies sit beneath the tree with their mouths gaping wide to catch the drops.

Personal anguish

Although plants are believed to join with humans in basic organic processes, they often stand as persons in their own

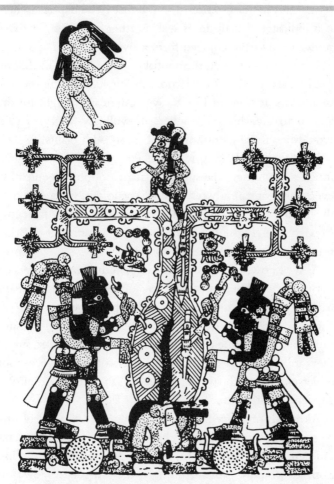

The birth tree at Apoala, redrawn by Peter T. Furst
from the pre-Conquest Mixtec screen-fold book Codex Vienna. After
Jill Leslie Furst, *Codex Vindobonensis Mexicanus I: A Commentary*
(1978). Courtesy of the Institute of Mesoamerican Studies,
State University of New York at Albany.

right. This has been implied in the first two chapters, where it is indicated that plants as well as other creatures may have souls or may have enjoyed former lives as men or women.

For plants, however, the contribution to human livelihood can be even more personal, more deeply felt, than in the case of animals. It is normal in Native American thought for the animal to give himself, or herself, willingly; a cry of pain would be virtually unthinkable. Not so with plants.

The anguished screams of the corn woman as her flesh touches the hot griddle suggest a degree of human empathy, even alarm, apparently reserved for the lower, vegetal links in the food chain. In highland communities of north central Mexico, merely the telling of such lore is sufficient to bring tears to the eyes of those who hear it.

As we know, plants, like animals, had the power of speech during their former lives. More accurately, perhaps, humans had the power of comprehending this speech, which may yet encode messages. As expressed by an early-twentieth-century Ojibwa, "When [the tree's] leaves shake and murmur, surely they are talking to one another. It is true that we cannot understand them today, but Nanibush, the great hero of old, conversed with them."

Although ordinary mortals may be denied the gift of understanding, Ojibwa shamans have extraordinary hearing and can detect such signals as the wailing of forest trees suffering from ax wounds. Not surprisingly, the old-time Ojibwa, in some communities at least, seldom cut down green or living trees.

Lore of this kind is to be found even in the larger, more complex societies, like those of the Aztec or the Zapotec.

According to an early colonial source, reporting from Aztec territory, "People thought that trees had been humans in a previous age—that they imitated or changed into trees—and that these had had a rational soul. . . . And thus when they cut them for human use, they prayed to them and gained mercy for having cut them. And when the trees creaked while being cut, it was said that they were protesting. [Then the tree was] consoled with many loving words, begging it not to be angry."

Even in the ancient days, so it is said, plants expressed feelings, as in the Zapotec myth which explains that trees wept when the world flood began.

Trees that must be cut are approached cautiously in many cases, or even provided with comforting appurtenances. Thus when a Tlingit lumberman used to take his ax to a tree, he would first pray to it, saying, "Black bear skins have been laid in the place where you are going to fall. Fall down on them."

In various traditions such kindness was especially important if the wood was being taken for ceremonial purposes. "O tree! I ask that you will fall easily," cries an old-time Blackfeet woman when chopping a tree to be used as the center pole in the Sun Dance lodge. Expressing the same kind of concern, a Delaware ritualist, when cutting out live wood to make the figurine for the Doll Dance, would talk to the tree, explaining why it was necessary to take a piece of its trunk.

The rationale—in a similar instance—is set forth in detail by a Pawnee narrator, who tells the story of a young man who had received ceremonial instructions from a beaver. Later, outside the animal's lodge, while the beaver was gnawing at a tree, the young man "saw that the tree was wavering and that it was a young girl. The tree seemed to scream when it was about to fall. The man noticed that it began to turn into a real woman. . . . In the night the man had a dream. He saw the woman he had seen in the tree. She spoke to him: "Brother, the timber you see are like people. Some are men and some are women. Be careful how you cut timber. You must first talk to the tree before you cut it. Some trees become angry at the people and send a lot of trouble to them. Either they cut their fingers or feet, or some accident befalls them. Occasionally the timber sends sickness among the people."

In some cases exquisite precautions are observed, even when the tree has already been cut. Among the modern Maya of the Guatemalan highlands it is reported that a woodsman, after felling a tree, covers the stump to save it embarrassment amid its fellows.

Whether for modesty or for protection against the elements, the need to be clothed is widely recognized. Courteous bark gatherers in British Columbia, while cajoling the plant that is to be exploited, refer to the bark as "your dress" or "some of your blanket." In Alaska, the gathering of birch bark is suspended during the winter, so as not to leave the tree naked to the cold.

But not only do trees and other plants betray human sensitivities, succumbing to pain, anger, and embarrassment; they literally bleed, or at least they did so in the ancient time. Moreover, blood appears to form a bond between plants and humans, serving as a common substance that flows in either direction.

In a myth from the Yupa of northern Colombia, the first

humans are said to have been carved from a tree that spurted blood when touched by the ax. Conversely, a myth from the Tepehua of central Mexico has the first plants formed from the blood of the sun as it sheds its human guise and rises into the sky for the first time. As the sun reaches the stars, the stars cut off the fourth finger of each of the sun's hands, and from the drops of blood that fall back to earth all the different plants spring up.

A similar myth from the North American Yuchi tells of a wizard in the ancient days who tried to make the sun travel too fast by rushing her. To prevent this, the wizard was ambushed by concerned humans, who beheaded the man and tied his head to the top of a cedar. The blood drained into the tree, giving the wood its color.

This mysterious "blood" of the cedar is matched in various lore: from the Crow of Montana, where the flesh in question is that of the box elder; from the Pipil of El Salvador, where the tree is the calabash; and from the Chorote of Paraguay, where it is the lignum vitae. In each case the tree drips blood or reveals the life-giving substance through its reddish color.

How, in conscience, can such plants be used? The answer is not always easy and may require a difficult choice. Writing of the creation lore of the Cahuilla of southern California, an authority on that culture describes a case in point: "The god Mukat decrees that the first fire will be made out of Ninmai-wit, the woman who is a palm tree. Her screams of anguish are pitiful, yet the people recognize the inexorability of her sacrifice as part of the order of the universe."

The question is raised again in a myth from the Ixil of Guatemala. A boy of the ancient time is sent out by his mother to chop kindling. He returns empty-handed, saying, "When I cut a tree it cries, the blood flows out, and then I get worried. So I can't bring any firewood."

A tradition recorded for the Mopan of Belize resolves the dilemma, albeit uncomfortably, in a story of the first man, who went out to cut the first tree. The tree called out to him, "Don't cut me down." The man made a small cut, and blood started to flow. Frightened, the man withdrew. But later a supernatural messenger came and advised him, saying, "That is the way all over the world."

· ·Part Two· ·

KINSHIP

4

Within the Family

Just as decency of the
body lies in hiding it,
decency of the soul lies in
covering it with humility.

—*Aymara proverb*

It does not require fantasy or the lens of a distant culture to observe that nonhuman species, among themselves, maintain social relationships based on sex or kin. Native personality theory, with its focus on animal "masters," "lodges," and "villages," merely sharpens the obvious.

It is equally true, and universal, that humans desire admittance to this other world.

Parent-child and husband-wife relationships, across species, are the bridges that are typically erected. In the former case, one "adopts" a pet. In the latter, a hunter "attracts" game—suggesting a relationship that is considerably toned down in most modern cultures.

Even in Native American societies the husband-wife, or

courtship, bond between species may exist as no more than a mere echo. In a love song recorded for the Inuit, a young man speaks figuratively: "I dreamed that I followed you, that I wanted you like a young seal, that you were wanted by me the way the hunter wants a young seal." Similarly, among the Colombian Kogi, a woman's lineage, inherited from her mother, is always named for a prey animal, while a man inherits the name of a predator from his father. Accordingly, each man marries a woman representing the animal that *his* animal would hunt in the wilds. If he is a Jaguar, he must marry a Peccary; a Puma must marry a Deer.

But among the Aguaruna of Peru, the relationship is taken more literally. Aguaruna men, it is reported, actually bring their wives along on hunting expeditions as sexual bait to attract the game. The belief is that the animal will wish to come court the human female. In northwest Amazonia the hunter himself takes pains to appear sexually attractive in the eyes of game animals, using facial paint and herbal perfumes; and in Panama, male herb-gatherers do exactly the same, because the plant spirits are female and are thought to appreciate being courted in this manner.

Hunting expeditions, as it happens, offer the principal opportunity to capture fledglings, cubs, and other offspring, which are brought home to be raised, always with the human in the role of the parent and the animal as the child. Such attempts to make a parent-child connection across species are more common than the efforts to establish the male-female bond. Yet, as in the case of animal "spouses" or "lovers," the relationship arouses mixed feelings in some cultures.

The anthropologist Emory Sekaquaptewa, himself a Hopi,

recalls a school "ecology" project, conducted by non-Indians, in which children of various backgrounds were to learn respect for other species by taking care of caged animals. Strangely, as it might seem at first, the Hopi children in the class refused to participate. The reason, evidently, was that these children found the experiment disrespectful. This does not mean that the Hopi have no pets. Dogs, for instance, are kept. But the pets are neither caged nor brought into the house.

The Alaskan Koyukon man who explains that his people have too much respect for animals to put them in cages "because we know the animal has a spirit" is expressing a similar view. Yet here again there is more than meets the eye. The Koyukon will in fact keep a particular pet, if it is thought to have personality traits that are valued in humans (whereas animals with disreputable personalities, such as the red fox, are avoided).

On the other hand, completely uninhibited expressions of the parent-child relationship have been reported from many native cultures—from the Chatino of central Mexico, for example, where each domestic animal is treated ritually as if it were a child, and a "birth cross" is placed under the altar for it; and from the old-time Delaware, who used to keep young birds, deer, and squirrels until they were fully grown, giving each one a Delaware personal name.

Among the Penobscot it is said that dogs were petted with long, caressing tones and given such names as Sauce, Hoot Owl, Clown, and Baby. For the Cahuilla it is claimed that dogs and other pets were kept for the very purpose of teaching children to treat animals with care and respect. Likewise, an ethnographer who has described the techniques used by the Shuar in taming birds and mammals writes that these procedures "help to strengthen the bond with nature."

Such practices, however, do not reflect the full range of thinking on familial relationships with the nonhuman world. For a more complete view, one must turn to the intellectual lore, especially the myths, or stories. In the case of the parental bond, which will be considered first, the typical myth turns the real-life situation on its head: instead of the human as parent, it is the nonhuman creature who becomes the mother or father—and therefore the mentor.

Adoption

"Seven old Buffalo bulls found the child and looked at it. They pitied it. One of them said, 'Let us raise it. We will have it for our son.' Then the first Buffalo began to wallow. As he wallowed, he licked the boy all over. Then another one licked him. When all seven had licked him, he was no longer a baby, but a boy."

So reads, in part, the opening of a Gros Ventre myth in which male buffalo become the "fathers" of an abandoned human child. When the proper time had arrived, so it is said, the "fathers" instructed the boy: "Go into the woods and cut a piece of cherry wood. Make it so long. Cut also seven sticks of cherry wood for arrows. Season these. Shape the wood into a bow and arrows. Then cut sinew, and twist it into a bowstring."

Thereafter the bulls themselves carried the boy into the midst of the herd and stood by as he killed meat. "The bulls loved the boy very much, and never became angry at what he did."

Such readiness to give instructions for the killing of one's own species is not rare. In fact it is a recurring feature—though not the only feature—of the North American adoption myth. Often, as here, the teaching is spelled out plainly enough.

Somewhat more subtle are the Bear Boy myths of northeastern North America, in which the human child is nursed by a female bear and acquires bear language by playing with her cubs. In an Iroquois version the boy converses with the bear mother and learns that hunters can detect the presence of a den by watching for vapor traces. In addition, the bear points out mistakes being made by careless hunters who pass by in the forest. One of the hunters is inattentive; another has made the error of eating too much hot food, so that he himself spreads telltale vapor. But when a good hunter comes along, the mother is suddenly submissive, saying, "There's no help for it. We've got to go." According to some—but not all—variants, the boy, when at last he has been returned to human society, becomes a successful bear hunter, drawing upon the knowledge he has gained from his bear mentor.

In other instances, apparently, the knowledge is absorbed through mere contact. According to a Delaware version, the Bear Boy simply lived with the bears without receiving any explicit instructions. Yet, in some way, when the experience was over, "he now had the power to kill any game."

The absorption of knowledge, or power, is demonstrated more fully in a Pawnee adoption myth, in which a man is sheltered by a bear who becomes his teacher. The method of transferral is explained as follows: "When they were about to part, the bear came up to him, and put his arms about him, and hugged him, and put his mouth against the man's mouth, and said, 'As the fur that I am in has touched you it will make you great, and this will be a blessing to you.' His paws were around the man's shoulders, and he drew them down his arms, until they came to his hands, and he held them, and said, 'As my hands have touched your hands, they are made great, not to fear anything. I have rubbed my hands down over you, so that you shall be as tough as I am. Because my mouth has touched your mouth you shall be made wise.'"

A similar technique is described not in a myth but in a prayer formerly addressed to the slain bear by Kwakiutl hunters: "Now you have come to take mercy on me so that I obtain game, that I may inherit your power of getting easily with your hands the salmon that you catch. Now I will press my right hand against your left hand [says the hunter as he takes hold of the left paw of the bear; he says] O friend, now we press together our working hands."

In the mythology of South America, animal mentors are less common and, where present, less likely to impart hunting knowledge. In myths of the Argentine Tehuelche, the infant hero Elal learns to survive as a vegetarian through the example of his adopted mouse mother: "The rodent was his support. It taught him how to eat plant food; it housed him in its nest of guanaco wool, and it showed him the paths through the forested land."

In Brazil and in the Guianas the adoptive parent is most frequently the jaguar, a dangerous father (or uncle) from whom the hero nevertheless acquires knowledge.

In a story told by the Krahó, one of the Ge tribes of east central Brazil, the jaguar finds an abandoned boy, who had been stranded on a cliff. "You can jump down; I'll catch you. You won't fall!" says the jaguar. "Let's go to my house. Now I'm your uncle, and you are my nephew. Let's go now, because you are hungry. I'll feed you."

From the jaguar the boy learns the secret of cooked food. "If it wasn't for the jaguar," concludes the narrator, "we would still be eating raw meat."

Thus the jaguar, like the buffalo, the bear, the mouse, and others, serves humanity as a wise instructor. No longer the "baby," as it must be in the human world, the animal becomes the knowledgeable "father," "mother," or "uncle" in the wider world of nature.

Marriage

Just as myths of adoption reverse the actual human–pet relationship—making the animal the parent and the human the dependent—the typical marriage myth transforms the hunter-prey relationship. Instead of the hunter luring his game, it is now the game animal who lures the human.

As the myths themselves will show, the imagined marriage can be dangerous if the new husband or bride is an animal master; beneficial if he or she is a food animal; or merely useless and frustrating if the spouse is neither.

The stories of useless marriages generally involve an unwary young woman who is enticed by a bird and suddenly finds herself in a strange, avian world. These are sad, disappointing myths, always implying that humans are incompati-

Scenes from the Bear Mother myth. Front and back views of an
argillite carving (inlaid with abalone), Haida, 1850–1900. In the front
view (top) the mother in the form of a bear is shown holding her
bear child, with a salmon in her teeth and a whale at her feet.
In the center a shaman, with the salmon as his spirit helper, attempts
to heal the bear child, who here lies in human form at the
shaman's feet. The bear father is at right. In the back view (below)
the bear father is seen at left, embracing the mother in human
form. Linden-Museum, Stuttgart, Germany.

ble with nature. And yet, in the beginning, one has hope.

In a myth of the Nez Percé of Idaho, the narrator explains that a young woman was attracted to a certain man on account of his good-looking legs and therefore followed him to his home country to become his wife. Along the way, as they were wading across a river, she became entangled in moss that the "man" had used to pad himself. On the far shore she discovered his legs were skinny—and heard him give the call of the blue jay. Too late. She now had to follow him to his lodge, where every evening he would bring back pitch gum for her to eat, "thinking that she, too, liked only that."

More spiritual in his appeal, the would-be condor husband of Quechua mythology promises to bring his human bride to a mountaintop world of "pure solitude and perfect silence." However, when the two have set up housekeeping, he brings her nothing but foul-smelling flesh from dead animals and rotten potatoes dug from people's gardens. "She wished for bread," so it is said, "but the condor was unable to provide it."

More miserable still is the heron's bride in a famous old myth of the Tariana of northwest Amazonia: not only must the young woman find her own food, but she is deprived of sleep, since the herons, being nocturnal, keep her awake through the night.

At the other end of the scale is the decidedly dangerous union between a human (always male) and a seductive animal master in the role of the bride. In South America, from Guyana to the Andes, the nonhuman bride who seduces the human is the anaconda, a master of fish, who lures the fisherman—especially the successful fisherman—and exacts a payment of labor or even requires that the man give up his life.

P A R A B L E / The anaconda wife

A man was living near a lake with his family. When he went to the lake, he always caught fish. One day he was fishing, and a pretty young woman rose out of the water. It was the anaconda.

She said to the man, "You've caught many fish in this lake. I am the ruler of the fish. Unless you favor me, you may not keep fishing. Come to my house and live with me."

The man found the young woman attractive, but he said to her, "I am married and have a family to feed. I can't go with you."

"The fish obey me. I rule them. You'll have no more fish if you don't come with me." Then she took the man on her back and said, "Close your eyes." She dived with him and brought him to her house at the bottom of the water. The man stayed there and was happy.

After a while the young woman said to him, "Go to your home now. But you must not wait for daylight. You must come back sooner."

From that time on, the man went to his family at night but came back before dawn. His son caught many fish.

One day the man neglected to return on time. He was still at home with his family when daylight came. At that moment he died. The lake dried up, and all the fish died, too.

—Anonymous, Tacana
(Bolivia)

The implication is that the human in this case has made too much use of the protected species.

Between these extremes is the familiar food-animal spouse, who—as in the case of the animal parent—enables the human partner to utilize the species in question. Shuar hunters, for example, say that they know the ways of peccaries because in the ancient days a Shuar was married to a peccary woman and lived for a long time among the peccary people.

Likewise, the North American Thompson learned the techniques of successful deer hunting on account of a Thompson man who married a deer. The marriage was unintentional on the man's part; he already had two wives at home. But he could not resist the spell of the deer woman. "For a long time I have loved you and longed for you," she said. "Now you shall go with me to my house."

In the house of the deer woman were "people" who wore deerskin robes. On the following day the man killed two of the deer, his own "brothers-in-law," who ran ahead of him and stood on a knoll, offering themselves. Later, when the meat had been eaten and the bones had been dutifully thrown into a body of water, the two brothers reappeared in their human forms. Thus the deer population was not depleted.

By contrast, the Deer Woman myths of Arizona and New Mexico make the bride the human and the husband the deer. Here again, however, it is the human who is lured, against her will. In a vivid Apache version it is said that the deer man "took her mind away and made her crazy." In the home of the deer the woman gives birth to deer children, eventually returning to her own people as a teacher of deer lore—only to leave once again and resume residence among the deer. As a member of the deer community, though still human, she forms a link between the two species.

Indeed, in a Navajo variant the Deer Woman calls out to her human brothers as she leaves for the last time, "Do not grieve for me. I shall lead game here. . . . Right around here you shall do the killing." Speaking of Navajo hunters as a group, the narrator concludes: "Up to this time, they have had a sister, they say."

But the relationship is not without conflict. In the case of Deer Woman, there is a moral dilemma that arises as a consequence of the story itself. In many of the variants the woman finds that her human brothers have shot and killed two of her own fawn children. According to an Apache version, having made this discovery, she becomes inconsolable, crying and fondling her dead babies all over their faces, legs, and bodies. Then she runs away as a deer, saying, "I will not be your relative anymore."

Thus even the beneficial marriage—between the unwitting human and the amorous game animal—can lead to estrangement between the species.

Human sentiment

In an Iroquois variant of the Bear Boy myth, the adopted child has feelings similar to those of the bereaved Deer Woman but cannot express them because, having lived so long among bears, he no longer remembers the words to use. He can only watch as the hunter who has come to take him home kills and butchers his bear family: "The boy was grieved to see his companions dead and cut up, but he could not speak to let his rescuer know how dear they were to him."

The matter does not always rest with an unspoken complaint. Often there is a suggestion—even in the case of the Apache Deer Woman—that a crime has been discovered and should not go unpunished. The outcome may be that needed game is withheld or placed off limits.

A Yupa myth from northern Colombia tells how the master of animals took a Yupa man to his house and changed him into a peccary, or wild pig, making him the keeper of the pigs. One day some Yupa men killed a herd of these animals, and the peccary keeper ran after them shouting murder. "Since I am the father of these beasts, you have killed your own brothers! Don't you dare to eat any of these pigs!" With that the hunters left the meat for the vultures and went away ashamed.

In a story told by the Tsetsaut of western Canada a man is said to have married a marmot woman, who brought him luck in hunting marmots. One day, however, he came home with a particular marmot, which caused his wife (who was now in human form) to cry and wail: "You have killed my brother! you have killed my brother!" Then she revived all the marmots her husband had killed previously, and they ran up into the hills.

The crime may even be treated as a capital offense, especially if the relative in question is one's mother. In yet another variant of the Bear Boy story, the child who had been adopted by bears became a successful hunter after he had reentered human society. Remembering his bear mother, though, he avoided hunting bears. One day, goaded by his human family, he did track and kill a bear. "But on his return home he fell on a sharp stick and was instantly killed."

The same fate caught up with a hunter of guanacos in an old myth from Tierra del Fuego. Unwilling to hunt and kill a certain guanaco, but unable to resist the demands of his own hungry people, the hunter fell to weeping. Finally, when the pressure had become intolerable, he ran after the guanaco and killed it. As he had known all along, the animal was his own mother, and soon thereafter he himself died.

<hr>

PARABLE / The boy who became a flock of quail

They say there was once a foolish woman, and she had a little boy. She left him by himself. When she came back he was nowhere.

She looked in the neighbors' cooking fire.

Then she found his tracks leading to a tree. He was singing:

> pitiful
> pitiful
> all alone
> it seems
> I'll be a quail
> *potopái*★

As he finished his song, one arm fell out of the tree.

He sang again, and a leg fell down. Again, and his head fell. All of him fell. Each time, *potopái*.

★Call of the quail.

That's why the Delawares always hated to kill quail: they're that woman's little boy. It's why I tell the story. It's an ancient one.

—Told by Josiah Montour,
Munsee Delaware (Ontario)

In another of the Fuegian myths, a woman helps prevent her brothers from killing a sea lion that had abducted her— because, even though the animal had stolen her, by now "the two had fallen in love." Yet, in still another Fuegian story, the brothers do kill the sea lion husband; and although the woman is at first horrified, she gradually calms down and forgets her beloved husband. "From then on," as it is said, "she ate the blubber and meat of the sea lion with as much pleasure as did her brothers."

It should be observed that in none of these myths does the animal itself express pain or indignation. It is always the human relative who cries out. The dilemma, evidently, is one for humans to resolve, if they can.

Humanity's place

Whether the subject is adoption or marriage, the stories are poignantly specific on the relationships between humans and their animal spouses, siblings, parents, and in-laws; and, as may be seen, the ties that bind are formed less by thoughts than by feelings. Nevertheless, a broader, more philosophical position can be drawn from the myths—and has been, both by outside observers and by native people themselves. The essential idea is that family ties promote respect.

With considerable precision the ethnographer Janet Chernela, reporting from northwest Amazonia, has described the natural community of human and nonhuman species in terms of an overall, equalizing relationship between brothers and sisters. With reference to the Uanano, one of the Tucanoan groups, she observes that the people "see themselves in a universe ordered into sibling units classifying humans, animals, and plants. Relations between members of these groups have limits within which each group can impinge upon others. No action occurs without a counter-action however: man does not act upon nature without repercussions."

More poetically, and with an ear for phrases that resonate in the modern world, Luther Standing Bear, for the Lakota, has described the same kind of unifying relationship in terms of an extended family of grandchildren. Recalling his own childhood experiences with animals, he writes: "All this was in accordance with the Lakota belief that man did not occupy a special place in the eyes of Wakan Tanka, the Grandfather of us all. I was only a part of everything that was called the world."

Such a statement reflects a sense of proportion that is echoed by ethnographers from all corners of the hemisphere; and for the most part the insights are derived directly from myths. Speaking of what can be learned from the old mythology of California, Robert Heizer concludes that "the attribution to animals of higher intelligence and human qualities and emotions was common"; and of the Cahuilla specifically, Lowell John Bean records that humans were at the "center" of the living world—in the sense of "having greater power than some beings, but less than others."

From British Columbia, T. F. McIlwraith, again drawing upon a mythology rich in human-animal relationships, has stated that "the Bella Coola do not regard birds and animals as being of a lower order than themselves, for all were created by the same power, at the same time; in many respects they consider that they belong to a higher plane than human beings."

In the same vein, an authority on the mythology of the Campa of Peru has noted that "in thought and in action the Campa places himself on a par with the rest of the animal kingdom, nor does he consider himself to be necessarily first among equals."

For many observers the fine line between equality and humility is actually crossed. Indeed, animals may often have "intelligence, knowledge, and power far beyond those of man"—in the words of George B. Grinnell, for the nineteenth-century Pawnee. Of the world view held by the Zuni, Frank Cushing, another of the nineteenth-century ethnographers, could state: "In this system of life the starting point is man, the most finished, yet the lowest organism; at least, the lowest because most dependent and least mysterious."

Finally, as unraveled by a Winnebago elder, in a traditional speech addressed to young men, the mystery—at least for a moment—seems clearer: "My son . . . Earthmaker made spirits up above and some he made to live on this earth; and again some he made to live under the water and some to live in the water; and all these he put in charge of something. Even the small animals that move about this earth the creator put in charge of some power. Thus he created them. Afterwards he created us human beings; and as he had exhausted all the powers to be disposed of, we were not in control of anything."

5

The Earth as Mother

The Moon is man and woman combined;
men see in her a woman,
women see a man.

—*Cora saying*

The earth is not always a mother, nor is it invariably female. In a whimsical tale told by the Selknam of Tierra del Fuego the earth takes the name of Kóre, a good-looking young man of a yellowish brown hue, who is said to have once made love to a guanaco woman. In remembrance of that time, the tawny-coated guanacos "still like to roll around on the ground, from which they have their color," the story explains.

By contrast, the folklore of the Cora, a tribe of western Mexico, makes of the earth a disagreeable old man, who can sometimes be heard to cry and complain.

Among the Quechua of Peru, earthquakes are attributed to the male earth-spirit, Pachacamac, whose name may be translated "earth lord." Likewise, among the Aztecs of ancient Mexico the earth was called Tlalteuctli, ":earth lord"; yet, fearsome as this spirit was and despite the masculine title *teuctli* (lord), the Aztec deity carried the additional name Tonan, "our mother."

Of course, the earth does not always have to be a mother, or a lord, or an old man, or a young lover. Like other objects in nature, the earth may be treated as perfectly neutral with regard to kinship, sex, and even personality.

Reporting in 1970 from the Quechua of southern Peru, the anthropologist Juan Víctor Núñez del Prado notes that according to local thought, "the sun stands still in the universe and the world is constantly turning, producing the phenomena of day and night." Equally sexless, and apparently lacking in personality, the earth is said to be "spinning around" in a version of the Piman creation myth recorded in the 1930s. In twentieth-century Potawatomi lore "the whole earth is moving"; and, once again grafting newer ideas onto the older mythologies, a latter-day Pomo myth has the Creator himself rolling the earth over, ordering dark and light to succeed each other.

In the same vein, a Winnebago mythmaker asserts that the Creator made the world as a sphere, then flattened it with his thumb to keep it from bobbing in the water. Nevertheless, the text refers to this newly created earth as "our grandmother."

Though sometimes male, or often sexless, the earth is indeed widely linked to femininity and motherhood.

Iroquois texts are quite specific in establishing authority for the kinship term. In a Cayuga version of the Iroquois "thanksgiving" address, the speaker announces: "And there is a way people will have to refer to it as related. This the earth: 'Our Mother, it is related to us.' " According to a Seneca version of the same address, "[The Creator] decided, 'It will be in the nature of a relationship when they want to refer to it.' He decided, 'They will say Our-Mother-who-supports-our-feet when they want to refer to it.' "

Again stressing kinship, Aztec mythology has the sun itself instructing the newly emerged humans on their duties and obligations, reminding them, *auh no yehuatl in amonan in tlalteuctli,* "and the one who is your mother is Tlalteuctli."

The Aztec text, recorded in the 1500s, is one of several that point to the antiquity of the earth-mother concept in the Americas, an idea undoubtedly dating from pre-Columbian times. Another is the lost manuscript of 1559 used by the Peruvian historian Bernabé Cobo, who reports, "they all worshipped the Earth also, and they called her Pachamama, which means 'earth mother.' " Still earlier is the pre-Columbian codex Nuttall, from the Mixtec culture of central Mexico, showing on its first page an ancestor emerging from the earth womb.

In contemporary Indian thought, especially in North America, some voices are skeptical of this mute, passive earth mother, creative only in the physical sense. At the same time there persists an age-old awareness of the idea's political—and moral—value in the continuing struggle for ownership of the American land. In other words, the image of mother earth is useful and deep-seated, even if, in modern contexts, it is too often sentimentalized and oversimplified.

Creativity

The objection is not to the earth mother itself but to the manner in which the idea has been received in the wider world. Stating the problem in personal terms, the folklorist Marta Weigle has questioned the view held by commentators who identify "the feminine" with nature and procreation, rather than with "women's continuing strategies for creativity and empowerment." The view that is being criticized is indeed simplistic, and Weigle's implied connection between nature spirits and women's lives is not irrelevant.

Native texts themselves suggest that the female earth may be none other than everywoman. At the Creator's command, the earth rose up "to live in human shape," proclaims a Menominee narrative on world creation, and "in her arms she held a child." In Peru, among the Aguaruna, a wife and mother sings, "Because I am a woman I am like Nunkui," thus identifying herself with the female spirit that inhabits the soil. Similarly, in the old days a Cheyenne woman who had lost her virtue could undergo a prescribed ritual and renew herself, "like the earth." In Winnebago instructional lore, a father would customarily advise his son, "Never abuse your wife. . . . Our grandmother, the earth, is a woman, and in mistreating your wife you will be mistreating her."

But there is a larger concept not always revealed in excerpts from native texts and often overlooked by outsiders enchanted by the simple fact of the earth as mother. With the admirable patience that is characteristic of her work, the Laguna novelist and literary critic Paula Gunn Allen has approached this issue cautiously, writing: "Lagunas regard the land as feminine. What is not so clear is how this might be so." Throwing tact to the winds, an Assiniboin woman in the 1960s put the matter more bluntly to a visitor who had come to interview her: "Oh, all that Earth Mother nonsense. Those anthropologists ought to write mysteries."

What Paula Gunn Allen makes clear—for the Laguna—is that the people do not set up a "primitive" equation between fertility and womanhood; rather, the Laguna "associate the essential nature of femininity with the creative power of thought." This follows from the idea of the Laguna earth spirit herself, called Tse che nako, "thought woman," a creator who inhabits the earth yet also stands apart from it.

Generally speaking, it is useful to make a distinction between the earth and the earth spirit. And it requires no great subtlety to do so. The native texts are often explicit on this point. In the mythology of the Jicarilla Apache, for instance, the creative earth mother is said to reside within the body of *her* mother, the earth.

Much the same is true for the Kogi, who regard the mother deity as living within the earth, while the soil on the earth's surface is merely her "daughter." Farther south, among the Quechua of Qotobamba, the earth is *allpa* ("earth" or "soil"), as distinguished from Pachamama, "earth mother," where the element *pacha* means earth in the sense of "world."

In a text from the Navajo, the native commentator explains, "You see, the one who became the inner form of earth, being a woman, was given charge of the care of things on earth and upward."

"Earth," then, is not necessarily the same as "earth mother," even though the two terms may be used interchangeably; moreover, the spirit in question is not always passive. Her work involves planning, or thinking ahead. In the lore of the Laguna and other Pueblo groups of New Mexico, Thought Woman prepares for the creation of life on earth, entrusting the actual tasks to a pair of sisters, who carry out her ideas.

In Kuna mythology the earth mother is said to have exerted her intellect in conjunction with a male consort. At the very beginning, these two conceived the future. In the words of a narrator, "There was no end to what they were thinking."

In one version of the Kogi creation myth, it is said that at first the "mother" was not even a person. Existing in the lowest depths of the earth, she was "not anything, nothing at all. She was *alúna* [soul, life, or desire]. She was the spirit of what would come, and she was thought and memory."

According to one of many versions of the Navajo origin myth, it was "the one called Earth Mother"—or simply "Earth"—who gave humans themselves the gift of intellect. The mother placed her hands on either side of our head; and then, "where her fingers met, where our eyebrows are, she ran her finger to here, to where the tip of our nose is. 'This will be your thinking, this you will think by,' it was said to us." From that time on, the earth was in charge of human consciousness, removing it and restoring it with the daily alternation of sleeping and waking.

"This earth is alive"

Nevertheless, for some native thinkers the creative power of the earth exists in its very substance, spontaneously generating plants and animals. Seeding, in such cases, is not required. A mythic text recorded from the Winnebago states that "our grandmother, Earth," simply "opened her body where her heart was and, suddenly, green leaves were to be seen."

According to a well-known myth from the Okanagon of British Columbia, a male creator merely rolled up balls of earth that were changed into creatures, enabling the narrator to say: "Thus everything living sprang from the earth; and when we look around, we see everywhere parts of our mother." In Iroquois mythology the Creator throws up a handful of earth, and living things fly off in all directions; thus the Creator can observe, "This earth is alive."

Often the living creatures, if vegetal, are said to be earth's "dress" or "blanket." "A blanket made of everything that grows" is mentioned in a Navajo account of the earth's formation. In a Kuna tradition the earth mother—called *nan tummat*, "great mother"—gives birth to her own "green clothing." More imaginatively, Zuni lore endows her with a "green robe full of moss" in the summer and a white robe of "frost flowers" in the winter.

In other traditions the vegetation is spoken of as her "hair" (Aztec, Hopi, Okanagon, Quechua, Winnebago). In Apache lore the "hair" protects her from the cold.

Mythmakers and ritualists often compile lists of the earth's body parts, usually identified with particular landscape features. One of the most complete, obtained from the Navajo, includes toes, fingertips, knees, soles, palms, shoulders, cheeks, eyes, and lips—not to mention a protruding mountain said to be "the tongue of earth's inner form."

The nurturing breast

Earth's anatomy suggests an intimate, caring relationship between inanimate nature and humanity. Humans are nursed, or suckled, at the earth's breast. "Pachamama has milk," explains a Quechua of Pinchimuro in the region of the old Inca capital of Cuzco. "On earth she suckles us. That's how we live our lives." (Notice once again the distinction between Pachamama, or "earth mother," and the earth itself.)

In view of the earth's nurturing qualities, humans may be regarded as earth's children, taking their name directly from her. As stated in a sixteenth-century text from central Mexico, the first ancestors of the Mexica Aztecs—the founders of the city of Mexico—were at one time newly washed infants. But "Mecitli suckled them. This Mecitli is Tlalteuctli ["earth lord"]. And so we today who are Mexica are not really Mexica but Mecitin [the plural of Mecitli and a lesser-known variant of the name Mexica]."

The nutrient itself is sometimes spoken of in figurative terms, as in Winnebago lore, where it is said of "Our Grandmother, the Earth," that "white blossoms, like life, sprouted from her breast."

Often, however, the breast milk is equated with corn. An ancestral, or spiritual, "mother," not identified with the earth, is envisioned as providing corn from her breasts in Iroquois, Lakota, and Zia lore. According to the Zia (of northern New Mexico), the mother planted bits of her heart in the earth, and when these had grown into corn, she announced, "This corn is my heart and it shall be to my people as milk from my breasts." In a legend of the Lakota, the woman declares, "My milk is of four kinds [meaning white, black, yellow, and variegated corn]; I spill it on the earth that you may live by it."

The actual practice of planting corn in mounds is widely linked to this basic idea. "You shall make the corn grow in hills like breasts," according to an ancient instruction handed down among the Iroquois, "for from the corn shall flow our living." Scrupulously, the Pawnee of the southern Great Plains made sure that every cornfield had an even number of mounds, since these were regarded as women's breasts and needed to be paired.

More fundamental than corn, earth itself is said to have been formed from breast milk in the mythology of the Amazonian Tariana, who assign the role of Creator to a young woman called Grandmother of the Days: "She took a rope and wound it around her head, laid the rope down, divided it in half, and pressed milk from her breast. Her milk flowed into the circle and made earth. The next day a great field had formed on that earth. Then she gave the earth to the women, so they could work it, and she said, 'With this earth you can live.' "

A related concept has been reported for another of the Amazonian tribes, the Tucanoan-speaking Desana, who imagine a region deep within the earth called *ahpikon-diá*, "river of milk." All the rivers on the earth's surface, which in Amazonia flow eastward, are believed to end in a great lake of milk that connects with *ahpikon-diá*, the source of earth's mysterious life-sustaining substance.

Seemingly less profound, but clearer, is the idea set forth by an early-twentieth-century Tahltan of western British Columbia, who could say, "The earth is animate and the same as our mother, for if there were no earth, there would be no people." The testimony continues: "The people are her children, and the animals also. She looks after them all, and provides food for all. The rocks are her bones, and water her milk. A child cannot live without sucking its mother's milk, and people cannot live without water."

Emergence

The mother-child relationship between the earth and its human charges is based not only on nurturing. In many cases it derives from the idea of earth as the original birth mother.

Ancestral emergence, or birth, either from soil or from water is one of the most widespread concepts in the Americas, reaching from northern Canada to Argentina. Often it is missed by outsiders if—as with the Iroquois—it is not incorporated into the myths of creation, standing aside as an event of the more recent (though still ancient) past. Today, in a changing world, the lore of emergence together with the lore of nurturing supplies a rationale for native land claims and for the related argument that native people have a vested interest in caring for the earth.

In its simplest form, the tradition states that the first humans arose spontaneously. The people came "out of the ground" (Nez Percé); "the people grew up from the soil" (Tarahumara); "the people came out of the hills" (Tzotzil); the first man "emerged from the earth" (Toba).

According to the Inuit of north central Canada, earth was repeatedly the birth mother in ancient times. Women who

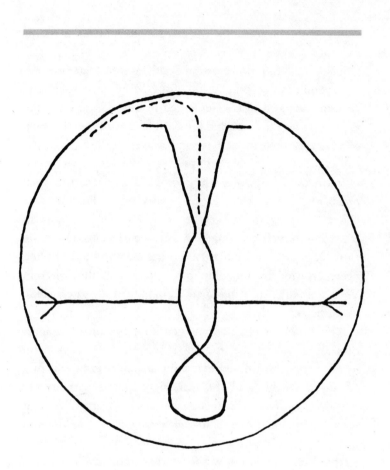

Figure representing Tamaiawot,
the earth, the mother of all; drawn by Pachito,
Luiseño of Pauma, California, 1905 or earlier.

wanted children just looked along the ground and gathered them up.

Traditions from northeastern South America state that the first people were caught like fish. More ceremoniously, ancestors are said to have emerged from a lake or from the ocean—in legends reported for the Tupari and the Kaingang of Brazil, for the Inca of Peru, and, as well, for North American Ojibwa and Pueblo groups.

In the mythology of the Maidu of California, earth was an incubator, which received tiny pairs of seedlike humans planted by Coyote. When the time was ripe, "the human pairs, long buried, burst out." According to Santee myth, the earth gave birth to humans and other creatures after having been fertilized by sunlight; in a tradition of the Sáliva of Venezuela the fertilizing agent is described as water falling from the sky.

Sometimes the place of emergence is a specific geographical feature, as with the Iroquois of western New York, who in the past have claimed that their ancestors grew out of a certain hill at the head of Canandaigua Lake. The Choctaw of Mississippi have also recognized a particular hill as their place of emergence, the so-called *nani waiya* in Winston County, at the headwaters of the Pearl River. For tribes of eastern Bolivia, the spot was formerly said to be a hole in the earth at the site of a rocky promontory called Mamoré, inaccessible to human climbers today.

Such lore provides the basis for an intimate and continuing connection with the land. In the view of the Choctaw, one does not abandon one's "mother"; thus the Choctaw remained in Mississippi—where their culture has continued to flourish—despite pressure to move westward to Oklahoma. The operative idea was that the people could not leave their mother, *nani waiya*.

An Iroquois view, expressed by the eighteenth-century Onondaga orator Canassatego, was recorded in the minutes of the famous treaty conference held at Lancaster, Pennsylvania, in 1744. Addressing the governor of one of the English colonies, Canassatego rebuked the English for basing their claim on a possession of merely one hundred years. "What is one hundred years in comparison of the length of time since our claim began? since we came out of this ground? For we must tell you, that long before one hundred years our ancestors came out of this very ground, and their children have remained here ever since."

The principle is codified in the traditional constitution of the Iroquois, which continues to be upheld by the native people of New York State: "The soil of the earth from one end to the other is the property of the people who inhabit it. By birthright, the Oñgwehonweh [original beings] are the owners of the soil which they own and occupy and none other may hold it. The same law has been held from the oldest times."

When the idea of the earth as nurturer is added to the principle of "birthright," a compelling moral argument develops, favoring native stewardship. Often cited in this connection is the argument of the nineteenth-century Nez Percé prophet Smohalla, who objected to the removal of his people from "the bosom of our mother." Smohalla's accusations ring out to the twentieth-century-world: "You ask me to plough the ground! Shall I take a knife and tear my mother's bosom?

. . . Shall I dig under her skin for her bones? . . . You ask me to cut grass and make hay and sell it, and be rich like white men, but how dare I cut off my mother's hair?"

Similar ideas enter into the current debate over whether the Black Hills should be returned to the Lakota. So far as non-Indians are concerned, the matter is non-negotiable. But traditionalists can find authority for their position in the words of Luther Standing Bear, who recalled that "of all our domain we loved, perhaps, the Black Hills the most." He goes on: "According to tribal legend these hills were a reclining female figure from whose breasts flowed life-giving forces, and to them the Lakota went as a child to its mother's arms."

PARABLE / The emergence

The story says that one morning long ago a lone man awoke, face to the sun, emerging from the soil. Only his head was visible, the rest of his body not yet fashioned.

The man looked about, but saw no mountains, no rivers, no forests. There was nothing but soft and quaking mud, for the earth itself was still young.

Up and up the man drew himself until he freed his body from the clinging soil. At last he stood upon the earth, but it was not solid, and his first few steps were slow and halting. But the sun shone, and always the man kept his face turned toward it. In time the rays of the sun hardened the face of the earth and strengthened the man, and he bounded and leaped about, a free and joyous creature.

From this man sprang the Lakota nation and, so far as we know, our people have been born and have died on this plain; and no people have shared it with us until the coming of the European.

So this land of the great plains is claimed by the Lakotas as their very own. We are of the soil and the soil is of us.

> —Told by Luther Standing Bear,
> Lakota (South Dakota)

Less imaginative in its phraseology but illustrating the same theme, the proclamation issued in 1983 by the Committee of Indian Peoples of Eastern Bolivia states, in part: "The forests are our dearest possession, and they presently are being destroyed by people from outside of our communities. For this reason we must demonstrate claim to them." And in defense of the land: "The land is ours in our own right, as it is the source of our livelihood and because it constitutes the most vital element of our existence."

The extent to which such claims have impressed the general public can be judged by the case of the Taos of New Mexico, who in 1970 convinced the President and the Congress of the United States to give them title to a site known as Blue Lake, together with 48,000 surrounding acres. It has been said that Blue Lake, also known as "lake of the summer pilgrimage," is a place of ancestral emergence. But the reticent Taos were never required to give a public explanation.

The people of the United States were evidently confident that the native governor of Taos, Querino Romero, spoke the truth when he vowed—after the episode had been concluded—that the lands would be "properly maintained and protected."

None of this means that native people are immune to the pressures of land development or have maintained uniformly pristine environments for their communities. It does mean that they can, and do, draw upon a reserve of traditional attitudes toward the earth, having kept what modern environmentalists would wish to instill in a largely uncomprehending public—the quality known in English as "a sense of place."

6

The Responsive Universe

Hold sacred all of the spirits.
—*Lushootseed commandment*

The larger whole, of which the earth forms merely a part, is sometimes referred to in native languages by the double term "earth sky." In Nahuatl, the language of the Aztecs, this may be written *tlalticpac ilhuicatl*, literally "earth, sky." In Quechua it reads *urin pacha janan pacha*, "world below, world above." As used in prayers, the term can be heard in such expressions as "Who made the sky and the earth?" (Nahuatl); "You said, 'Let there be earth and sky'" (Quechua); and "Earth and sky are everlasting" (Crow).

But a single word may also suffice. In Lakota the term that means either earth or the female earth spirit, *maka*, also designates the larger concept, which has been translated "world" or even "universe."

As with the separate parts of nature, the world in its entirety may be invested with personality. In the ritualistic sand paintings of the southwestern United States, earth and sky are shown side by side as mother and father (Navajo) or combined as a single person having "arms," "blood," and "soul" (Luiseño). In an old text of the Quiché Maya the world is referred to as *ah raxa laq, ah raxa tzel,* "lord green-plate, lord blue-bowl," meaning, once again, earth and sky.

Not only the entirety of space, but the intangible dimension of the universe—time—may be personified. "When I was small," recalls the Navajo traditionalist Left Handed, "I used to wonder what it meant when they said, 'a year.' . . . I always thought that the year must have arms and legs and a head"; and when "my folks" mentioned a certain month, "I thought it was something that moved or walked about." In fact, according to the ceremonialist Hasteen Klah, a well-known contemporary of Left Handed's, "each month had its own name and character"; and in the view of Sandoval, another learned Navajo contemporary, each month, in addition to its name, had a "heart" and a "headdress." For example, the fourth month (January) has ice as its "heart" and the Milky Way as its "headdress."

Among the Maya, units of time are regularly personified and evidently have been since the Classic period of more than a thousand years ago—especially the days, each of which is called "lord."

In the lore of the Guajiro the character Mensh, known also as "he who has always existed" and "the one who is forever," is time itself. Among the Tehuelche of Argentina, Time is said to be Night's lover; and in Huastec lore the female earth is moved by her male companion, K'ih, "time," a kind of wind, or movement, that has no form.

Regarded as persons, aspects of the universe may enter into a relationship with humanity that becomes even closer than the familial bonds suggested by such expressions as "mother earth" and "father sky." Some writers have used the term "harmony" to designate this highly figurative form of kinship. But a single term, useful as it may be, runs the risk of oversimplifying a complex set of ideas that varies from culture to culture. Among the recurring themes, elaborated in different ways, are the imagined ability to speak and listen at far distances, a feeling that one inhabits the larger structures in nature just as one inhabits a house, and, ultimately, the identification of one's own person with the natural world.

Listening

"Earth, help me in my prayers," asks a Potawatomi boy, seeking knowledge that will guide him through manhood. In a hunter's prayer from northeast California, the supplicant calls out, "You, rocks! You, mountains! Give me my deer." And in a prayer for the well-being of society, an Inca ritualist could say, "Pachamama [earth mother], take the Inca king, your child, in your arms."

At times, however, the spirits in question may be listening when their help has not been requested, as with the Mazatec of Mexico, who say that the subterranean little people, or owners of the earth, know everyone's name and hear all that is said on the earth's surface.

Clearly, more than the earth beneath one's feet is meant

when the northwest California ritualist announces, "All the world will hear me"; and when the Lakota singer opens the annual Sun Dance, saying, "A voice I am going to send, hear me, all over the universe [literally, "earth," *maka*, but in the larger sense]."

In North America, appeals to the great world were often made on behalf of newborns or of children receiving their names. In an old-style Ojibwa name-giving feast, the name giver is reported to have held the child and asked: "All you manidos [spirits] in the east, all you manidos in the south . . . , west . . . , north . . . , in the earth . . . , in the air, bear witness that I give this child the name of ———."

In a similar ceremony of the Wishram of Oregon, the ritualist would explain, "We want the mountains, the rivers, the creeks, the bluffs, the timber to know that this [child] is now named ———. We want to let the fishes, the birds, the winds, snow and rain, the sun, moon, and stars know."

For the Arapaho child at puberty, the sponsor prayed: "My grandfather the sun . . . , those that shine above at night, and the animals of the night . . . , the morning star . . . , animals that move on the surface, animals under ground that inhabit the water, listen, be attentive. This one standing here asks of you a name that is good."

An even fuller list of world powers was invoked by the Omaha priest, who stood at the door of the lodge where the newborn child lay, and called out: "Sun, Moon, Stars . . . , I bid you hear me. Into your midst has come a new life. . . . Winds, Clouds, Rain, Mist . . . , Hills, Valleys, Rivers, Lakes, Trees, Grasses . . . , Birds . . . , Animals . . . , Insects . . . , into your midst has come a new life."

In Arikara myth, an entire people emerging as newborns from the earth hear "the voice of Vegetation speaking to them, making the people welcome into the world of living things, offering friendship and companionship." Thus a sense of community with the world is openly expressed.

A significant result is that nature may align itself with human sentiment—especially in moments of anguish, when the large-scale elements, earth and sky, may be felt to react sympathetically. For the Inuit it is reported that straw, or hay, may not be harvested when there has been a funeral, because the earth would suffer keenly if something of itself should be killed so shortly after a person's death. In a myth of the Fox of the midwestern United States, it is said that a man mourning the death of his brother "gulped, sobbing, and the earth moved and quaked"; and in a ritual lamentation, also from the Fox, the affecting words read: "The sky will weep, the sky, at the end of the earth, the sky will weep."

The greater home

Just as the world magnifies human emotions, it may also represent the purely physical realm of human living space— likewise on the grandest of scales. As such, the locale may be earth, sky, or a combination of the two.

In earthly terms, the Iroquois of New York used to speak of their entire territory, stretching a distance of some three hundred miles, as the great "longhouse" of the confederated nations. At Niagara Falls, the Seneca were keepers of the western "door," while the Mohawks were keepers of the eastern "door" on the Hudson River. Within this "house" were figurative partitions; also separate "fires," each of which represented one of the five original nations—Seneca, Cayuga, Onondaga, Oneida, and Mohawk.

In British Columbia, the Bella Coola looked to the sky for the "house" that resembled the ordinary dwelling on earth yet was boundless in size. Called "the place of myths" or "where everything began," it was conceived as the home of the sun, or, more precisely, the home of the spirit within the sun.

A similar sun's house plays a role in Navajo lore, where it is said to consist of four great rooms, decorated with rain, vegetation, animal life, and precious minerals.

In the great house imagined by the Bribri of Costa Rica, sky and earth are held together as a unit. Here the earth's surface represents the circular floor plan of the traditional Bribri residence, and the sky is the conical, thatched roof. It was the Creator, Sibú, who gave the world its houselike shape in the beginning. In the words of a Bribri narrator: "After he had made the floor, then he put on the sky for a roof, just like our own house, and that's how he made the [great] house."

For the Guaymí of Panama the great house is similar, except that the ground floor corresponds to the base of the underworld, and the earth's surface represents the floor of the loft.

In Costa Rica, people say that the stars are the knots that tie the roof of the great house of Sibú, while the tips of the roof poles, just above the apex, represent the star cluster known in English as the Seven Sisters, or Pleiades.

Among the North American Pawnee, the world's rim, or horizon, was considered to be the circular "wall" of the great house, with the sky as its "roof," representing the traditional domed earth-lodge. And since anyone who inhabited an ordinary house was said to be "inside," the universe as a whole was called the "inside land."

Insofar as it projects, rather than integrates, the human condition, one might be tempted to regard such lore as merely self-centered. But any generalization ought also to take into account the opposite idea—which, instead of placing humanity at the center of the world, miniaturizes the universe, and thus, in a sense, brings it home.

The smaller world

In exact opposition to the Iroquois scheme, which expanded the longhouse to the ends of the Iroquois realm, the Inca of Peru condensed their empire, figuratively speaking, to fit within a circumscribed seat of government. Since the territory of the Inca was divided into four quarters, so was the capital city, Cuzco, laid out in four wards; and within each ward lived representatives of its many provinces, house by house in geographical order. "The result of this arrangement," writes an early chronicler, "was that anyone who contemplated the wards and the dwellings of the numerous and varied tribes who had settled in them beheld the whole empire at once, as if in a looking glass or [on a map]." Since the actual empire reached to the limits of the known world, the capital could be described as a model of the earth's surface.

In humbler fashion, but equally grand in its design, the North American Pawnee encampment mirrored the sky, with lodges set up in three divisions, representing the Milky

Way, the eastern heavens, and the western heavens.

In many cultures the meeting house, or even the family residence, stands as a replica of the greater world. This was true for the Pawnee, who regarded the dome-roofed lodge as a smaller universe. It is also true for the present-day Kogi, who set up four hearths to mark the sunrise and sunset points for the longest and shortest days of the year; and for the Desana, who speak of the fence that surrounds the circular house as "the limit of the universe."

For the Panare, a Cariban tribe of western Venezuela, the center post of the house represents the center of the "world"; and the same is true for the Yekuana of eastern Venezuela—another of the Cariban groups—who, in addition, recognize various features of the sky world within the thatch and timbers of the conical roof, including the Milky Way and the spirit homes of animal masters.

Perhaps the most eloquent commentary on the Native American dwelling has come from priests and elders of the Great Plains, a number of whom have articulated their philosophy for the benefit of outsiders. Among these is the Arikara priest Four Rings, who offered the following explanation to the ethnologist Melvin Gilmore in 1924: "The structure of the dwelling house . . . should be symbolic of the structure of the world. As the world extends about us like a great circle, so should the house be circular in ground plan. The circle of the world is a unit, but it consists of four quarters. In the structure of the world the sky appears like a dome above. So in the structure of the house there shall be four main posts . . . dedicated, one to each of the four quarters."

Readers of John Neihardt's *Black Elk Speaks* will recall the

KINSHIP · · 113

familiar testimony of another of the Plains holy men, Nicholas Black Elk, who in 1931 criticized the square reservation houses provided by the wasichu (or "fat takers," i.e., Europeans in America). The original version of Black Elk's remarks, preserved not in *Black Elk Speaks* but in Neihardt's notes published in 1984, reads, in part: "You see today that this house is not in a circle. It is a square. It is not the way we should live. . . . The power won't work in anything but circles. Everything is now too square. . . . You take the bird's eggs and put them in a square nest and the mother bird just won't stay there. We Indians are relative-like to the birds. Everything tries to be round—the world is round. We Indians have been put here [to be] like the wilds and we cooperate with them."

To summarize, it may be said that the human species, ideally, lives in relation to the shape of the universe.

World essence

But humanity also bears a relationship to the world's composition. Whatever basic stuff the world is made of, humans and other creatures must share it. Heat, light, wind, water, mist, and soul are among the qualities mentioned in the various talks that have been recorded. Sometimes, however, the term in question seems best left untranslated.

Among the Cahuilla the word *'iva'a* designates a substance—or, better, force—responsible for the creation of all matter. Humans, we are told, stand at the midpoint of the *'iva'a* scale, having more of the essential substance than some creatures but less than others. The seemingly contradictory notion that not all things, at least not today, possess *'iva'a* is perhaps explained by the belief that *'iva'a* was very intense at the beginning of the world and has gradually diminished with time.

No time constraint, apparently, limits the Hopi concept of *navala*, which refers to a kind of liquid essence. *Navala* is possessed by each person; and, in the form of rain, it becomes tangible in the surrounding world.

More pervasive is the *nek purpalet*, "world of spirit," spoken of by the Panamanian Kuna. The invisible *nek purpalet* provides each person or object with vital force and at the same time extends outward in all directions. A similar idea has been reported for the Luiseño of southern California, neighbors of the Cahuilla. Formerly the Luiseño spoke of the encircling night sky as "our spirit," or "soul."

Both pervasive and tangible is the *nilch'i*, the so-called holy wind, of the Navajo. *Nilch'i* refers either to the atmosphere in its entirety or to air in motion. In the words of one Navajo philosopher, "Wind was creation's first food, and put motion and change into nature, giving life to everything, even to the mountains and water."

The idea of a supernatural wind, or breath, is not confined to the Navajo. In the language of the Campa the word *tasórentsi*, a noun derived from the verb "to blow," is used to identify a class of spirits that have the power to transform one thing into another, typically with a puff of breath. As observed by the anthropologist Gerald Weiss, a longtime student of the Campa and of other cultures of eastern Peru, "The universe as it exists today is partly the result of many such transformations."

A three-panel design conveying the idea of the life-force that animates
the universe; pencil drawing by Murú, Southern Barasana,
Vaupés Territory, Colombia, 1968. The hourglass figures in all
three panels represent maleness; the three "flowers" or
"suns" of the central panel represent femaleness.

Similarly, among the Chimane of Bolivia, it is said that the transformer, Duhvít, changed the ancient people into animals by blowing his breath. He simply walked up to them and exhaled, and they became what they are today.

According to testimony volunteered by holy men of the Lakota, breath, as a medium of exchange, may promote a sense of universal kinship. In the words of the twentieth-century elder Lame Deer, "It suddenly came to me that if I mingled my breath with the sacred smoke [from the ceremonial pipe], I would also mingle it with the breath of every living creature on this earth." As expressed nearly a century earlier by the prolific Lakota philosopher George Sword, "The spirit that is in the smoke goes with it into the mouth and body and then it comes out and goes upward. When this spirit is in the body, it soothes the spirit of the smoker. When it goes upward, it soothes the god. So the god and the spirit are as friends."

Such statements complement—though they are not quite the same as—the Lakota idea of the great spirit as a unifying force flowing through all creatures and material objects. "There was no such thing as emptiness in the world," recalls yet another well-known Lakota, Standing Bear. "Even in the sky there were no vacant places. Everywhere there was life, visible and invisible."

The concept of omnipresence is echoed in a culture far removed from the Lakota: the Sáliva of Venezuela, who once spoke of an invisible deity called Puru, the originator of all natural forces and all matter. The ethnographer who inquired into this lore in the early 1930s reported, "When I asked them the reason for their not [ever making representations of Puru,] they said, 'Nobody has ever seen Puru, he is like this,' and they pointed out the invisible air."

A similar deity, from a culture much given to picturing gods, is the Ipalnemohua of the Aztecs, never represented either in painting or in statuary. The name means, literally, "he, she, or it by means of whom one lives," or, freely, Life Giver. According to one of the old texts, Life Giver's "home" was "everywhere."

PARABLE / Chiminigagua

They have an account of how the world was created, and they explain it by saying that when there was darkness, *by which they mean nothing existed*, light was kept in a large object far away, *and to give this a name they called it* Chiminigagua, and from there it flowed out.

So this object, or Chiminigagua, in which the light was kept, started to dawn, showing the light inside it, *for by this they mean what we call God*, and from this first light it began to create things.

The first were two large black birds, which it sent out from the place where they had come to life, telling them to spread wind, or breath, from their beaks. This wind was all bright and shining, and when they had done what they had been told, the world was lit the way it is now.

—Fray Pedro Simón, paraphrasing a
lost Muisca text (Colombia)

Although allusions to the concept of world essence can be detected in lore from Aztec Mexico, from twentieth-century Venezuela, from Arizona, and from elsewhere in the hemisphere, the most important evidence comes from the Great Plains and, to a lesser extent, California. The idea of interrelatedness, especially, is a hallmark of Plains thinking.

Anyone acquainted with the native literature of the Plains will have encountered dramatic, yet typical, statements on world kinship from such cultures as the Lakota ("I am related to all spirits the world over"), the Pawnee ("You, birds in the air, and you, animals upon the earth, we are related"), and the Omaha ("All life was considered as one and related").

This is a harmonious kinship, one that puts the human being in tune with the whole environment. It may even be expressed as a form of merging, or integration, as suggested by the lore of domestic architecture and settlement planning, already mentioned—or by the organically minded dead man in the old Pawnee story, who comes back as a ghost, saying, "I am in everything; in the grass, the water."

Or it may result from an act of concentration, in which the universe is felt to be listening, even sympathizing. Examples from Plains and other cultures have been given above. One of the best known may be quoted here, in conclusion—the prayer to the seven spirits recorded by Alfred Kroeber for the Yokuts of California. As understood by Kroeber, the words were recited "not so much for the achievement of any specific wish as for the general fulfillment of good fortune," rising above "any petty concrete desire": "Do you see me! See me, Tüüshiut! See me, Pamashiut! See me, Yuhahait! See me, Echepat! See me, Pitsuriut! See me, Tsukit! See me,

Ukat! Do you all help me! My words are tied in one with the great mountains, with the great rocks, with the great trees, in one with my body and my heart. Do you all help me with supernatural power. And you, day, and you, night! All of you see me, one with this world!"

PART THREE

RESTRAINT

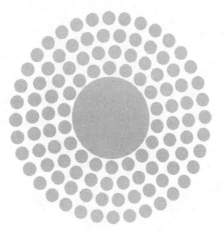

7

The Consumer as Ritualist

Fulfill good customs and
reap the benefits.
—*Aymara maxim*

Matter-of-fact, plainly stated conservation measures are known to most, if not all, cultures. But if the plea to take only what is necessary has an inarguable logic about it, it may also seem wearisome and too familiar.

For all but the most dedicated, restraint for restraint's sake makes an easily broken rule. More effective than the bald injunction to save for tomorrow is the pressure exerted by inner forms of plants and animals and by other supernaturals, who demand a morality higher than greed and hold out the necessary threats to enforce it.

Let it be clear that morality is not absent, even when veiled by ritual or wrapped in myth. The Tlingit hunter who prays, "Spirit Above Me, I need to eat the animal I kill," is conscious of a transgression, asking that he be excused because, as he explains, "I don't kill it for nothing." Similar thoughts are revealed by the Kwakiutl berry picker, who addresses the plant as her "means of mercy," asking for food "that I may eat, that I may keep alive."

There may even be a hint that humans would have been unwilling to exploit other species had they not been instructed to do so by higher powers. With reference to the legendary heroes Sweet Medicine and Erect Horns, the Cheyenne ritualist asks permission of the forest and all vegetation before cutting a tree, saying, "Today we are here to do what those two men of ancient times *told us we ought to do*" (italics added).

And even if one's failure to conserve is unavoidable, there may be a sense of regret. Noting the wasteful manner of carving a canoe, a Yekuana traditionalist has explained that in the ancient days, if the people had a twelve-meter tree, "they cut ten canoes from it! They didn't throw the inside away like we do. They didn't waste it. First they carved one canoe, very carefully. Then another and another and another, until they got down to the biggest one at the bottom. [Nowadays] we just throw all that away and make one canoe."

For such an infringement, there may be a remedy. In the words of another Yekuana, "To make *conucos* [i.e., gardens] we have to cut down, to kill many trees, and the invisible masters of these can turn against us and cause illness, bad luck, and even death. Through the Garden Ceremony we admit our guilt to the invisible masters of these trees and ask them for their favor. The song cleanses us of that guilt."

Worst of all, surely, are the cases of exploitation merely for cash. In a story obtained from the Paiute of Nevada the shame is forcefully expressed: a trapper, it seems, found his traps completely empty one day, except for one which held a large coyote; "when the trapper was about to shoot," goes the story, "the coyote told him to stop, and said in Paiute: 'My friend, we as people have found it necessary to warn you against trapping us, taking from our bodies our skins, and selling them for your happiness.' "

But even if the techniques of restraint are built on a moral foundation—which includes guilt and a genuine concern for other species—these techniques must be carefully crafted if species and their habitats are to be protected from the thoughtless user year in and year out.

Increasing the cost

At its simplest, restraint on the part of the harvester means giving back or taking a little less. There need be nothing mysterious about such an act, and the reason for it can be openly acknowledged. When the Menominee of Wisconsin gather wild rice, they make sure that some of the rice falls into the water so that there will be a crop the next year. Nothing could be more obvious.

But in other instances there is more to reseeding than meets the eye. In the old days, when a Seneca had located medicinal herbs that he wished to gather, he would first build a small fire. After the flames had died, he would throw a pinch of tobacco on the embers, praying, "I will not destroy you but plant your seeds that you may come again and yield fourfold more." Then he would dig the plants, break off the seed stalks, and drop the pods into the hole, gently covering them with leaf mold, saying, "The plant will come again, and I have not destroyed life but helped increase it."

Whether the Seneca gatherer had actually increased the plant stock would depend upon a number of factors, including the necessary condition that the seed be ripe. What can be said with certainty is that the man had increased the cost to himself. Moreover, one would not gather herbs indiscriminately if a time-consuming ritual such as this were required in every case.

Consider the corresponding Cherokee procedure reported a hundred years ago by the ethnologist James Mooney: "In searching for his medicinal plants the shaman goes provided with a number of white and red beads, and approaches the plant from a certain direction, going round it from right to left one or four times, reciting certain prayers the while. He then pulls up the plant by the roots and drops one of the beads into the hole and covers it up with the loose earth."

Here, obviously, there can be no question of actual reseeding. But once again the cost to the gatherer is not inconsiderable.

In fact, reseeding, even as an empty gesture, is not usually a part of herb collecting. The business of gathering plants is generally laborious, however, as reports can show from cultures as widespread as the Delaware (prayers before gathering), Hopi (sprinkled cornmeal with prayers to the sun), or Ojibwa (sunwise procession around the plants).

Certain gestures may strike the uninitiated as especially meaningless— as when the Koyukon returns wood chips to the forest or the Munsee father orders his children to return a pair of antlers to the woods. Such efforts, evidently, are echoes of the bones ritual by which the hunter ensures the immortality of game animals. But no such rationale is given for the return of the chips. And in the case of the antlers, the deer has not even been harvested; it has merely shed. Yet here once again there is human cost.

On the whole, bones rituals are in line with native theory on the preservation of parts that are thought to regenerate. But even so, the labor may exceed mere saving or depositing. It may include keeping the eyes as well as the bones (Naskapi); the eyes may need rubbing with charcoal (Ojibwa); the bones may have to be sprinkled with pollen (Navajo) or covered with a wedding robe (Hopi).

To the outsider, the ritual may be not only inexplicable, but fascinating in its detail—as in the case of the Maidu rabbit hunters of central California, whose technique has been reported by the ethnographer Paul-Louis Faye. "The head hunter and the other hunters planned the hunt," Faye writes. But "it was necessary for them to speak in a whisper lest the rabbits hear them. When the first rabbit was killed, the head hunter picked it up, and pressing it tenderly against his chest, petted it and spoke soft words to it. All [the other] hunters sighed while he was going through this performance."

Conciliatory rituals, often outwardly sentimental, are not uncommon in far-western North America. Their avowed purpose (though the explanation was omitted from the Maidu account) is to ensure that the inner form, or spirit, of the game animal will go back to the others of its kind with a good report on the hunter who has been so considerate. Thus the animal's fellows will want to enter the same snares.

For the Yurok, Alfred Kroeber has described an even more luxuriant ritual of the same type. As the lore is recorded, a young deer on the advice of older deer will "try" a particular hunter, lie down in his snare, and be taken to his house. There the deer should be consumed respectfully. None of the flesh should be dropped on the floor; after the meal, every scrap must be stored away carefully. The "hands" of the deer must be ritually washed in a basin and rubbed with fragrant, chewed pepperwood leaves. After two days the deer returns to its home. "How did you like that [man's] house?" its elders ask. "He is good. He acts rightly. Smell my hand." The others sniff it. They like the fragrance and go frequently into that man's snares. But not more frequently—one must conclude—than the hunter and his family have time to spend on so lavish a reception.

Economizing

In addition to rationing the harvest by increasing its cost, there is the more direct approach of merely taking less, even when more seems readily available. Often the question of proper restraint can be answered by a homily or a rule of thumb. Succinctly stated, among the old-time Cahuilla, no stand or colony of a particular plant could be eradicated.

More ingeniously, among the Cherokee it used to be said that an herb gatherer had to pass up the first three plants he found. Then, when he came to a fourth, he could pluck it and go back for the other three. Evidently this prevented the harvesting of three or fewer specimens.

Slightly different is the Delaware injunction never to take

the first specimen you see. In the Delaware case the plant has to be not only spared but given a small offering of tobacco.

Nearly the same as the Delaware practice is the ritual observed by the Navajo herbalist when collecting "deer-plant medicine" (*Conioselinum scopulorum*, a white-flowered member of the parsnip family). The collector approaches a large specimen and prays, "I have come for you, to take you from the ground. . . ." But then, in a seeming contradiction, he digs up another, smaller specimen, for which the explanation is that "you never take the plant to whom you pray."

In neither the Navajo nor the Delaware ritual is there an open acknowledgment of the theory of species masters—by which harvestable plants and creatures are thought to be under the control of leaders. The idea comes out, however, in testimony recorded by the Pawnee author James Murie, who details the procedure for cutting small trees to make a ceremonial enclosure. First the ritualist approaches a particular tree and makes a smoke offering. "The tree selected must be one of the largest and finest of its kind," writes Murie. "It is not to be cut but entreated, as if it were the grand chief of the forest, the idea being that by this ceremony permission is secured to cut the necessary small trees."

The practice of honoring—and sparing—at least one specimen may be complemented by the requirement that only a portion of the exploited plant be taken. Again, this may be formulated as a simple, workaday rule: don't strip it bare (Cahuilla); or, more specifically, if you need the root, take a piece of it and leave the stem undisturbed (Ojibwa).

But with ritual comes deeper motivation. Reflecting a Delaware belief, Nora Thompson Dean used to say that she preferred to strip bark from the east side of the plant, because that's where the morning sun had struck.

For the Cherokee, likewise, James Mooney could report that the bark was always taken from the east side of the tree, "and when the root or branch is used it must also be one which runs out toward the east, the reason given being that these have imbibed more medical potency from the rays of the sun."

Animals as well as plants should be harvested with care; and here, too, the practice may be accepted as a conservation measure pure and simple. "So as to make more sheep for the next hunting" is the reason given by a Hopi for the custom of releasing one male and one female whenever mountain sheep were surrounded by a harvesting party.

Restraint in harvesting animals is sometimes linked to strictly mundane concerns, as in the report that Cree men enjoy prestige and even political power by dint of careful hunting that avoids excess; or in a very old report which states that the Iroquois once made war against the Illinois and the Miami because these tribes were exterminating beavers, females as well as males.

But here again, where female animals are accorded respect, there may be a hint of ritual—as when the Shuar hunter takes only the large males from a herd of peccaries, apologizing to the shoats and the females with words of consolation.

Among the Navajo the practice of sparing females is reinforced by myth: a spirit fawn, it seems, appeared to a hunter of the ancient time and announced, "If you are walking on an unused road and see the tracks of a doe, or if a doe catches up with you from behind, that is I. And knowing this you will not bother me."

As might be expected, the Bear Boy myth of northeastern North America has also been used to discourage the killing of females. In a Maliseet version, the narrator tells how the adoptive bear mother carefully protected the human boy through the winter; then, in the spring, "when the hunters came up, the boy begged them not to kill his 'mother,' and they spared her."

Fallowing

Rather than sparing the individual, certain measures work to spare the habitat, at least temporarily. In its most elementary form, the technique of fallowing—if an agricultural term may be extended to include rest periods for game lands—amounts simply to hunting out a territory and moving on to another. Thus the land left behind has a chance to replenish itself.

More systematic is a procedure once known to the Cahuilla, who occasionally discontinued the gathering of fruit for one year to "let the ground have more seeds for plants another year."

When fitted into a schedule, the method qualifies as rotation. As is well known, the Cree and other eastern Algonkian groups work only a section of their hunting lands in a given year, permitting the fallowed portions to recover. According to some reports, each territory is divided into quarters, with hunting and trapping confined to just one quarter per year.

As with other techniques, fallowing may be enforced by supernatural powers. In the case of the Ojibwa of Parry Island, a community of southeastern Ontario, the people used to change their hunting grounds not for the sake of conservation itself but because the "shadows" of the animals had

Woman Fishing in Spring,
print by Leah Amituk, after a drawing
by Akenesie Novalinga, Inuit of
Povungnituk, Quebec, 1979.

grown wary and were keeping the game away.

Still more indirect is the procedure that fallows the game lands of the Ka'apor of eastern Brazil. It works in this manner: menstruating women and women who have recently given birth must keep to a ritualistic diet of yellow-footed tortoise meat; therefore the men, who must constantly bring home tortoises, hunt in wider and wider circles as the species is depleted. Since the men are hunting other, larger game as well, the entire range is subjected to a system of rotation, allowing the nearer circuits to be replenished for future use.

Time, rather than space, may dictate a fallowing regime; and, again, ritual plays a role. For example, among Tucanoan tribes, seasonal hunts are prompted by the stars. Each game animal is identified with a particular constellation and may not be hunted until its own star group has risen above the horizon.

In some instances the private ownership of land is a key to fallowing, with conservation measures enacted not for the living but out of respect for either the dead or the unborn. In the old days, among the Shasta of the Oregon-California border, if a man died who had owned hunting lands, his parents kept all other hunters away for one year. The avowed reason was that it would hurt the family to see another man in their son's place. In the case of fishing grounds the respite was two years. In British Columbia, among the Kwakiutl, women used to manage their privately held clover-root grounds, taking care never to deplete the crop. No one else could touch such grounds, and to sell them or give them away was forbidden, because to do so would be to rob unborn descendants.

Still another fallowing technique is to randomize the harvest, that is, to pick hunting or gathering grounds at random, so as not to overuse any single region. Tucanoan shamans, who plan tribal hunts, are reported to do this consciously whenever they believe a particular species is endangered.

In certain other cultures, phenomena of nature appear to dictate random protection. An unusual example is on record for the Maidu, who are said to have avoided hunting and gathering for an entire season in any region where a shooting star had apparently struck the earth.

Positive, rather than negative, advice proceeded from the phenomenon known to the Canadian Montagnais and Naskapi as *tceka'ceko pi'cema*, "sun illumination," meaning spots of sunlight cast on the earth through a canopy of clouds. The spots, supposedly, were the areas where the hunter would find game at that particular time.

The Naskapi, like other northern peoples, used another technique that has been linked to randomization, at least by some outside observers. Known to ethnologists as scapulimancy, this method involves the use of an animal's scapula, or shoulder bone, which develops lines and spots when heated over a fire. The broad surface of the bone is then read as a map, with the disfigurements showing areas where game should be sought.

As with similar procedures, it cannot be proved by outsiders that scapulimancy serves a conservation purpose. The ritual is never described by native people as a saving technique, and since the rules for its use are not fixed, there can be no hard evidence that the tool is a true randomizer. Although the value of ecological rituals lies in their mysteriousness—since the hidden motive then remains beyond the reach of argument—we may conclude that here we have plumbed the depths of mystery, where value itself, presumably operative at some level, becomes elusive.

Punishment for waste

With the help of ritual, commonsense restraints may be practiced willingly. Yet threats are sometimes necessary, whether actually stated or merely implied.

The simple pressures of human society are often cited as a deterrent, as in the case of the Hopi man remembering from his boyhood that he and his playmates practiced shooting at birds and small animals. "But," he recalls, "we were told never to kill any creature that we did not intend to eat."

Parental displeasure, as a deterrent, is strongly implied in the words of a Lushootseed man, who recollects, "I shall never forget [my father's] disappointment when once he caught me gaffing for fish 'just for the fun of it.' . . . 'My son,' he said, '. . . you must respect them. You must not kill them just for the fun of it.'"

Less gentle is the scolding described by Nora Thompson Dean, remembering her Delaware childhood and, in particular, the time her young brother killed a crane for sport: "It fell to the ground like a huge pillow. My mother was in the house and she ran out and she said, 'Oh, you should not have shot this bird.' She said, 'Now then, you are going to have to pick this bird, and cook it, and eat it. We don't kill things for nothing.' So he did. He had a thundercloud look on his face." (Though not inedible, the dark, tough flesh of the crane was hardly a delicacy for the old-time Delaware.)

Harsher punishments than this are reported from much

larger societies, as from the Inca, who forbade the killing of guanays and other seabirds, on pain of death. The Maya of Guatemala, likewise, invoked the death penalty against those who killed the rare quetzal. In both cases the birds were protected for economic reasons, the guanay for its mounds of excrement (valued as fertilizer) and the quetzal for its brilliant green plumes (used as money).

Supernatural, rather than civil, punishments are typical of smaller societies, as with the Parry Island Ojibwa, who caught only what was needed when ice-fishing, lest a large snake appear in the fishing hole. Another of the admonitions, or taboos, was that children must not string berries; otherwise birds would quickly eat the berries from all the bushes. Still another, also from Parry Island, threatened that if a man killed a porcupine and threw away the meat, the animal's "shadow" would harm his children.

Indeed, animal souls and animal masters are often the enforcers of wise use. The annoying moose fly, for instance, is said by the Naskapi to be the master of fish; it hovers over the catch to see whether any are wasted. For the Guajiro, the master is the female deity Pulowi-of-the-sea, who simply destroys the overeager fisherman.

Amusing, yet cautionary, parables recorded for the Shuar remind the hunter that he runs the risk of being kidnapped if he tries to take more than is absolutely necessary for human survival. In one of the stories a man who killed too many *wáshi* (spider monkeys) was transformed by these animals into one of themselves—just so they could tell him what a great hunter he was. In another, the man who overhunted was kidnapped, and he himself was made master of the monkeys as insurance against their extinction. This was logical because a species remains viable so long as its master lives, and since human souls are immortal the group's survival could then be assured. (The theory, presumably, is not content with the concept that animal souls, too, are immortal—perhaps because an animal's soul can be extinguished, according to Shuar belief, if its brains should be eaten.)

PARABLE / The man who became monkey master

[There was a hunter who] kept on hunting by himself. The monkey master, who had given him tobacco, had said, "Watch. When you have caught many, you must catch no more." But he paid no heed.

When he came to more monkeys, he said to himself, "It doesn't matter what I was told, because they can't take revenge on me now." Just one little monkey was left alive, and it reproached him, reminding him that its father had been the one who had taught him to hunt.

Troops and more troops of monkeys came into view. He killed them, and when his darts were gone he killed with his hands. Then they made him the master of their troop.

Since it is said that monkeys become extinct when the troop master is killed, they placed the man's blowgun so that he could walk on it from tree to tree, and when it broke, he fell and was killed; then they asked him to be troop leader. "How can I be leader if I am dead?" he asked.

But it was his spirit that was leader. Therefore the Shuar say monkeys do not become extinct, because their master cannot be killed—for the master is not a monkey but the spirit of a Shuar.

—Anonymous, Shuar (Ecuador)

Punishments are most commonly meted out for the excessive harvesting of food animals and food plants. But species that seem to have little or no economic importance may also be protected, at least by the threat of shame. In a case drawn from life, not myth, two Huastec Maya boys are reported to have heard the sound of weeping while out shooting doves for sport. Alarmed, they ran home to their mother, who told them that this was the earth crying because her creatures were being killed.

Similarly, an Ojibwa—at least formerly—could suggest that one ought not to step on flowers while out walking, "for flowers are like little children." In another of the old-time Ojibwa admonitions, the killing of crickets was warned against, with the prediction that a cricket "messenger" would inform its fellows, who would thereafter descend as a group and eat everything.

Somewhat harsher is the fate of the man in the Lacandon Maya story who burns ants and destroys their nest. His just punishment is meted out by the ant master, who sends wasps to sting him.

In the words of the Arikara priest Four Rings, counseling

respect for even "worms and other humble forms of animal life dwelling in and under the ground": "We are taught to consider and to remember that the most lowly creatures have their proper place and work, and the world would not be perfect without them."

· · 8 · ·

The Value of Wilderness

No one's home is earth.
—Aztec warrior's proverb

Only the great earth
lives forever.
—Kiowa warrior's proverb

The practice of permitting habitats to replenish themselves
after a period of use has a long-term counterpart in the recog-
nition of wild, or natural, areas. If lands are kept permanently
off limits, they become more than mere recovery zones.
They may qualify as sanctuaries.

In modern contexts the methods used by native people to
protect land in this manner suggest little that can be linked to
traditional theory. A thousand acres, for instance, were set
aside in 1991 by the Chippewa of Lac du Flambeau in northern Wisconsin. The area in question, at the edge of the
Chippewa reservation, is to be kept by the tribe as a wildlife
preserve in cooperation with the international group known
as The Nature Conservancy. Wetlands are among the in-

cluded habitats; among the species to be protected are beaver, bald eagle, osprey, and great blue heron.

This seems quite new, and in certain ways it is. Yet the idea of establishing sanctuaries echoes a reality that has a long record in the Americas. Sanctuaries themselves have always existed; and the very idea of wilderness is by no means alien to native thought.

Among the Iroquois, at an early date, the "cleared space" was contrasted with the "wilderness" of "thorny ways" and "falling trees," and the threshold was spoken of as the "wood's edge." For the Tarahumara, even today, the wilds (*kamiche*) are to be distinguised from the cultivated lands (*wasachi*); and in former days, among the Maya of Yucatán, the "trees" and "rocks" of the wilderness were contrasted with the "well" and "grotto" of civilization, while Aztecs spoke of the "water" and "hill," meaning the human community, as distinct from the "place of gorges" and "the place of rocks."

Nevertheless, the historians Richard White and William Cronon make a valid point when they argue that "the very word wilderness in the sense of a natural landscape unaffected by human use has little meaning for most of aboriginal North America. To assert that Indians lived on pristine 'virgin land' not only ignores the human influences . . . but also 'naturalizes' Indians in a way that denies both their histories and their cultures."

The same protest is lodged by the native writer Standing Bear, whose contribution to this theme has been reprinted again and again by non-native writers on nature topics: "Only to the white man was nature a wilderness and only to him was the land 'infested' with 'wild' animals and 'savage' people. To us it was tame. Earth was bountiful and we were surrounded with the blessings of the Great Mystery."

To reconcile the data, which do indeed seem contradictory, it helps to draw a distinction between the perception of wilderness, on the one hand, and, on the other, the use of the earth as a natural garden. In line with the former notion, sanctuaries were—and are—often created, usually for ritualistic reasons or in response to the exigencies of war. In the latter case, the earth was subtly managed in ways that continued to fool outside observers (even through the middle of the twentieth century) into thinking they were contemplating "virgin" wilderness.

Purity and power

Whether wilderness exists in nature or only in the mind, the *idea* of wilderness is a romantic one for non-Native Americans, as it may be for Native Americans as well. Often it is associated with getting away from the home fire and into a more rarefied realm.

Cree hunters, when setting out on expeditions, think of themselves as leaving the unclean settlement and entering the pure, spiritual domain of the forest. The Naskapi, similarly, avoid the meat of supposedly impure domestic animals, preferring the clean *notcimí:umi:tacím*, or "forest food." In Yucatán, Maya ritualists shun the village well when preparing for the Rain Ceremony, obtaining "virgin water" from a natural well deep in the woods. And in the words of the Yaqui poet Refugio Savala, "men of wisdom" reject sin and "follow *seya aniya* [literally, flower world, i.e., wilderness]," which Savala associates with "godliness."

For the Yaqui, whose Mexican homeland has lately been extended into Arizona, the concept of *seya aniya*, also referred to as *huya aniya*, "forest world," has not only spiritual but political overtones. Contrasted with *pweplum* (from the Spanish word *pueblo*, meaning the human community), the *huya* is the realm of the unseen ancestors who still preserve, uninfluenced by Christianity, the old Yaqui "religion of the woods."

In Yaqui thought the power of the "woods" is a source of continuity and strength for the Yaqui people in a changing world. Presumably the idea is recent, at least in its present form, since the Yaqui did not live in villages before the arrival of Spanish missionaries in the seventeenth century. But there is no reason to doubt that the *huya*, in which the old-time Yaqui were settled in scattered homesteads, was always a place of mystery.

Indeed, the mysteriousness of the wilderness—even the terror of it—is a quality deeply entrenched in native lore. In the words of an anonymous Aztec writer of the 1500s, "the forest . . . is a disturbing place, fearful, frightful. . . . There are no people, it is desolate." Likewise, the "thorny ways" and "falling trees," cited above as features of the Iroquois wilderness, were not meant as comforting images. Even in recent years, Yucatec Maya have thought of the bush as a place of dangerous, uncontrollable beings, as have the Shipibo of Peru and the Yekuana of Venezuela.

An inquiry into Iroquois attitudes in the 1950s revealed that people on the Tuscarora Reservation in western New

York continued to think in terms of forest and clearing. Cleared land was contrasted with "national land," or that part of the reservation which remained as woods and swamp—a place haunted by supernatural beings.

One result of this kind of thinking is that wild or remote areas may be placed off limits. Careful distinctions are observed, and evidently the protected zones are the ones for which the best case can be made for unusual power.

In the mountain country of the Colombian Kogi the highest elevations are held sacred, with alpine lakes shielded even from human stares. According to a native explanation, "This is the Land of the Mother; the lagoons are the openings of her body. This is why we should not look at them."

For the old-time Penobscot, the summit of Mount Katahdin in northern Maine was shunned, because mountain spirits, capable of inflicting harm, were said to live there. (Today the place is protected in a different way, as part of Baxter State Park.)

In the territory of the Shasta, dangerous mountain spirits called *axaíki* were spoken of as a cause of disease. Wherever possible, trails avoided places where *axaíki* lived. To the same effect, certain caves in the hill country of central Honduras were said by the Jicaque to be the home of the important animal master Tsëncley Jamon; humans were not to come near under the threat of death.

In south central California, in the territory of the Cahuilla, signposts in the form of rock pictures warned people away from sacred sites, which were thereby kept off limits. Such sites were in fact reserved by shamans for their ceremonial activities.

In Brazil, among the Tukuna and the Ka'apor, old gardens become de facto wild areas protected by human ghosts or animal spirits. The Ka'apor tend to avoid hunting and collecting in such spots, said to be "places of bones," and even bar certain trails with brush in order to prevent the ghosts from finding their way to the homes of the living. In theory at least, these former gardens are more than fallowed. They have been removed from human use, as with cemeteries generally.

P A R A B L E / The garden of the *nachií*

[A man named] *dUë'* decided one day to go to a long-uninhabited *tapera* [house site], to gather *vará* fruits. His wife wished to accompany him, but he would not let her, for he knew that there were *nachií* [shades of the dead] at that very place. Gathering the fruits, he delayed more than he intended, and as the sun was already low, he resolved to pass the night at the *tapera*. When darkness had set in, he heard a noise of many people approaching. They were the shades of the dead coming to the site where the house once stood, and suddenly *dUë'* realized that he was there once again in the house as he had been in former days. But *dUë'* escaped, taking refuge in the burrow of a giant armadillo. One of the *nachií* wished to dig him out, but when it had almost reached *dUë'*, the man rattled his quiver. His pursuer, thinking that the noise was that of a hornets' nest, fled. Another *nachií* tried to finish digging him out, but *dUë'*, with the same trick, made him scamper away, as he did all the rest, too, who dared try it. Suddenly, at dawn the house again vanished, and the shades, transformed into little animals, dispersed in all directions.

—Anonymous, Tukuna
(Brazil)

Sanctuaries may be established even where game is known to be plentiful, as along the headwaters of creeks in eastern Nicaragua, formerly said to have been guarded by a giant serpent. Similarly, an area on the north side of the Klamath River in California, reportedly rich in game, was once shunned on account of a woman-panther that was said to behead any man who trespassed there.

The reasoning is not always covert. In some cases a master spirit will control a particular zone for the stated purpose of guarding species. Such is the case with the Kuna, whose territory includes reserves where trees may not be cut for fear of offending dangerous spirits. Conservation districts are also known to the Yekuana, who must consult a shaman before cutting canes used in basketmaking. The canes, it is said, belong to masters known as *yododai*, who plant the canes and check on them regularly. Certain stands, apparently favored by the *yododai*, must remain permanently unharvested, too dangerous even to approach.

But wild areas need not always rely on nonhuman protection. The exigencies of that most human activity, war, may also serve to shelter wildlife and its habitat.

No-man's-land

The forest is a place where "one is slain by stealth, one is abused, one is brutally put to death. . . . There is calm, constant calm, continuing calm." So reads one of the definitions elicited from Aztec speakers for a dictionary project in the mid-1500s. In the case at hand, the danger specified is anything but supernatural.

As we learn from the traditional Aztec chronicles, one of the "calm" locales in question was the highland zone around the twin peaks Popocatepetl and Iztactepetl, which separated the realm of Montezuma from the hostile Huexotzincan nation to the east. On one occasion, in the year 13 Rabbit (A.D. 1518), it is recorded that a group of Huexotzincan ambassadors was about to leave the court of Montezuma. "And they were ready to go," relates the native historian, and "they counseled together, and when they had decided on it, the one called Ixtehueyo said, 'Indeed, we comrades must flee. We must go tomorrow night.' "

The account continues: "Then the ruler [Montezuma] heard about it, and he gave orders for [the Huexotzincan ambassadors] to be placed under surveillance when the time came for them to leave. Then they went off to be ambushed in Amaquemecan. Well, it was for this purpose, then, that they were being trailed, and they were assassinated there at Cuauhtechcac [near the high pass between Popocatepetl and Iztactepetl]."

The geographical term Cuauhtechcac may be freely translated "place where victims meet their death in the woods."

The extent of the Cuauhtechcac danger zone is not recorded. More specific data, however, have been obtained for

similar zones separating hostile nations in what is now the
United States. Between the Mohawk and the Mahican—also
in the 1500s—the neutral zone extended from Schoharie
Creek on the west to the Hudson River on the east, a distance
of nearly thirty miles. Although this was nominally Mahican
territory, Mahicans did not dare to maintain settlements
there, for fear of Mohawk raids.

In California, as recently as the nineteenth century, a complex network of borderlands covered the entire region, con-
fining dozens of tribal and local groups to carefully circumscribed living areas. Wars were fought over hunting grounds,
fishing rights, acorn groves, and other seed-gathering sites.
Conflicts arose even within ethnic territories, as between
Chumash villages (over seed gathering) or among Miwok
groups (over acorns). Lands close to a border could, in effect,
be off limits for both sides.

Battlefields themselves, where recognized, were necessarily
closed to other activity. In Aztec usage, one of the words
meaning "wilderness" or "wild open spaces," *ixtlahuacan*, was
also a synonym for "battlefield."

In a modern application of the presumably ancient principle, the Kuna of Panama took steps in the 1980s to set up a
nature park straddling the highway that leads from Panama
City into the Kuna reservation. During the 1970s, farmers and
cattle ranchers, seeking new lands to exploit, had already
broken through the legal boundary of the reservation. The
newly established "Kuna park," as it has come to be called,
would comprise five thousand acres at the most vulnerable
point, serving as a buffer zone to prevent further incursions.
Yet the avowed purpose of the park, much applauded by

international organizations, was to protect the rain forest.

Here among the Kuna, evidently, is an application that reverses the traditional order of priority: whereas, usually, strategic, or military, needs came first, with land preservation as an inevitable outcome, the Kuna have put preservation first, meeting strategic needs as a result.

Natural gardens

But whether to achieve a ritualistic, strategic, or frankly preservationist goal, the setting aside of untouchable areas, by itself, does not ensure a continuing relationship between humans and nature. A larger view is required.

Surveying the whole environment, one must see the "wilderness," if it may be called that, as indistinguishable from the home and the workplace. Or, to put it in another way, the workplace must extend indefinitely into the wilds. This ideal is never fully realized, and often enough it has been betrayed. Yet it serves as a guide.

The underlying concept is of the forest or the prairie as a kind of garden, stocked with useful plants, animals, and other resources, completely untended by human hands.

The idea is reinforced by lore such as that of the Yekuana *yododai*, the supernatural masters who "plant" the canebrakes. Or of the Navajo deity White Bead Woman, who keeps jars filled with seeds. With reference to the alternating prevalence and scarcity of species, a Navajo elder explains that "White Bead Woman can use only one kind of seeds during a season for the people's use. These are the seeds used for food." Furthermore, "It would cause her sorrow if the people did

A *nuchu,* or tutelary spirit, standing guard at the gate of the Kuna
Park, Comarca de San Blas, Panama, 1983. Photograph by
Patrick Breslin, Inter-American Foundation, Arlington, Virginia.
Courtesy of Mac Chapin, Cultural Survival, Arlington.

not eat the ripened seeds of plants whose seeds she planted for them."

Useful plants may be sowed not only by deities but by animals—or by their spirit forms—either in remote areas or close to home. Navajo say that medicinal herbs growing in mountain pine forests were planted by deer in the ancient time. Likewise, deer and peccaries are said by the Ka'apor to plant the brocket-deer manioc and also the wild morning glories that grow at the edges of clearings.

Among the Campa the small mammal called *oáti* (the tayra, *Galictis barbara*) is the proverbial planter. Papaya trees growing in Campa settlements are supposed to have been planted by "him."

Not just species but entire habitats can be thought of as deliberate creations, as with the grasslands of central Peru, said by the Campa to be what is left of *oáti*'s fields, from a time long ago when he cleared the forest for cultivation.

And just as nature may imitate the gardener, the gardener may imitate nature. As suggested by a study conducted in Brazil in the early 1980s, a suspiciously large proportion of trees in the "untouched" forests of the Amazon basin are useful to humans. Is this accidental? In fact, the research also shows that 11.8 percent of the forest acreage in Brazilian Amazonia, excluding wetlands, was planted by native people. Brazil nut, bamboo, and babassu palm (which yields an oil-bearing nut) are among the most important species in this category.

Moreover, the figure of 11.8 percent may underestimate the total situation, since it does not take wetlands into account and does not include the "island" forests occurring in savanna lands. Such "islands" in the territory of the Cayapó are said by one investigator to have been created by the Cayapó themselves, who—it is claimed—build up the soil before planting the trees.

One must be cautious, however, before giving humans, as opposed to nature, more credit than they deserve. In 1992 a carefully documented refutation of the "island" research, including testimony from Cayapó who entirely disavowed the concept, appeared in the pages of the journal *American Anthropologist*. The new research cast doubt on an exciting scientific "finding" that had been widely heralded as showing how Amazonia could be reforested and thereby saved for the good of the world.

The Amazonian "island" research remains in doubt. But uncontested, if more modest, investigations in North America suggest that stands of plum trees in New York, chestnut (formerly) in Ontario, and black walnut in California should indeed be attributed to the influence of native people.

Information of this sort is often less appreciated than it ought to be. And yet it is not entirely new in the public record. Early English reports from Virginia mention stands of mulberry trees and connect these to human activity in and around native village sites. Likewise, the seventeenth-century settler Daniel Denton observed Indian-created grasslands in New Jersey, which served "no other end except to maintain the elks and deer, who never devour a hundredth part of it, then to be burnt every spring to make way for new."

If the human activity is unnoticed, this is because it blends with the natural landscape, which may be referred to—as it is by some researchers—as an "agroecosystem." In such a landscape, as among the Huastec of eastern Mexico and the Bora of northwest Amazonia, farms have no permanent boundaries and cannot be clearly distinguished from the forest.

Among the Lacandon of southern Mexico, who inhabit a complex agroecosystem, the whole landscape is utilized. Yet here, too, the use is unobtrusive. In a Lacandon garden of less than half an acre, as many as seventy-nine different herbs, shrubs, and trees have been counted, all intermingled. One clear benefit is that by imitating the natural diversity of the forest, the gardener suffers fewer losses from pests and diseases that attack a single species.

Even where fewer species can be cultivated, the practice of intermingling may still be carefully upheld. In traditional Iroquois gardens, bean and squash seeds were planted with the corn seed in every seventh hill, or, in some gardens, in every hill. The reason given was that the spirits of these "three sisters" were inseparable. One result was that the bean vine could use the cornstalk as its support.

Domesticated animals, it might be thought, are not part of the arrangement, since the people in question are widely known as hunters and gardeners, not herdsmen. Nevertheless, the system may include large mammals, often as a planned element of the gardens. To attract peccaries, an important source of meat, the Ka'apor plant more manioc than they can use. For the Bora the edge of the clearing serves as a hunting blind. In Costa Rica, tapirs are drawn to the gardens of the Bribri, who, according to myth, receive instructions from the animal master to plant extra cane and bananas for his charges.

One of the most unusual systems is to be found in the so-called blackwater region of northwest Amazonia, where animals—fish in this case—are the principal "crop." Human manipulation is here in abeyance, with restraint as the guiding principle.

Unlike the "whitewater" streams in most parts of the world, which deposit nutrients when they overflow their banks, the sterile, acidic blackwaters have nothing to contribute to the land. Rather, the water itself, during flood seasons, gathers in nutrients in the form of vegetable matter, insects, and insect larvae, which drop from trees. As the floods rise, twice yearly, the fish swim out into the forest, grow fat from the food, and spawn.

So poor are the soils that if the forests are replaced by conventional gardens and pastures, the food yield is less than can be had from the fish. Taking advantage of the natural system, then, the Tucanoan peoples who inhabit the region forbid the cutting of trees along the rivers and prohibit fishing in designated floodplain areas presumed to be spawning grounds. As in the case of sanctuaries elsewhere in the Americas, the floodplain sites are protected by animal masters, or fish "elders," as they are called in the blackwater region, who threaten human intruders with death.

It is said by the Tucanoans that the fish attend "dances" at the spawning grounds. On their return trip from these "dances," the fish may be caught by human fishermen without penalty so long as immature specimens are allowed to go free. The practical result is that fish provide almost all the animal protein in the Tucanoan diet.

Such relationships between human and nonhuman species do not strain the environment and can sustain life indefinitely for all parties involved. Yet they do strain the human weakness for change and for rapid, if illusory, gain. The old, fragile relationships were perhaps always endangered, even if modernization in the newest sense of the term must be blamed above other causes.

As reported by Janet Chernela, an anthropologist who has studied the Tucanoan fisheries closely, young people today are not learning the names and locations of the floodplain sanctuaries in the blackwater country. The lapse is no doubt attributable to modern schooling, which, as elsewhere in the hemisphere, takes children out of the home and undermines native values.

But the sanctuary concept, as a feature of native land use, is not doomed if it can be adapted to outlast the skepticism of the larger world. The Chippewa preserve at Lac du Flambeau, backed up by legal safeguards, stands as an example of unimpeachable land protection in the eyes of even the most unsympathetic observer, as does the Kuna project in Panama, which draws upon the support of international conservation groups. Even native religious values may be upheld in this context, as in the case of the sacred Blue Lake of the Taos, which, as we have seen, was voluntarily transferred to the Taos nation by the United States government. At the same time, the study by outsiders of whole-environment utilization, or agroecosystems, suggests patterns of multi-crop gardening and, in general, a diversified use of the land, that may enable the larger society to learn ways of making the human community more like the "wilderness."

· · 9 · ·

Control over Life

If a man fears spirits, how much
more must he fear women, who
create both men and spirits?

—*Aymara saying*

As part of the traditional Zuni house blessing, a ritualist prays that the house may be "full of people grown to maturity," that the "offspring may increase." Envisioning rain and abundant harvests, he hopes that the "house may be full of little boys and little girls," that the "children may jostle one another in the doorway."

But these words of the Zuni prayermaker in praise of human fertility are contradicted by the Zuni mythmaker, who—on a different occasion, certainly—sees a grim future world that has "overflowed with children."

"To beget children is a great virtue," proclaims a Lakota traditionalist. "A Lakota's spirit is honored in the spirit world in proportion to the number of children he has." Nevertheless, as is well attested, the old-time Lakota advocated one of the most restrictive birth-spacing policies of any Native American culture.

There is a conflict, evidently, between fertility and restraint, and in some cases, opposite emotions may come to the fore simultaneously. This is especially true when the question of twins arises. In many native cultures, twins are regarded as marvelous in the literal sense of the word. But even if wanted, twins may suffer hardships; and more often than not, folkloric methods are applied in the hope of preventing multiple births.

With regard to human fertility in general, the ultimate conflict is neither social nor personal. Rather, it is a clash between human society and the natural world. It may be expressed in human terms, as with the Yucatec woman who worries: "Now when the land gives less corn than it did, there are so many children to be fed." Or, shifting to the nonhuman point of view, the collision of interests may be revealed in a command from the masters of species.

For the Lakota it was the buffalo master who enforced the rule of chastity, threatening to punish any man who had a child by a woman outside his household. For a man of the Yekuana tribe nowadays, merely to have a wife at home with a young child is to court the displeasure of the cane master, who would harm the infant if the new father dared to gather canes for basketmaking. Human fertility, obviously, is not viewed with favor by masters of the animal and vegetal realms.

As in the cases just noted, fathers may do their share of the worrying. Yet whatever line of reasoning is pursued, the crucial issue is women's, not men's, fertility. Marriage patterns can always be rearranged to accommodate fewer men if need be. In fact, as the social theorist Marvin Harris has observed, "The biological reality is that most males are reproductively superfluous"; and numerous native traditions, too, acknowledge this point, with the result that women are burdened with both blame and honor.

Painfully instructive is a tale widely told by Jivaroan men, including those of the Aguaruna tribe, in eastern Ecuador and northern Peru. The story harks back to a mythic past when the superfluous males were dispensed with at birth and women lived only to incubate daughters.

A version recorded in 1970 by the young Aguaruna man Fernando Túyas explains that in the ancient days woman's pelvic opening was too narrow to permit childbirth. As a result, the husband had to cut out the infant with his machete, unavoidably killing the mother.

The story goes on. To compensate for the loss of adult females, all male infants were killed at birth. Among newborns, only the females were allowed to live. Husbands, evidently immortal (since this was the ancient time), raised their female children to become their own brides. The system changed, however, after a helpful mouse taught a certain woman the techniques of birthing and gnawed the woman's pelvis to make the opening wider. From then on, women were able to give birth normally—and to lead full lives. But the husband of the woman who had been instructed by Mouse was annoyed, because the new arrangement meant he would have to practice birth control (which for Aguaruna men means abstinence). Men today, concludes the narrator, accept this restraint philosophically, saying, "If Mouse had not taught that woman, we [mortal] men today would not exist. Only the women would be reproduced."

Though told from a male point of view, the myth suggests that an environmental necessity—birth control—is connected to self-fulfillment, even life itself, for the woman. And this, too, is openly acknowledged within the native community. As a Tewa mother, whose children were well spaced, once remarked to a neighbor woman who obviously was not practicing family planning methods, "You don't have good times."

The hardships of fertility

For both men and women, restrictions linked to sexuality begin with the onset of puberty. Certain cultures, especially those of Mexico and Central America, seem to have minimized this linkage, although the restrictions themselves, notably on food, were observed by adults nevertheless, always with ceremonial overtones.

Western North America and eastern South America are the regions where, traditionally at least, evidence of procreative ability goes hand in hand with food restrictions and the periodic lowering of nutrition. Puberty, menses, pregnancy, and childbirth are (or were) the times of greatest sensitivity.

The general rule is that the person under constraint must eat lower on the food chain. Game meats and fish are disallowed. Typically, among the native peoples of northwest Amazonia, diets observed by men during boys' initiation rites and by women during menstrual periods are limited to water and manioc, with ants or termites as the only animal food.

But although men are widely affected, the restrictions on women are more frequent, even proverbial. In an old Winnebago folktale, the culture hero Hare tricks his grandmother into thinking she has her period so that he can eat all their meat himself. Like trickster stories generally, this little tale probably amused the native audience. But it should not be taken to mean that the custom was lightly regarded, especially in the case of girls at their first menses, for whom isolation and complete fasting were required.

A heightened awareness of the danger is reported by Alfred Kroeber for the Sinkyone of California, among whom (according to Kroeber) the young woman "fasted, kept awake, and kept her hair over her face in order not to blast the world with her disastrously potent glance." For the Alaskan Tlingit, Frederica de Laguna has written that the woman's first menstrual seclusion ideally lasted two years; she would then "emerge from the dark cellar or room with the admired transparent complexion, but with legs almost too weak for walking."

During pregnancy and immediately following childbirth the meat restriction is often intensified to include a ban on hunting. Even the gathering of plants may be curtailed. The young Yekuana father who says he will not cut canes for fear of offending the cane master is expressing a traditional point of view. A more modern line of reasoning is expressed by the Navajo man who, though in need, refuses to hunt while his wife is pregnant because "it is inappropriate that I should take life just now when I am expecting the gift of life."

Closer to the Yekuana position is the old Hopi view that hunting during a wife's pregnancy can damage the child while still in the womb or cause blood to run from its nose at birth. At Laguna pueblo, in New Mexico, birth defects used to be attributed to the same cause.

In some cultures the pregnant woman herself is said to poison her husband's chances for hunting success. Such was the case with the ancient Huron of Ontario, where hunters with expectant wives suffered "many misfortunes," according to an old missionary account. Similarly, among the Cahuilla of more recent times, men whose wives had just delivered were kept from tracking game because of the possibility of contamination from the afterbirth.

"I want only one baby"

Whether nature is perceived as hostile to human childbearing or whether the pressure comes from within, humans throughout the Americas have contrived very specific methods to regulate birth. Some of these techniques are more effective than others.

On the Great Plains, women are said to have carried special charms, or amulets. As with all contraceptive devices, specific details are hard to come by. The use of such charms among the Assiniboin is merely rumored. For the Arapaho it is recorded that women attached small containers of "medicine" to their belts, fumigated themselves with burning herbs, or relied upon a combination of both methods. Better information is available for the Blackfeet of Montana, where it is reported that women used to wear a beaded amulet in the form of a butterfly, either at the waist or at the neck. Another Blackfeet charm was the snakeskin, worn either as a girdle or as a necklace.

More widespread are the precautions taken after conception in order to ensure a single birth. Among the Cubeo of Amazonia, for instance, both men and women believe that continued intercourse during pregnancy will add to the number of children growing in the womb. Failure to exercise restraint could cause the woman to burst from an accumulation of fetuses.

Well known is the account of the Hopi woman—told by the Hopi memoirist Don Talayesva, speaking of his own mother—who, after consulting a native doctor during her pregnancy and learning that she carried twins, advised the doctor, "I want only one baby." "Then I will put them together" was the doctor's reply, and he gave the woman an amulet made of twisted white and black wool. The patient wore this charm as a bracelet, and in time the two fetuses, so it is said, were "twisted into one child." Yet the child itself, when born, was regarded as especially blessed, having been formed from two persons.

Mixed feelings about twins have also been recorded for the Mojo and Bauré cultures of Bolivia, where the mother of twins is said to have been held in the highest esteem, especially by her husband. Yet the twins themselves were forced to marry other twins or remain single.

Likewise, the birth of two children among the old-time Kwakiutl of British Columbia was greeted with awe and reverence; the two were spoken of as if they were salmon in human form and were thought to have the power to communicate with this important food animal. However, the parents of newborn twins had to refrain from borrowing their neighbors' utensils, so as not to cause the lenders themselves to have twins. Moreover, the Kwakiutl woman during pregnancy would rub her body every fourth day with hemlock branches as a charm against a multiple birth.

In southeast Colombia a pregnant woman's husband had to

stop eating plantains. In New Mexico the woman herself avoided walking too close to sleeping dogs. In southern California the expectant mother took care not to eat eggs with double yolks—always for the same reason, to keep from having twins.

Without fuller information (which is almost never forthcoming), one should not judge such methods too harshly. Though it may be safe to predict that they will not find modern applications, they may in fact yield a needed result in their own setting, either indirectly or in combination with other techniques. For better or for worse, they help keep alive the attitudes that create a climate of restraint.

Honor and continence

Customs that suggest sexual freedom, not restraint, have been reported from Native American cultures of both continents. Yet the weight of evidence with regard to relations between men and women falls on the side of propriety. For various reasons, familiarity between the sexes, not to mention intimacy, is often deemed inappropriate, dishonorable, dangerous, or even ridiculous.

At the highest levels of communal activity—in war and in statecraft—sex is routinely banished. Either it compromises the dignity of leadership or it actually drains the vitality of those upon whom society depends. Among the outrageous transgressions of the proverbial "foolish people" of Apache lore is a decision made in council to engage in sexual relations; the mere idea is sufficient to provide the theme for a parable.

P A R A B L E / The foolish men call like crows

One of the Foolish People called a big council. They agreed that
they would break up the council just about dark and each man
would go home and have intercourse with his wife. They were to
do this when they heard the sound of a crow and each man was to
make this sound as he got home and did it.

They broke up the council and every man hurried for his camp.
Some hadn't even got back to their camps when the crowing
started. And pretty soon all you heard was crowing.

—Anonymous, Chiricahua Apache
(Arizona and New Mexico)

Similarly, "chagrin and horror" are the emotions described
in a Winnebago tale as councillors discover their chief cohab-
iting with a woman on the night before a war party.

In the view of the Aztecs, the downfall of their predeces-
sors, the Toltecs, was linked to the excessive sensuality of the
Toltec leaders Huemac (who demanded a woman with an
ample figure) and Quetzalcoatl (who broke his vow of abstinence and became drunk with his sister). A later king,
Moquihuix, who challenged the authority of the Aztecs, suffered a crushing defeat in the wake of scandals regarding his
sexual proclivities. Montezuma the Elder, the ruler who built
the Aztec empire, was saved from taking a sexual liberty, so

it is recorded, when the woman he desired fainted at his approach. Less fortunate, Montezuma the Younger high-handedly took a woman for his own use and later lost the empire to the Spaniards.

Equally rigorous (and more heavily reported) are the absti-nences demanded of those who exploit the earth, either as hunters or as planters. In many societies, the annual round of exploitation is developed into a ceremonial calendar, marked by rituals requiring sexual continence. As tersely expressed by an old-time ritual leader of the Pawnee, "Do not go near your women, and prepare for our ceremony."

In certain Maya communities the matter has not always been left to chance. In Belize, a Mopan Maya man used to be obliged to stay up all night in the company of his friends the day before clearing his cornfield. One of the avowed purposes of the vigil was to make sure the planter did not sleep with his wife.

The effects of such ceremonial continence have seldom been measured. Yet statistics from at least one native group, the Chatino of central Mexico, show that the birth curve dips in the winter, meaning that fewer children are conceived during the highly ceremonialized season of cultivation.

In the case of the hunter, the hunt itself is thought to be futile unless preceded by abstinence. If the hunter has slept with his wife, his blowgun will not shoot straight (Peru); if he has not abstained for three days, he will miss his quarry (Cali-fornia); a man "in love" can spoil the hunt (Mexico); and even a man who has had an erotic dream will fail to find game (Colombia).

Fertility itself gives rise to sexual restrictions, directly associated with adolescence and childbearing. For the young woman between the ages of puberty and marriage, chastity was at one time a widely established (though not universal) norm. In the old days a Tlingit girl had to sleep on a high platform, with the ladder removed after she had gone to bed. A Kwakiutl bride, so it is said, would be sent home to her father if her husband discovered she was not a virgin. By the same token, the Aztec maiden was admonished, "Don't give yourself carelessly." Extreme and unusual was the perpetual chastity of the Inca "chosen women," designated from childhood as brides of the sun.

The onus did not fall exclusively on the woman. Among the Shawnee of eastern North America, it was at one time averred by the Shawnee themselves that young men became eligible for marriage at the age of twenty-five, at which time the man "is not even a little aware of the way in which he should have sexual intercourse with a woman." So reads a section of the traditional Shawnee Laws, requiring that the groom be taught the proper technique by his mother. Among the Panare of Venezuela, even in recent times, young men were obliged to do without women, practicing socially approved masturbation.

Restrictions need not end with marriage. Among the Ojibwa, a maple log was placed between the young married couple for the first four nights, in order to teach them restraint. For the Shawnee, once again according to their Laws, restraint was necessary to the "health" of both the woman and her husband.

For married couples of all ages, the diurnal cycle no doubt provides one of the most common inhibitors—as in the old

Anambé folktale from Amazonia, where the heroine refuses
to sleep with her husband, explaining, "It isn't night yet." A
refinement is observed by the Nambikwara of southern Brazil, who discourage marital relations even at night if the moon
is shining.

After the birth of a child, continence becomes obligatory
in many, if not most, cultures. The duration ranges from one
month (Tewa of New Mexico) to one year (Delaware of
New York) to two years (Nambikwara)—and longer.

Among the nineteenth-century Lakota, six years was said
to be the "law." Those who flouted it lost respect in the eyes
of their neighbors. A well-known Cheyenne custom was that
a public vow must be made by the father at the birth of his
first child, promising not to have another for seven years, ten
years, or even fourteen years. Fulfillment of such vows was
considered a mark of strong character. In the words of George
Bird Grinnell, a nineteenth-century friend and student of the
Cheyenne, "the people talked about it and praised the parents' self-control."

Medicines

For men, sexual abstinence may be the only contraceptive
available. Suppressants occasionally play a role, as in the lore
of the Aztecs, who recognized the herb *acueyo* (unidentified)
for its supposed ability to dampen desire. The Shawnee, apparently, had a similar remedy, since it is recorded that their
overly virile young men could be "doctored." But such no-
tices are rare.

For women, actual contraceptives are widely reported,

even if studies on their efficacy remain scarce, and details, in any event, are often kept secret. The subtlety of such methods can be fairly judged from the information obtained by the missionary-ethnographer H. R. Voth, who writes, "When explaining to me the nature and uses of 'big-maiden blossom,' *wupámanci* (*Castilleja linariaefolia*), my friend and informant of the Hopi medical profession once said that a decoction of this was also sometimes used against excessive menstrual discharges and to prevent conception, as it 'dried up the menstrual flow,' as he put it. Another informant, in speaking about Hopi drugs, mentioned two other herbs, both called 'not child-bearing medicine,' *ka tíhta-nga*, as being used for the same purpose. One of them is said to be so strong that 'it twists the uterus all up,' causing the death of the woman. To prevent such a fatal result, the two herbs are used together for the purpose mentioned, one partly neutralizing the strength and severity of the other."

Evidently the Hopi drugs affect the procreative, or estrous, cycle to the point of stopping not only ovulation but also menstruation. This appears to be typical of American Indian contraceptives. It is possible, though, that lighter doses merely suppress ovulation, as with the modern birth-control pill. In any case, varying periods of sterility are reported for different drugs and different dosages. For many women the suppression of menstruation acts as a useful indicator, showing that the drug is still working.

Wondering whether adverse menopausal symptoms could accompany a menstrual suppressant, one investigator asked a Campa woman whether this was the case and received the answer that it was not. Such medicines, nevertheless, are strong.

Many of the drugs are said to cause permanent sterility, even without repeated doses. Yet there are antidotes, which apparently restore fertility after a duration of months or years.

Two celebrated herbs known to native women are the *piripiri* of the central Andes and the stoneseed of the North American Great Basin. *Piripiri*, a name used in the Quechua and Jivaroan languages, refers to one or more species of umbrella sedge, or *Cyperus*. The rootstock of this plant is drunk as a cold-water "tea," inducing sterility for a year or longer, depending on the dosage and the woman's age.

Stoneseed (*Lithospermum ruderale*) is prepared in the same manner. A dose daily for six months, so it is said, ensures sterility thereafter. Although its use has been recorded from one community only—a Western Shoshone settlement in Nevada—stoneseed was repeatedly tested by non-Indian researchers during the 1950s, evidently under the impression that this was a popular Indian contraceptive. It is not. And yet its effectiveness was verified. Tests showed that the estrous cycle in laboratory mice was suppressed by *Lithospermum*.

Nevertheless, in the quest for a modern oral contraceptive, stoneseed fell by the wayside (presumably because chemists had trouble isolating the operative compound), and the well-known "pill" was developed from another herb, *Dioscorea*, not known to have been used for birth control by native women in the Americas.

One other species of *Lithospermum*, *L. incisum*, has been reported as a contraceptive for the Navajo; and, as mentioned, *Cyperus* is used by several groups in South America. But no single species or even a single genus predominates. For the United States alone, Daniel Moerman's comprehensive index of thirty-one contraceptive herbs includes no genus used by

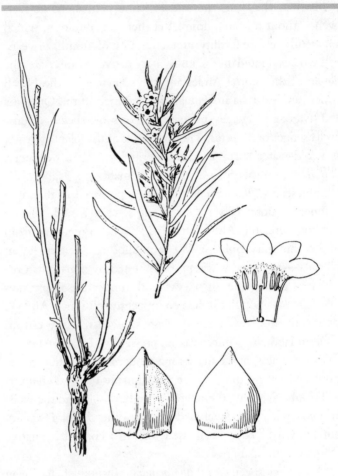

Stoneseed *(Lithospermum ruderale)*, drawn by
Jeanne R. Janish, with the flower cut open and two
views of the seed (greatly enlarged).

more than two Native American tribes, though plants as widespread as tansy, yucca, and spring beauty appear on the list. The reason, probably, is that even this "comprehensive" roundup is skimpy, owing to the difficulty in getting data— or, to put it frankly, the reluctance of women to share their knowledge with male anthropologists.

Obviously, Native American birth-control methods, whether chemical or behavioral, can work for the individual. The larger question is whether these same methods can hold human population in check and thereby work for the whole environment. The answer would seem to be yes, and many investigators have theorized that such is the case.

But population control makes for a treacherous study. Often there is a hidden detail in the picture. A Tarahumara mother, for instance, may warn her daughters not to have children too rapidly. She clinches the argument by pointing out that there is no one to carry so many infants and toddlers. But the case is not closed. The same ethnographer who has reported this much goes on to reveal that the Tarahumara family averages seven or eight children.

The example of the Chatino, who practice sexual continence during the summer, looks more convincing. Statistics actually show that the birth curve dips in winter. However, the researcher who worked up the data discloses that children born in the dry winter months are less likely to survive, because this is the season when airborne dust particles spread diphtheria and other diseases; and thus, by pushing births into the moister, healthier summer season, the abstemious Chatino may be preserving, or even adding to, their total population.

Equally deceptive is the chain of cause and effect that seems to include sexual continence and presumably ends in birth spacing. While continence, widely proclaimed, may appear to delay a woman's second child for two or more years, there is a hidden factor in breast-feeding, and also in the lowered fertility brought about by the new mother's ritual diet. Lactation itself suppresses ovulation, and most women nurse each child for several years. Therefore, with both lactation and harsh diets taken into account, sexual continence might not be necessary.

Yet some studies have shown that starchy, low-protein diets favor the return of ovulation; and, as we have seen, the diets required of new mothers are often meatless. So continence may be useful after all, and the meat restriction may be seen as a conservation measure, rather than as a means of limiting population.

Although in theory birth control may be sufficient to bring about a needed result for society, and indeed its techniques are ingenious and of undoubted practical value, it is a subject tortured by ambiguity. Birth control works and it does not work. It is wanted and it is not wanted. At the very least, assuming that it is wanted, even needed—and viewed against the alternative—it offers hope.

PART FOUR

DEATH

10

The Argument
for Death

Do not murmur when you suffer in doing
what the spirits have commanded,
for a cup of water is provided.

—*Ute saying*

Envisioning the prompt return of the deer he had just killed,
the Navajo hunter, in former times, would address it hopefully, saying, "From this day may you lead the other game
along the trails, that I may hunt." To make sure that the
animal would be seen again, the hunter, praying, would offer
it a small jewel, in order that "we may continue to hold each
other."

With the same purpose in mind, the Yokuts eagle catcher
would talk to the eagle before trampling it to death, saying,
"You will have a new body." Equally aware of the animal's
value, even if without the hunter's sense of responsibility, the
Kwakiutl man who had chanced upon a dead squirrel would
give it a ceremonious burial and pray to it, "Now let the

supernatural power of your body come over to me."

Evidently, in some contexts at least, the continued presence of animals, even after death, is much desired. One does not wish them to be gone (or, if they must return "home," the journey is merely to facilitate their prompt return). Yet in the case of humans, once death has occurred, the wish to have them gone may become an urgent priority.

While wishing to "hold" the spirit of the deceased game animal, the Navajo traditionalist uses prayer and song to drive off the ghost of the human dead. Similarly, addressing the deceased friend or relative, the Delaware prayermaker instructs the corpse, or its ghost: "Go on in your spirit life. Do not ever think about us or remember us."

Virtually the same injunction recurs in prayers to the dead recorded for the Aztec ("You will think no more of what lies here"); for the Fox ("Do not think of looking back"); and for the Tewa ("We have made steep gullies between us. Do not, therefore, reach for even a hair of our heads").

Putting words into action, the Kaingang of Brazil used to scatter herbs to frighten off the recent dead. The Cubeo of Colombia burned pepper for the same purpose. Zuni mourners cut off the "road" of the dead by darkening it with black cornmeal.

Banishment, however, does not always mean that reincarnation is avoided. In fact, the rebirth of the human dead is widely accepted as inevitable. Yet in many cases, the deceased returns not as a human but as an animal.

For the Yucatec Maya, human souls may come back as newborns. Or, they may enter the bodies of animals. The same belief, by which humans are changed into animals, has been reported for the Inuit of western Alaska and also the Inuit of north central Canada.

Among the Nambikwara of Brazil it is said that deceased women and children merely disappear with the wind. Only the men are reincarnated—as jaguars.

Selective reincarnation may operate on a time scale, as with the Tarahumara, who say that the dead return as humans, but only three times, the fourth time becoming moths. Alternately, reincarnation may be dictated by the life that was lived or the death that was suffered. Thus the spirits of Kwakiutl hunters become wolves; Aztec warriors killed in battle turn into birds and butterflies; the spirits of Tlingit drowning victims become otters.

The reverse process, apparently, does not occur. Or, better to say, it is not wished. Animals, though they may have humanlike inner forms, are not reincarnated on earth as humans.

In other words, it is humans, not animals, who must disappear.

Invoking the kinship of the whole environment, humans counsel one another to accept this permanent death, or disappearance, either because all things die, or, more optimistically, because all things are living.

The darker view is taken by the Omaha elder who advises, "We see death everywhere. Plants, trees, animals die, and man dies. No one can escape death and no one should fear death, since it cannot be avoided."

More comforting, perhaps, are the words of the Modoc woman who observes, "Water evaporates, trees die. I used to think it was too bad to get old and die; but I see everything and everything grows to maturity and then dies. So now I think it is all right. Trees mature, and they fall, and new trees spring up."

The Modoc woman's hopeful sentiments are echoed by a Pima narrator, citing the example of the hero-god Elder Brother, who "went and stayed with the life of the earth. Where his dead body lay, small children used to play on him."

Evidently death is necessary, at least for humans. Why? The answers are various, and often they are not expressed. The question is openly asked, however, in a widespread narrative type, half myth, half debate, in which two or more characters solve the problem once and for all. Interestingly, the death of nonhuman species is almost never argued in this kind of story. The topic is *human* mortality, often with an explicit warning against overpopulation.

In the beginning

The debate takes place in the mythic time before humans were created or at least at a time when the culture hero—the figure who establishes rules and customs for a particular people—was still on earth. Someone asks: Shall humans live forever?

Often the culture hero argues the affirmative, challenged by a hard-minded doubter. The doubter, of course, wins, sometimes with little or no effort. In a myth of the Guajiro he simply points out to the culture hero, Maleiwa, that "the earth is so heavily populated, there is no room for even one more person." Thus diseases are needed to bring death, so "there can be more space for the people who remain." Heed-

ing this advice, Maleiwa establishes measles and other ill-
nesses. Yet to this day the people excuse him, blaming the
doubter who influenced his mind.

Rare are the stories in which the people themselves wish
to limit their lives. An example comes from the old-time
Serrano of California, who told of the hero-deity Kúkitatc,
who had once proposed, "When people die, they shall come
back." But the people themselves said, "If they come back,
the world will fill up, and there will be no room. We will get
rid of Kúkitatc." To save the earth, they took the deity's life,
allowing him to become the celebrated "dying god" of
southern California mythology.

In the myths of western North America as a whole, more
often than not it is Coyote who advocates human death,
generally in a debate with one or more other animal-people.
Humans, not yet born, are unable to challenge him. If there
is no death, he argues, "There will be too many people"
(Sinkyone); "There will be many people, too many"
(Tubatulabal); "This little world is not large enough to hold
all of the people, and if the people who died came back to life,
there would not be food enough for all" (Caddo).

On occasion, Bear, Raven, Mole, and other animals are
known to argue for human death. In a story of the Gros
Ventre of Montana, Bear explains that there would be "not
enough for everyone to eat. There will be more pleasure and
happiness in life if all die." Hard-minded Raven, in a
Thompson tale, decrees, "Let them become sick and die."

Mole's argument, in a Modoc myth, mentions the common fate of humans and other species. In answer to the
question "How long do we want human beings to live?"

The first couple, Cipactonal and Oxomoco,
casting kernels to decide human fate;
painted by a sixteenth-century Aztec artist,
from Libro Quarto of Bernardino de Sahagún,
Códice florentino.

Mole replies, "I want them to grow old, and get cold when they sit down, and shake and die. Flowers, trees, and everything living must die or the world would get too full."

Citing the needs of his own species, Frog, in a Cherokee version, speaks out against resuscitation for those humans who have already died. "If all of them live," he argues, "it will be so crowded that they might step on us."

The argument advanced by the frog is more commonly assigned to insects, a group proverbially interested in saving itself from human trampling. As Black Beetle explains, in a Pima variant, "I think that when someone has lived a long time he should die and go away and never come back here again. That way the earth will never get overpopulated and no one will crush me." The same position is taken by grasshoppers, grubworms, dung beetles, and ants in stories from the Choctaw, Cherokee, Seri, and Kiowa.

Confronted with the prospect of human increase, the earth mother herself, if gently, takes the hard-minded position. "I have been created small," she explains in a Winnebago myth, "and if all the people live forever they would soon fill up the earth. There would then be more suffering than there is now, for some people would always be in want of food if they multiplied greatly. That is why everything has an end."

In a myth of the Cochiti of New Mexico it is told that a child died just as the people were emerging from the earth. They went back to "our Mother" in "Shipap [the underworld]," to ask what had happened, and the Mother said to them, "The child is dead. If your people did not die, the world would fill up and there would be no place for you to live. When you die, you will come back to Shipap to live

with me. Keep on traveling and do not be troubled when
your people die."

For the lives of the elders

Difficult as it may have been, the verdict by spirit powers to
permit human death leaves the even harder choices to humans themselves. In most mythologies the gods and the animals are excused from contemplating such questions as whose
life should be put first or who should remain unborn. With
little or no help from myth, and without the social sanction
provided by prayer, the individual—often the woman—must
act in private.

P A R A B L E / The origin of permanent death

After the first death, the hummingbird was sent to get clay, in order
to make a more durable human. Then the cricket was sent to get
lightweight balsa wood. Finally, the beetle was sent to get stones to
mix in with the new creature to give it firmness.

And so they started to make a human who could withstand death.
The cricket returned right away with the lightweight wood. And
the hummingbird came with the clay. But the beetle never showed
up. Its job was to bring the stones, but it never came back.

After a long wait, and it still had not returned, they decided to
make the human being out of clay. Having no stones, they just used
clay, and those balsa sticks. Then they blew the breath of life into
it, and the human being was finished.

And then Etsa [the sun] said, "Did I not ordain that humans be made also of stone? Was it not my wish that humans be immortal? Had I not determined that even old people would become children again? I had indeed determined that humans would be immortal. But now I say they must die." He pronounced this solemn judgment: "Now let full-grown men and newborn children die. Let young men die who have not yet had children, and young women who have not yet married."

Whatever is made of earth and fragile clay, must it not break? The earthen bowl, though it is made well, does it not break? We ourselves are made the same.

—Píkiur,
Shuar (Ecuador)

In one kind of case the action taken favors the elder over the younger. That is, the life of a parent or of an elder sibling takes precedence.

Revealed in a sixteenth-century Aztec medical text is a decision to save the mother: "Here also let something rather amazing be told. When the baby adhered there within its mother, if the baby had died, the midwife inserted an obsidian knife within the woman. There she dismembered the baby; she drew it forth piece by piece. Thus the parent was yet relieved."

Evidently Aztec surgery would have been capable of Caesarian section to deliver the distressed child before its death—but presumably without recovery for the mother.

A decision to spare the father is reported by an ethnographer of the Venezuelan Sáliva: "The second-born of twins must be instantly put to death by the mother. This custom finds an explanation in the native concept of the soul. The natives believe the individual has only one soul. When a child is born, the father loses part of his soul. When two children are born at the same time, the father has to suffer a double loss, and this double loss from his own soul might cause his death."

Among the Brazilian Bororo the fate of either parent may be at stake if the mother or the father has had a "negative" dream during the mother's labor. In such an event the child must be ritually put to death in order to avoid the fulfillment of the dream.

A decision may also be made for the elder of two siblings. The conflict arises if the mother becomes pregnant with a second child while nursing her first. In such a case—as reported for the nineteenth-century Pima—the fetus would be aborted in order to protect the welfare of the nursing child, which the mother loved more, so people said, "because she could see it."

Such subtle lines of reasoning, however, do not always come through in the available ethnography. By and large, the reporter understands no more than that the action is taken and that it is, or is not, done openly. In fact, in many societies the matter is kept secret, and in a few it has been criminalized.

Among the Chimariko of northern California the penalty is said to have been death at the hands of the guilty party's husband (the culprit is always a woman); in ancient Mexico, death by hanging; among the Creek, fifty lashes. For the twentieth-century Cheyenne the death of the fetus, if intentional, is defined as homicide and may be punished by banishment. Within the meaning of Cheyenne law the unborn fetus is a legal personality and a member of the tribe.

But native theory has many variations.

As viewed by the Huichol of Mexico, the fetus does not become "complete" until just before birth. At first, in the mother's womb, it is mere flesh. Then, after the passage of five months, the female deity Tatéi Niwetúkame (Our Mother) sends it a picture of its face and of its human garments. At seven months the pregnant woman feels the fetus moving, but it does not yet have its fontanelle, which is the life essence, or soul. This it receives from Our Mother five minutes before birth. Then, finally, it is complete.

For the Chatino, another of the Mexican groups, the process of becoming human takes longer. According to Chatino belief, each person has a mind, a heart, and a stomach. The stomach is formed at the moment of conception and determines the person's sex. The heart, or living soul, is set in place when the umbilical cord is cut; and the mind, or "storehouse," is not formed until the infant's first cry.

An even greater delay is indicated by the Brazilian Ka'apor, who say that the child does not "wake up" until it has been given a name. Before naming, the child is "asleep," that is, spiritually unformed.

Such theories, widely reported, could easily be cited as a rationale for dismissing the unwanted child. Instead, they seem to provide a stimulus for giving extra care to the child that is wanted.

Among the Cubeo, for instance, the newborn child does not have human status until its body has been painted red. Thus the newly delivered mother, who has given birth in the garden, brings the baby into the house and paints it immediately. Evidently for the same purpose, the Tukuna child is immediately painted with the black dye genipa.

In societies as diverse as the Campa, the Modoc, and the Delaware, the newborn is thought to be not yet completely in the human world or, in a sense, still attached to the ghost world. Therefore the Campa parent sets up a barrier of branches to keep the child's soul from returning. The Delaware parent, in the old days, used to dress the infant in adult clothing in order to fool visiting ghosts who might be tempted to steal the child.

Nevertheless, against a background of strong motivation to protect the lives of newborns, abortion and infanticide have been reported from more than a hundred native cultures in the Americas, ranging from the Canadian Arctic to Tierra del Fuego. Often denied by native informants, and poorly understood by outsiders, the methods include physical as well as chemical procedures, which can be only sketchily described for lack of detailed information.

Among abortifacients, or herbs that cause expulsion of the fetus, the sweet flag, *Acorus calamus*, has been reported for the Delaware, the Menominee, and the Mohegan. A "tea" made from the root is taken orally, or the root may be chewed. Roots or tops of the wild sage, *Artemisia frigida*, have been used in a similar manner by the Pawnee and by various Siouan groups including the Omaha and the Ponca.

Less drastic are the so-called emmenagogues. These cause menstrual flow after the first missed period and before the second, at which time the embryo is not yet implanted in the lining of the womb. Abortifacients may be taken for the very same purpose, but generally as a women's "health" measure and without risk of social disapproval.

A large number of emmenagogues were known to the Aztecs, including preparations made from the maguey plant, the rubber tree, chili peppers, and several unidentified herbs known as *cihuapatli*, "women's medicines," used for the stated purpose of simply bringing on one's period (not unlike the modern "French pill").

Physical techniques include pressure applied to the abdomen during pregnancy and the smothering or shaking of newborns. Abandonment of newborns has occasionally been reported. But it should be emphasized that such methods run counter to the avowed wishes of the cultures in question. Popular feelings are vividly expressed in widespread folktales like The Deserted Children and the story of Thrown Away, in which unwanted offspring survive against all odds to become young heroes and heroines.

For the lives of the young

Folktales may also protect the interests of the aged, as in the story told by the Chiricahua Apache in which a blind and deaf old woman is abandoned by her people as "good for nothing." Mountain spirits hear her weeping, pity her, and sing to restore her sight and hearing. Having cured her, they send her home to her people to teach the ceremony she has just received.

But another kind of tale, in which the old person yields to the needs of younger members of the community, is perhaps more common. A Delaware story puts it this way: "One morning the old folks told the young people that they were tired of living, and they went out where it was marshy and the old lady sat down and said, 'You can always think of me when you see this,' and there stood a weed instead of the old lady. And the old man sat beside her, and *he* turned to a weed. And those young people lived on by themselves and had plenty of meat."

In a similar episode from a Cahuilla tale, an old man chooses to become a palm tree because he "felt that his time was about gone" and he "wanted to be a benefit to his people."

More realistic, a Montagnais story from eastern Canada tells how an old man was abandoned when the people moved camp. "He was so old he could not walk, he had to be dragged. 'I've become too much of a burden. Leave me here with a little food,' he said." In response, the others constructed a platform of the type used to cache meat, adding a roof and walls. When it was finished, "the old man was placed inside. No one wished his death. He was simply left behind."

Similar instances from life, not fiction, have been reported from the Arctic, the Great Plains, the Great Basin, Central America, Amazonia, and elsewhere.

In cases of extreme infirmity, however, abandonment may be judged inhumane. Sometimes, as reported by the anthropologist Robert Redfield, for the Maya of Yucatán, "the soul has such difficulty in getting free from the body that the dying person is whipped with a rope, to bring the soul's release." Likewise, according to an early ethnographer of the Wintun of California, "When a person is manifestly sick unto death, the Corusies [i.e., a Wintun group] sometimes wind ropes tightly around him to terminate his sufferings."

A detail is added in a similar account from the Mískito of Nicaragua, who are said to have first tested the dying person's vitality, placing him or her in an awkward position. If the body remained motionless, the person was put to death.

But while the death of the aged may be less emotionally charged than the death of the very young, it can never be easy. Tender regard—and, more important, genuine respect—for the aged is one of the traits most widely ascribed to Native American cultures, and with much supporting evidence.

In many, if not most, communities, abandonment and euthanasia are said to be rare, and more than a few investigators have been told that such practices do not exist. One cannot know what course of action, if any, may lie in the mind of the aged Koyukon chief who is heard to comment, "I have camped many times beneath spruce trees, roasting grouse over my campfire. So there is no reason to pray that I might live on much longer." Or of the Tlingit elder who sings, "The world is rolling around for all the young people. So let's not love our lives too much, hold ourselves back from dying."

Reviewing the lore of the two continents, one must conclude that native cultures are profoundly impressed by the truism that death falls most heavily on the aged and on the very young. And by a second truism, that human death is mandated—whether by "nature" or by the "earth" or by nonhuman species. The culture that tries to deny this may be headed for extinction, since, as we hear in the myths, "there would not be food enough" or "there would be no room to stand."

The reality, as expressed by the Fox ritualist, concerned for the health of his community, is that the watchful spirit blesses not the individual but the group. It is not "you" to whom the spirit says, "You please me." Rather, "It is us and future generations." Moreover, "No one of us who exist as mortals here, shall exist as a mortal forever. As many of us as blink have death, all of us who call each other mortals. If any one thinks, 'No, not I; I shall always exist as a mortal,' he surely dies. He surely comes to death. For he, the manitou [i.e., the spirit], has fixed that which will happen to each one of us."

11

Reduction of Ancestors

He who cannot govern his own house
can scarcely govern at large.

—*Quechua saying*

Individuals may die, but the human community has a life of its own. Its various parts, which are its families and groups of families, continue to function as a unit from generation to generation, suggesting that the community, or social body, may be regarded as a personality in its own right.

Accordingly, the Iroquois speak ritually of their society as if it were a woman, referring to it as "she." If a chief dies, "she" grieves. Similarly, a Navajo tradition states that some (though not all) of the Navajo clans were originated by the deity Changing Woman, who formed them by rolling up bits of flesh from the surface of her skin.

In the case of long-settled communities, built around a

central town, the town itself may be regarded as an organism, typically with a "root," a "navel," or a "heart."

Among the Chatino of southern Oaxaca State, the community of Yaitepec has not only a "heart." It has "eyes," "ears," and "mouths," which are the paths leading into the village. At Zuni pueblo, in New Mexico, four "arteries" lead outward from the "heart," reaching to the four cardinal points, east, south, north, and west.

In the florid imagery used by the ancient Mexican ruling classes, the Aztec capital, Mexico City, was the "root, navel, and heart of this whole worldly edifice." Somewhat more modestly, it was *atl xictli*, "water navel," referring to the city's location on an island in the middle of a lake.

Cuzco, capital of the Incas, was also a "navel." Or at least this was the translation of the obscure word *cuzco* given by one of the native chroniclers. For the modern Tewa pueblo of San Juan, in northern New Mexico, the true center of the village is said to be *nan echu kwi nan sipu pingeh*, or "earth mother earth navel middle place," which consists of a circular arrangement of stones in one of the village plazas.

But the life of the community, even if identified as an independent personality or organism, does not continue automatically. Thought and effort are required on the part of its human inhabitants. For the tribes of the Mississippi Basin of North America, a sacred bundle, or portable altar, must be maintained within the community and carefully guarded at all times; otherwise, as the Lakota were warned in the ancient days, "you will cease to be a nation."

Among the Aztec city-states either a bundle or an idol represented the life of the town. For the Aztec nation of

Cuitlahuac Tizic it was the idol Mixcoatl. "If I gave up Mixcoatl," said the Tizic ruler on one memorable occasion when his city was besieged by the Mexica Aztecs, "what would befall my children in times yet to come?"

A comparable source of power for the Inca residents of Cuzco was the shrine called *sapi*, "root," said to have been part of an enormous *quinua* (*Polylepis* sp., a tree of the rose family). In the words of the historian Cobo, this was the root "from which Cuzco issued and by means of which it was preserved"; therefore the people "made sacrifices to it for the preservation of the said city."

As envisioned by the keepers of bundles and "roots," the ruin of the community would be signaled by a population decrease resulting from war, drought, or disease. So unfortunate a community, in Aztec parlance, was said to "lie in darkness." An unmanageable *increase* in population is never included among the disasters to be warded off by sacred charms. Myths, not charms, provide the insurance against such a calamity, which in many mythic traditions is treated as though it had been forestalled in the ancient days.

The problem of too large a community cannot arise, so the stories relate, because the population was definitively reduced in the ancient times by the elimination of certain ancestors. As a result, the proper number of families, clans, or other social groups was fixed; and these in turn establish the proper relationship between the people and the land.

In some cases, patterns on the earth, created by encampments or settlements, show that the separate parts of society are living together as they should. None of this would have been possible, however, without the mythic reduction of clan forebears—reassuringly placed in the distant past, beyond the reach of controversy.

The emergence halted

Not every native history includes an emergence story; and many that do, make little of it. Nevertheless, the tale of human beings pouring out onto the earth's surface is probably the most widespread account of how the human community originated. The full story tells not only that the event occurred, but that it was brought to a stop.

Sometimes it is said that the people, while climbing up on a rope or a ladder, began to fall back, so that only a certain number emerged, while the remainder stayed permanently inside the earth. In other cases the hole becomes suddenly plugged, to the same effect.

According to a Choctaw version, the passageway was closed by the "good spirit" named Aba, imprisoning many people inside. Later they crept out through tiny holes here and there—but in the form of ants.

The Zuni, while emerging on a ladder made of grasses, became reduced when some people fell off and were changed into underworld monsters. Much later, during an earthquake, the monsters came out through cracks and murdered a few of the people who had settled on the earth's surface, further reducing the population.

Occasionally a tribe will use emergence lore to account not for their own origin but for that of a neighboring group. Here too, understandably, reduction plays a role. In the view of the Machiguenga, who live on the eastern slopes of the Peruvian

Andes, the highland people to the west and south were able to emerge only partly, having been stopped in their tracks when the passageway was blocked. As in the case of the Zuni, those who remained underground were transformed into demons.

Another kind of myth, one that puts a brake on population and at the same time points to the source of human increase, has been widely recorded in both North and South America. Generally the key figure in stories of this sort is the so-called Stopper Woman, who prevents the emergence from going forward when she becomes stuck while trying to crawl through the opening. The problem in most, if not all, cases is that she is pregnant.

In a Mataco variant from Argentina it is said that the armadillo put its ear to the ground and, hearing noises below, began to dig. When it had broken through, humans emerged. All the nations came out. Last were the Mataco; but while they were emerging, a pregnant woman became stuck in the hole, and the emergence ceased. This is why the Mataco— lamentably, so it would seem—are few.

Expressing neither satisfaction nor regret, the Kiowa of Oklahoma say that their people emerged from a hollow log far to the north, progressing in a continuous stream until a pregnant woman tried to squeeze through. It was she who blocked the way for those who remained behind.

For some South American groups the emergence proceeds from the upper world, rather than from the earth. But since a hole in the sky is the means of entrance, the Stopper Woman again has a role to play. According to the Warrau of Venezuela, her body remains wedged in the opening even today, and it is this that prevents mortals from being able to see into the sky world.

In other stories the pregnant woman never quite gets to the entrance. She is so heavy that she falls back, again putting a stop to the emergence.

As envisioned in old variants from the Lakota and the Mandan of the northern Great Plains, the heavy woman broke the vine that the people were using to climb upward, thus causing a separation between those who had already emerged and those who were forced to remain underground. As far away as Venezuela, the Yaruro tell essentially the same tale, adding the significant information that the Creator was opposed to the emergence even before it began.

An exhaustive review of reduction myths would include other types as well: flood myths in which the entire population is reduced to a single couple, or fire myths in which one or more survivors take refuge under the earth. Fire myths, naturally, lead into emergence stories—as in the case of the Brazilian Tapirape, who used to tell of two couples who hid under the ground in the form of birds, then emerged after the fire to give birth to the human race as we know it today.

Clans and living space

An initial reduction in population necessarily eases pressure on the land. But for how long? Unless human society is divided into manageable units, it may sprawl uncontrollably.

Of course, human sprawl may not be seen as a problem for societies blessed with vast spaces to fill. For the Navajo there would seem to be no limit to the possible number of social units, or clans. More than sixty have been counted. According to one tradition, the earliest clans to be established were formed from ears of corn "turned in every direction, and this is the reason the Navajos never stay in one home like the Pueblos, but wander always from place to place."

Other groups are more cautious. For the old-time Pima of southern Arizona, five clans were sufficient, and these were neatly grouped into halves, or moieties, with three clans on one side and two on the other.

According to one version of the Pima emergence myth—in which the supernaturals Coyote and Elder Brother play leading roles—Coyote is said to have found out in advance that the people were about to emerge from the earth. Elder Brother warned him not to go near until all had come forth. But Coyote did not heed this advice.

Instead, as the text relates, Coyote "looked down the opening to see the humans struggling upward like a long line of ants ascending a tree, and the sight provoked him to laughter, which caused the opening to close up, preventing many people from reaching Pima land. Five clans had come out, and it is supposed that those that were shut in belonged to yet other clans."

In a comparable story told by the Guajiro the culture hero stands by as the people emerge, dividing them into eight clans. Those who stupidly come late are turned into birds and other animals.

Neither laughable, as in the Pima case, nor stupid, as with the missing Guajiro, the excluded ancestors in Ojibwa, Inca, and Yuracaré versions of the story are frankly dangerous. In the Ojibwa myth the five clans are said to be descended from six supernatural beings who emerged from the ocean to mingle with preexisting humans. One of the supernaturals, it seems, was a looking monster and was made to return to the "great water" because his glance inflicted certain death. Therefore only five clans were founded.

In Inca lore the supernaturals were four "wise and powerful" couples, who emerged from the ancestral cave and mingled with the preexisting humans, whereupon their leader, Manco Capac, assigned living space to each of ten *ayllus*, or territorial clans. One of the four male supernaturals, however, was judged too powerful by the other three; and to save themselves the three tricked him into returning to the cave of origin, where they sealed him in with a boulder.

The Yuracaré variant, from nineteenth-century Bolivia, has it that the deity Tiri closed the cave after the ancestors emerged, in order to "prevent a great chief from coming out," and a serpent has guarded the opening ever since.

P A R A B L E / The eight jars

In the beginning God formed a being called Sulayibi to finish making humanity for him. This creature set to work constructing eight jars of clay; and from these, human beings would be born.

The different jars produced beautiful sounds, representing different personal qualities: industriousness, intelligence, kindheartedness, and others.

When Sulayibi had made the eight jars, God asked to see the

work. But Sulayibi refused, three times. The fourth time, he gave God permission; but at that instant the eight jars broke, signifying death—though shortly beforehand an owl had cried, proclaiming death.

That's how the earthen jars, where human life arose, came to be broken.

After the breaking of the jars—which God himself had wanted to happen—Sulayibi succeeded in reconstructing just four of the jars, for originally there had been eight.

Then, to distinguish each clan, God took corn kernels, giving them different names, couple by couple, and in this way God established just two distinct [groups of] clans. . . .

—Told by Guillermo Nelson,
Bribri (Costa Rica)

Reduction lore may be found even in a society where clans do not exist. This is a quibble, perhaps, because in place of the clan—as with the Aztecs—one finds a localized group that functions in much the same way. The Aztec *calpulli*, or neighborhood unit, is not actually the subject of any surviving origin myth. Yet the Aztec ancestors were reduced, nevertheless.

To achieve the needed result, the production of elders, at first unsatisfactory, was simply revised. At or near the cave of emergence a supernatural mother, so it was said, gave birth to four hundred ancestral Aztecs. Then, without comment, she took them all inside the cave and gave birth again, this time to just five (four males and a female). Inspired by the sun, the five made war on the four hundred, killing all but "a few." Or all but three, according to a slightly different version.

Reduction, let it be granted, does not always yield a lasting effect. Nor does the revision of an original scheme necessarily downsize the population.

In an Iroquois myth it is told that "in ancient times a people dwelling in a certain country, having become very numerous, decided to divide their hunting grounds into equal parts." One man trespassed, however, and in the war that resulted his entire family was killed, while he himself fled to a cave and entered the earth.

The story so far would seem to confirm the general pattern. But in the next episode we learn that the exile, while under the earth, marries into the porcupine people and becomes the father of many children. After fifteen years he and his new family emerge and are given status as a distinct clan.

In the absence of native commentary we cannot know whether the Iroquois mythmaker is simply taking a realistic view of the world, or whether the Iroquois people at the time the myth was devised had good reason to be unconcerned about overpopulation (at least for themselves).

In certain cases, however, reduction myths that might otherwise be ambiguous are clarified by a mythmaker who openly expresses the need for population control.

As explained by the late Bororo narrator Akirio Boróro Keggeu, the event in question took place in the ancient days when "the population had grown so rapidly that Méri, the sun, became worried and began to think of a way to reduce

it." His method was to bridge the river with a soft, fragile wood, then order the people of the village to cross over.

When the bridge was filled from one end to the other, the wood broke and the people fell into the water and drowned. Only one man was saved, a cripple who had lagged behind. Lonely, the crippled man called the drowning victims back to life in seven groups, one group at a time. He accepted only those who brought him gifts, killing those who did not. Any who had drowned in the turbulent part of the current revived with curly hair; those who had fallen into the still waters had straight hair: thus the origin of seven clans divided into moieties (the curly-haired and the straight-haired).

A moiety system, by which a society is divided into two parts, need not have the same number of clans on each side. But the two "halves" should be roughly equal in number of individuals. An imbalance, presumably, was the cause of an argument between the Creators Mukat and Temayawut, brother deities who represented the two Cahuilla moieties, the Wildcats and the Coyotes. In the ancient time, when the brothers were creating humans, Temayawut, for his part, began making too many, so it is said. Mukat protested, pointing out that "the earth was not large enough to hold them."

In subtle ways the relationship between clans and living space may survive—or be sorely missed—even in native communities that appear to blend in with the larger, non-native society. Such was the case with the Grassy Narrows band of southwestern Ontario, an Ojibwa group that was moved to a new reservation in the early 1960s. Unforeseen by the planners, the new houses, which were bunched together in the manner of a modern suburb, created problems for the people.

One member of the band explained the situation in these words: "When we moved here, we were packed in. That was bad. But what was more bad was that the clans were pushed together. There was no sense of clan area. It isn't so much that we were pushed together, as that our clans were mixed up. It is too late now. The damage is done."

Patterns on the earth

The kind of "damage" referred to by the Ojibwa speaker has a long history in the Americas. Relationships between people and living space do not remain constant; they are often disrupted. Even those societies that insist upon precise land allotments may suffer changes over the years; or the same society may exhibit precision in one region and not in another.

For the nineteenth-century Crow it has been recorded that the tribe's clans always occupied fixed positions in the camp circle. Yet half a century later there were no fixed positions at all, and the circle itself was set up only on special occasions. For the Omaha, circles and clan positions are reported for hunting encampments, while in the permanent village the lodges were simply "huddled together" without regard for clan order. Likewise, in Incan Peru (except for Cuzco and some of the other large settlements) the towns were "jumbled."

If social groups fit together in patterns nonetheless, and if these can be seen in the mind's eye, there may be no problem for the community as a whole. But the situation is undoubtedly clarified—and the community helped—wherever soci-

ety confines its imprint to a recognizable pattern on the land.

Often this is achieved through a kind of geometry. Inter-clan relationships, social halves (or moieties), and even simple lists of clans and neighborhood groups translate into settlement patterns that may take the form of lines, squares, rectangles, or circles.

One of the commonest arrangements is the line of dwelling places that follows a beach or a river course. As described by Alfred Kroeber for the Californian Yurok, all of the tribe's habitations "stood either on the Klamath River or on the shore of the ocean. All land back in the hills away from the houses served only for hunting deer, picking up acorns, harvesting seeds, and gathering firewood . . . , occasionally camped on, though never for long periods. All true settlements formed only a long winding land; and along this waterway Yurok life was lived."

In Oregon, British Columbia, and southern Alaska, as well as in California, linear settlements were the general rule, with parallel lines forming villages of several "streets" wherever the population warranted.

According to a myth of the Cahuilla—who, like other Pacific Coast groups, maintained a linear arrangement—Náal ("ancestor") was the one who established the basic pattern, giving the lineages "their different homes, traveling over the country, naming the places and the animals and the things they should eat, marking boundaries with boulders and with lines drawn on the earth."

Quite different from these often meandering lines are the four-angled figures created by social groupings in Peru, Mexico, and the North American Southwest. Among Aztec communities in ancient Mexico a fourfold division seems to have been standard—as in the case of Tenochtitlán, the more powerful of the twin boroughs that comprised Mexico City. The Tenochtitlán *calpulli* groups, of which there may have been seven or more, were evidently fitted into the four divisions.

Careful planning is suggested by a passage in one of the sixteenth-century Aztec chronicles, describing the origin of the city of Cuauhtitlán, a community about twenty miles north of Mexico City: "When the elder Xaltemoctzin started on his temple, he used it to lay out the city of Cuauhtitlán in four quarters. It was from this that he patterned it, building it to the four directions from the corners of his temple."

In a similar fashion the Inca capital, Cuzco, was built around a central square, from which four great highways led north, south, east, and west to the four quarters of the Inca empire. Within the city itself, *ayllus* belonging to the "upper" moiety lived to the north of the square; *ayllus* of the "lower" moiety, to the south.

On a more modest scale, the pueblo of Zia in northern New Mexico duplicates the Cuzco pattern, with neighborhoods north of the central square assigned to the Wren moiety; those on the south, to the Turquoise moiety.

Geometrically more perfect than the sometimes ragged squares and rectangles of the Zia and other town-dwelling groups are the circles and ovals reported from Brazil and from central North America. In these beautiful arrangements each clan has its assigned place on the rim of the figure, which may be replicated as a great square of four circles (Lakota) or as a system of concentric circles (Blackfeet, Bororo, Cheyenne). Or, in some cases, the rim may be connected to the center by spoke-like paths, forming a wheel (Canela).

The Settlement from a Distance,
lithograph by Pudlo, Inuit of Cape Dorset,
Baffin Island, 1982 or earlier.

Cheyenne camp circle, after
G. Dorsey 1905a.

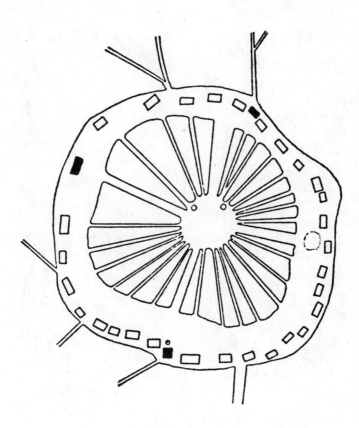

Plan of a Canela village, after
Nimuendajú 1946.

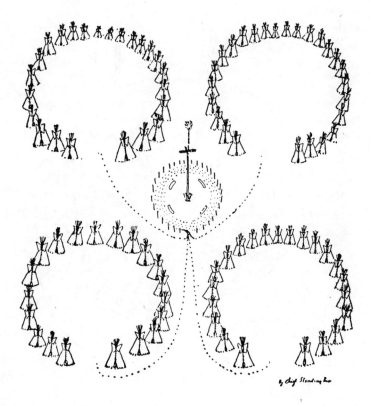

Lakota encampment
(the four villages), after
Standing Bear 1933.

Observed by the nineteenth-century anthropologist Alice Fletcher, the circle "made a living picture of tribal organization and responsibilities. It impressed upon the beholder the relative position of kinship groups and their interdependence, both for the maintenance of order and government within and for defense against enemies from without."

As we have seen, the reduction of ancestors is often regarded as the initial step in the establishment of this kind of "interdependence" and "order." It is not the final step, however—at least, not always. For some societies a continuing policy of reduction, though never stated, may be understood as a necessity.

The effect of social patterning on population control—not in the mythic past but in the present—depends upon the complexity of the social system and whether it can function beyond a certain limit. One society that has been studied with this question in mind is the mid-twentieth-century Tapirape, for whom there are data both on patterning and on reduction.

Among the Tapirape—until recently—each individual belonged not to a single clan but to a paternal kin group, determined by one's male ancestry, and, on the mother's side, a kin group descended from females. The village itself made an oval pattern, with nine houses arranged around the rim and a tenth house in the center. Female kin groups, together with their husbands and children, occupied the rim houses. The center house was for men only.

Further complicating the Tapirape system, there was a moiety division among the men, and within the two moieties there were three age classes. Different tasks were assigned to each age class. In addition, the whole community was divided into "eating groups," which acted as food cooperatives.

Such complexity necessitated a community of at least two hundred people in order to fill the places in the interconnected groups. But more than two hundred would have exhausted the resources of the local environment; and excess individuals who might have split off to form a new village could not do so, because a small community of, say, fifty or even a hundred people could not have functioned.

As a result, small families were valued, and specific measures, including infanticide, were put into practice. Each woman, for instance, was expected to have no more than three children and no more than two of the same sex. If a mother with two daughters, or two sons, gave birth to a third, the newborn was immediately buried.

Such practices, needless to say, are not enshrined in the mythology of the Tapirape. Nor are they spelled out in any other Native American mythology. In short, they were never meant to be given as gifts to posterity.

Nevertheless, the principle of reduction, even if veiled in symbolic language, stands as a permanent challenge. Told as a story, it hangs in the air as a problem. The ancients, one may say, have counted upon human compassion and ingenuity to find the specific solutions appropriate for each society.

12

The Human Payment

The great sun is the
only living thing.
—*Kiowa warrior's proverb*

Side by side with the wish to protect the innocent from death
is the uncomfortable realization that the individual is a tem-
porary unit in a greater scheme. As we have seen, society is
an organism in need of reduction to keep it from growing too
large for its allotted space. Yet even more basic is the realization that all of nature is a limited energy reserve, maintained
through a system of withdrawals and payments.

The word "payment" in this sense can be found in languages as different from each other as Aztec, Chorti, Desana,
Quechua, Navajo, and Zuni. In Aztec the verb is *moxtlahua*,
literally "to pay one's debt." In its extreme form the concept
is expressed by the term *tlacatica moxtlahua*, "to make the

human payment," more precisely, "to pay one's debt by using humans."

Missing the idea completely, outsiders who have reported (or overreported) the practice have given it the name "human sacrifice," which has come to be synonymous with all that is alien to civilized life. In the eyes of Christian Europe, during the early years of contact, "human sacrifice" was held as a proof of Satanism and a justification for conquest.

Typical is the account of the seventeenth-century writer George Alsop, reporting on the "warlike" and "naked" Susquehannock tribe of Pennsylvania and Maryland. "They Sacrifice a Childe to [their god]," he explains, "in an acknowledgement of their firm obedience to all his Devillish powers and Hellish commands."

Though toned down, the reports did not cease even in later years. Toward the end of the nineteenth century it was recorded that among the Bella Coola of British Columbia "children of the poor are bought from their parents to be made sacrifices. The blood is drunk and the flesh is eaten raw. The souls of the sacrificed go to live in the sun." Testimony along the same lines, from South America at least, has been forthcoming through the twentieth century.

Some of these accounts need to be considered carefully. The information on the Bella Coola, for instance, though published in a scientific journal, is hardly an eyewitness report. It was collected in Germany from the lips of a Bella Coola who visited Europe in 1885–86 and who may well have been describing one of the native theatrical performances typical of the cultures of the Pacific Northwest. As for South America, it is probable that in some cases the use of monkeys for food has been misinterpreted by missionaries who did not inquire closely enough.

There is no question, however, that the practice of paying one's "debt" existed, and perhaps still does exist in a few remote communities. Nor can there be doubt that it existed on a large scale in Aztec Mexico; and, as we have learned from the recent decipherments of Maya writing, it was more prevalent in southern Mexico and Guatemala than had previously been thought.

But it is necessary to understand that human sacrifice in the Americas, though widespread, has been common only as a philosophical concept. It is the idea, not the practice, that is paramount in native cultures.

By command of the sun

It will be recalled that in the Aztec myth of the reduction of ancestors, the five who made war on the four hundred, killing all but "a few," were inspired by the sun. It was the sun who gave them darts to shoot, and when the task was accomplished, the five victors "served the sun and gave it a drink."

Again, in the reduction myth of the Bororo it is the sun who worries about overpopulation, contriving a scheme to drown the people, so that they can be revived in more manageable numbers. Yet the Bororo, unlike the Aztec, have no tradition of human sacrifice as the term is understood by anthropologists and the world at large.

The same is true of the Mexican Huichol, who also look to the sun as a kind of regulator. The sun, according to Huichol mythology, saved the earth from overcrowding by

The Woman Who Lives in the Sun,
lithograph by Kenojuak,
Inuit of Cape Dorset,
Baffin Island, 1960.

ordering the trickster Kauyumari to place teeth in the women's vaginas. As a result the men of the ancient time, when they attempted intercourse, were desexed.

In an apparent reminder of the sun's intentions, an old riddle of the Cashinahua of western Brazil asks, "What is it that burns people when it gets up?" The answer, of course, is "the sun." The Cashinahua's neighbors, the Sharanahua, from whom no riddles have been reported, preserve the same idea in the expression "It is eating," which refers to the sun beating down while one is working in the garden.

The sun is not always successful, however, even when its intentions are perfectly clear. In a myth of the Venezuelan Yupa, a man who has traveled to the sky world is discovered by the sun, who tries to eat him. Fortunately, he is protected by his friend the moon, who stands in front of the helpless human, keeping him from the sun's clutches.

Equally circumspect, though in a different way, some mythologies aver that the sun used to eat humans but doesn't do so anymore. "Sun was a bad man formerly, and killed people," reads an old tradition of the Tahltan of British Columbia. "When people look at him now, sometimes they get sick. He is hard to look at. This is because he was formerly a bad man."

Providing fuller details, a story of the Brazilian Shipaya explains that in the ancient days the sun lived as a man among humans, while actually maintaining the people as a source of food. He would secretly kill someone, then grill the flesh for all to eat. At first the people were not suspicious. But when they discovered the ruse, they killed the sun. Without his light, however, they "suffered from dire want, because in the darkness no one could hunt or fish." Finally, one of the sun's children took his father's place, and he, so it is said, "is the sun today."

The Shipaya, like the Cashinahua, the Sharanahua, and the Tahltan, have no history of human sacrifice. Nor do countless other groups with similar lore, such as the Kaska (the sun was formerly a flesh eater), the Chumash (the sun to this day is a cannibal who stuffs babies into his headband), and the Isleta (the morning sun comes to get "sons and daughters of the people"). Clearly it is the idea itself that counts, rather than the practice.

Bringing and taking

Sun lore from various traditions presents not only the facts— in a metaphorical sense—but their interpretation.

The "facts" tell us that the sun is pitiless and calculating, asking for human lives, often on a daily basis. The explanation, in part, is that the sun needs victims if it is to continue in its course. As the sun himself states, in one version of a well-known Navajo myth, "I am glad when a person dies, as that is what keeps me moving." In some variants the sun stops until he is "paid." "I will travel," he says, "if I am paid with the lives of the people of the earth." Usually his pronouncement is connected to the origin of human death. As the Navajo mythmaker Sandoval expresses it, "He had claimed the lives of all the living in payment for his light."

Essentially the same story is told by the Hopi. Confronted by the stubborn, immovable sun, so the myth relates, "the [people] said, 'We will give you something.' They buried a child. Its spirit came up, then the sun moved on. [Later they] gave him another child, one which was not sick; [they] killed and buried the child. Then the sun went on."

Need it be said, human sacrifice in the literal sense has never been reported for either the Navajo or the Hopi. And certainly not for the Inuit of the far North. Yet an old Inuit myth, collected by the Danish-Inuit ethnographer Knud Rasmussen, emphasizes the inevitability of the process in question.

"At first there was only darkness, and no death," begins the text; then "two old women began one day to talk to each other. 'Let us do without the daylight, if at the same time we can be without Death!' said the one; doubtless she was afraid of death. 'Nay!' said the other, 'we will have both Light and Death.' And as the old woman said those words, it was so— Light came and with it Death. . . . With Death came the Sun, the Moon, and the Stars."

But the sun, like the moon and the stars on a smaller scale, can also be a bringer of human life.

As a Lakota has observed, "Without these life-giving rays all would be death." In the words of a Tewa prayer on behalf of a newborn, it is the sun and the morning star that "help this child to become a man." Similarly, addressing the sun with a newborn girl in her arms, the Hopi midwife prays: "Your beautiful rays, may they color our faces; being dyed in them, somewhere at an old age we shall fall asleep old women."

Yet in Hopi mythology—as opposed to prayer—the sun demands payment in human flesh. Correspondingly, the Navajo sun who requires human deaths is also regarded as the father of many children; and in Aztec lore the sun is spoken of as a "father" (and even a "mother") to humanity in general.

Evidently the sun as flesh eater and the sun as life giver can exist together in a single philosophy. Or, to paraphrase the Inuit myth on the origin of the sun, light and death are joined in a single enterprise.

PARABLE / The sun and the cornbread

One time in the night a man came in the house where there was a woman sitting and asked for something to eat. He wants her to give him some bread to eat.

She answered she had no bread or anything. Again he asked. But she said, "No, I have none."

"Yes," he said, "you have some bread." But she did not know it.

"Take some if you see it," she said, and the man reached over and picked up a loaf of cornbread from by her side. He cut it in four quarters, and every cut he made drew blood from the bread.

Then he ate that bread.

They say that man was the sun traveling back. And every child the woman had after that died right away. The sun had made his bread out of something that ought to have remained to give life to the children.

—Anonymous, Munsee Delaware
(Ontario)

Attempting to explain the native position for audiences out of tune with myth, twentieth-century anthropologists have offered variations on the essential idea, using phrases that echo modern concepts.

In the words of Gerardo Reichel-Dolmatoff, speaking for the Desana, "The principal energy of the sun . . . constitutes mainly a huge closed circuit in which the entire biosphere participates. The Desana imagine this circuit as having a fixed quantity of energy that flows eternally between man and animal, between society and nature. The quantity of energy being fixed, man must remove what he needs only under certain conditions and must convert this particle of 'borrowed' energy into a form that can be reincorporated into the circuit."

Gerald Weiss, referring to the philosophy of the Campa, states the matter in somewhat simpler terms: "There is no such occurrence as the creation of something out of nothing, but only the transformation of something out of something else."

Claude Lévi-Strauss, for Native America in general: "Indigenous philosophy may even contain the idea that human beings, animals, and plants share a common stock of life."

And again for Native America, Bruce G. Trigger, delivering the Distinguished Lecture in Archeology at the 1990 convention of the American Anthropological Association: "While it is important to understand Aztec prisoner sacrifice in ecological and functional terms, it is no less important to recognize it as being one specific elaboration of a set of beliefs that extended from the Tupinamba of the Amazonian forests as far north as the Iroquoians of the northeastern woodlands of North America. This cult, or network of cults, involved sacrificing prisoners to the sun in the belief that this was necessary to maintain the cosmic energy flows upon which all life on earth depends."

Or, as simply expressed in an old song of the New Mexican Isleta—one of the great majority of American cultures for whom the sacrifice of humans in the Aztec sense does not exist—"The sun brings human lives to the earth and also takes them away."

Paying the earth

For those whose livelihood depends directly on the earth, as well as for hunters who must deal with the animal master, the concept of payment is more than an abstract idea. It is a duty.

Prayer, always the hopeful mode of expression, suggests that in the case of the agriculturalist, his or her debt may be discharged with something less than human life. In Arizona and in New Mexico a beautifully crafted "prayer stick" (a straight branch tipped with feathers) may be "sacrificed." Less elegantly—as among the Chorti of Guatemala—a valuable animal serves as the offering.

Addressing his words to the earth herself, the Chorti farmer prepares to slit the throats of a chicken and a turkey, proclaiming, "We bring it here, our poultry; it is your payment, and with it we entreat you. Look on us with open eyes, and give to us what we eat with open hands." A similar ritual is indicated in an old parable of the Cora, in which an offering of cornmeal soup is poured onto the earth with the hopeful declaration, "This and no more."

Thus prayer draws the line, placing human life off limits. It is myth—conveniently set in the ancient time—that permits the question of payment to be fully explored.

In a mythic text from the Tepehua of eastern Mexico a mother who has buried her stillborn child discovers corn sprouting from the grave. In a myth from Peru a woman who asks the sun for food is impregnated by the sun himself. She bears his child, but corn and other crops do not appear until the infant has been dismembered and the pieces of its body sown in the fields.

A not untypical story from Honduras makes the child himself beg to be sacrificed. "Listen, Papá," pleads the little boy, "if you kill me, you'll eat yams and chayotes. They'll grow right here. . . . From my blood I'll give you sweet manioc, malangas, bananas, chayotes. I'll be born again so that crops to eat can grow from my blood, and tobacco from my body." In a parallel story from southern Brazil, it is a girl who asks her mother to bury her alive. From her body grows the world's first manioc.

Though there are exceptions, the general rule in Native American mythology is that the sacrificial victim is female if the culture is one in which women are the planters; male if men are the planters. In North and South America, east of the Rocky Mountains and the Andes, women do most of the garden work; and in the related myths, crops arise from the body of the woman. In Mexico and Central America a man or a boy fills the same role, both as real-life worker and as mythic victim.

The very young and the very old—of either sex—often appear as either the victims or the beneficiaries. In a myth of the Mexican Mixe, it is the children who profit (though not without guilt) after killing their aged grandfather. The old man had insisted that they help him with the gardening. Irritated by his demands and seeing that he was weakened by work, they killed him and buried his body. Afterward, as they were boiling beans, a voice from the pot called out to them, "You killed your grandfather, you're eating your grandfather."

In stories recorded for the Cherokee, Creek, and Natchez of the southeastern United States an old woman is the one who is put to death, and her body becomes a source of crops for young children. In a Natchez version she instructs her two little girls to kill her and burn her. From the ashes come corn, beans, and pumpkins.

Where the situation is reversed, and the victim is a child, certain myths from Mexico make it clear that the sacrifice must not be wasted. It must be directed to the earth. In a version from the modern Nahua of Puebla State, it is told that an old woman threw her daughter's baby away, but he survived. Then she threw him into the river, but he did not drown. Finally she buried him, and cornstalks grew up. Drawing upon the same idea, a tale from the Huichol tells of exasperated parents who threw their baby out of the house instead of "planting" him as they should have done. They suffered the consequences when their stored corn suddenly disappeared.

These events, naturally, are said to have occurred in the ancient time, and they are confined to the give-and-take between humans and food plants. Latter-day equivalents, which stretch the concept to other kinds of earth disturbance, have been recorded from the central Andes—in the form of hearsay, the modern successor to myth.

In the Andes, irrigation projects or any kind of construction may require "payments" of coca leaves or slain animals. For large engineering works, human "payments" are rumored. In one case, reported by an anthropological team in southern Peru, a woman of Paucartambo in the Department of Cuzco made efforts to find out whether it was true, as she had been told, that her missing son had been buried under one of the piers of the newly constructed bridge over the Vilcanota River. Such sacrifices are said to be required by the deity Pacha, who, in the words of an ethnographer, "is very jealous of the integrity of the earth."

Bargaining with the animal master

Like the agriculturalist who sacrifices a prayer stick, the hunter in the North American Southwest may offer either a prayer stick or a pinch of "prayer meal" (special cornmeal used for ceremonial purposes). A Zuni hunter who sacrifices in this manner is said to "make payment."

Among the Popoluca of southern Mexico, hunters make similar offerings of natural resin, or incense, called copal. In this case the gift is presented so that the animal masters will *not* demand a payment in human life.

More substantial sacrifices are made regularly by hunter-farmers in Central America, who set aside a portion of their garden for either the master or his animal charges. On the simplest level, this is merely a technique of domestic economy: the extra produce attracts game, which can be easily harvested. The deeper meaning is that a process of give-and-take has been set in motion, which obligates both the donor and the receiver. As explained by a Bribri hunter, in order to get the tapir "we must exchange banana plants."

Humans who hold up their end of the bargain may thereby prevent the animal master from demanding the heavier price. Among the Honduran Jicaque the story is told of a coati who complained to the master, "The farmer caught me eating his corn and killed me!" But the master replied, "It's all right. You were ruining his corn. He keeps my beloved animals nice and fat. He has the right to kill one to eat. Don't bother me with that farmer."

In theory at least, the more drastic price is demanded often enough, and in some cases it is taken in advance—or taken regularly as a kind of retainer fee. Numerous cultures harbor the belief that human diseases are sent by animals or their masters in order to protect the animal side of the equation from an overweighted human population. The price, typically, is exacted from the very young.

Among the Cubeo, for instance, the anaconda—widely regarded in Amazonia as an animal master—is said to become enraged at the birth of a human child. In the words of a Desana shaman, "The Master of Animals, in his personification of an anaconda, is furious when women bear children. The fish, too. Also the jaguars of the forest." The consequence, it is said, is human disease directly caused by the animal spirits.

Likewise, among the Havasupai of Arizona the mountain lion and the wolf are said to contaminate the carcass of the slain deer, causing not the hunter but his infant child to fall ill. Similar theories have been reported from numerous other groups, including the Cherokee (diseases were invented by animals when human population became too "thick"), the Creek (specific animals made specific diseases), and the Navajo (there are thirty-two diseases, each caused by a specific animal).

The animals are not always so subtle. The indirect method of sending a disease may sometimes be replaced by a more brutal counterpart. In a myth of the Zoque of southern Mexico it is told that a man who had been pointedly invited to visit the animals' underground home saw that "they roasted the buttocks of men who like to hunt and gave the roast meat to others to eat."

For the Guajiro it is reported that the female animal-master, Pulówi, has a husband, the rain spirit, who travels over the earth on her behalf. He carries bottles with him and brings back human blood for his wife to drink.

In some cases, and for reasons of their own, the animals may be selective—as with the Tucano, who say that if fish are taken from restricted areas the "ancestors" of the fish will take infant children. One child is taken for each fish.

But in other lore the animals need only drop the hint. The sacrifice is then volunteered by humans or their representatives. For the Desana the essential idea is that shamans make hunting possible by offering young lives to the animal master. Parents who suffer the consequences blame the shaman, saying, "He pays for our food with the lives of our children."

As expressed by one Desana commentator, "It is an exchange of deaths." In other words, just as the dead tapir enters the house of the hunter, the dead child enters the house of the tapir. In this way an equal trade is achieved.

Or—once again in a mythological setting—the hunter himself may take the initiative. In a story told by the Cree of eastern Canada a man is said to have returned empty-handed day after day, always to find his little son waiting for him. Blaming his bad luck on this, he shot the boy with his bow and arrow and thereafter was able to kill game.

The need for payment on the part of an immediate family member may be recognized even in prayer—though with an escape clause.

In a typical prayer, or formula, sung by hunters of the Aguaruna tribe the singer promises the spirit powers that his wife will have a miscarriage if he is granted a spider monkey or a deer. But the words he uses are these: "Make me find deer. To the Nunkui woman I will give a miscarriage . . . , I will give a miscarriage for monkey fat." The trick, calculated to fool the animal masters, is that the hunter is identifying his wife with the earth spirit, Nunkui, who would naturally be immune to miscarriage. As the quintessential woman, she can suffer no imperfection. Thus there is a will to obey the rules, and a will to break them.

Though there may be cheating (in the hope of evading the immediate consequences) the underlying assumption is that a meaningful payment is necessary in order to achieve the balance that permits human life. The cultures in question—the Aguaruna, the Desana, and others—are evidently acquainted with human sacrifice. They do not *perform* it. Rather, they *acknowledge* it as an expected part of doing business with nature. This is not to say, of course, that the principle is highly

valued. It simply means that it is dealt with, indirectly no
doubt, and without consistency, which, in its clumsy way, is
the only acceptable method of approaching a subject that
most societies—rightly so—are unable to place squarely on
the human agenda.

RENEWAL

13

The Angry Earth

There is a hole at the end
of the thief's path.

—*Lakota proverb*

You are buried in the hole
which you dug for yourself.

—*Ute proverb*

Even if people can restrain themselves, allowing natural resources to be held in reserve, and even if "payments," or
sacrifices, are made, there is still uncertainty about the future.
How long will the earth endure the presence of humans?

By their mere existence, human beings defile the land.
They use it up. They "eat" it, in the words of the Mayo of
northwestern Mexico. Can something be done to lessen the
harmful effects?

One answer is that human beings can make amends for
their offenses. Another is that they may exert themselves to
prolong the earth's life. Still another is that they may restore
the earth to its youthful condition.

Each of these approaches is represented in Native American testimony, and to some extent the solutions are intertwined. But the preliminary step, perhaps, is to make amends. In the words of an old Ojibwa myth (in which a presumptuous human attempted to control the winds), "you," the perpetrator, must "undo your foolishness."

As part of the effort, it helps to have an understanding of the earth's own point of view as expressed both in formal mythology and in everyday folk belief.

An examination of native lore from various cultures reveals that those creatures who injure the earth by and large are humans. "Don't urinate on me!" warns the earth spirit in a typical passage from the lore of the Hopi. The warning, of course, is addressed to human beings. Earth seldom if ever complains of animal urine or pounding hooves or tree roots striking deep into the soil. Humans are the species guilty of defilement.

Defilement, moreover, takes in a broader range of injuries than is implied by the modern word "pollution." Simply working the soil, widely viewed in European thinking as a healthy communion with the earth, may be seen differently in a Native American context. Agriculture, even for those who willingly practice it, can be a form of abuse. The Mazatec say that the planting of crops "mistreats" the earth. Or, in a phrase used by the Bribri, it "kills" the earth.

One can imagine, therefore, that the earth reacts unfavorably. It may abandon its role as nurturing mother and become a scold. Or, instead of simply waiting to receive "payments," it may cry out and demand them.

The weeping woman

As we have seen repeatedly, the coming together of philosophy and folklore is one of the essential features of Native American thought. Ideas often gather around a folkloric figure, which may have existed in local mythology for a very long time and which may subsequently become the rallying point for differing, even contradictory, points of view.

One of these figures, known widely through North and Central America, is the dangerous woman who lives apart from the human community, haunting woods, swamps, caves, or riverbanks. Though she keeps to herself, she yearns for company, crying out eerily. Sometimes she is said to be looking for children; sometimes, adult males, especially hunters.

For the old-time Penobscot of Maine, she was Skwákcwtemus, "swamp woman," described as having been dressed only in moss, with long, flowing moss-hair covering her body. When people heard her moaning and crying in the depths of the forest, they took care to keep their distance. Both adult males and children were at risk. Hunters, forgetting their better judgment, were tempted to seek this woman out. Children, if they wandered from camp, might be snatched and carried off.

A similar female spirit was known to the Okanagon of British Columbia. It was said that she haunted the woods and lured hunters with beautiful sad wailing. For the Chumash of California the dangerous woman was a feline spirit called *maxalaw*, or, in Spanish, La Llorona, "the weeping woman." People said that she cried from the trees like a newborn baby.

Whenever her voice was heard, it meant that someone would die.

Among the Hopi, at least formerly, she was Tíkuiwuhti, a terrifying supernatural dressed in either a white bridal robe or a large white antelope skin. Considered a deity of game animals and of children, she was known by her long-drawn-out moans. Sometimes hunters reported seeing her campfire at a distance.

The Chumash description of the "weeping" voice and the Hopi emphasis on the all-white costume suggest a link with the well-known Mexican form of this terrifying spirit, almost always known as La Llorona—"the weeper" or "the weeping woman"—and generally said to be dressed in white.

The Nahua of central Mexico call her either by her Spanish name, La Llorona, or, in their own language, *cihuachocani*, "woman weeper." All in white, with long, black hair hanging down her back, she glides over the earth or the water, moaning *aaaaay, mis hijos!*, "alas, my children!"

Tarascan people of Michoacán State report that she comes right up to the people's houses. Again dressed in white, she is called La Llorona, or La Guaricha, "the ghost." Her appearance serves as a warning that someone is about to die.

La Llorona is also known in Mexican communities in Arizona, New Mexico, and southern California. In Los Angeles it is reported that she is constantly searching for children and believes that all children are hers.

Southward, her range extends into Central America as far as Panama. Among the Bribri of Costa Rica she is said to have lost many children and now lives in caves beneath waterfalls. To hear her voice is to know that a small child will die. "I am weeping," she is reported to say, "and one day you will weep just as I do."

In some of the twentieth-century accounts, La Llorona is made to appear repentant. According to a Nahua report, she drowned her newborn children and now weeps with regret. The Zapotec say that she ate her own child; and now, tormented by the painful memory, she wanders at night, wailing.

Although it cannot be proven that Christian influence is responsible for these pious modern versions, it may be pointed out that in the oldest records—from the sixteenth-century Aztec—the weeping woman exhibits no guilt whatsoever.

In the Florentine Codex, an early colonial document prepared with the help of Aztec scribes, the familiar figure appears under the name Cihuacoatl, "woman snake." "The clothes in which this woman appeared were white," reads a portion of the text. Moreover, "at night she would cry out and wail."

The description continues: "They also say that she carried a cradle on her back, the way a woman carries her child, and she would appear in the marketplace in the midst of other women, lay the cradle down, and vanish. When the other women noticed the abandoned cradle lying there, they would look inside and find a stone like the point of a spear, [the instrument] with which they used to put to death those whom they sacrificed. By this they knew that it was Cihuacoatl who had left [the cradle]."

As reported by the sixteenth-century Spanish missionary Diego Durán, the statue of "the goddess Cihuacoatl was of stone. It had a very large mouth, wide open, with ferocious teeth. It had a huge broad headdress and a woman's costume with skirt, blouse, and mantle completely white."

Native sources do not identify either Cihuacoatl or La Llorona with the earth. Nor does the weeping woman in any of her other aspects appear as an earth deity or a nature spirit—at least, not in modern folk belief. The connection is openly made, however, in an old Aztec myth that accounts for her origin.

Recorded in the mid-1500s, probably in Spanish—but preserved only in a French translation from the same period—the story relates that the terrifying woman who cries at night was at first a sky dweller. In those days there was nothing but sky above and water below. Called Tlalteuctli, this "goddess" who would become the earth was covered with eyes and mouths at every joint of her body, and in each of her mouths she had biting teeth "like a wild beast."

When the other gods had brought Tlalteuctli to the surface of the water, they created earth's features from her flesh: "from her hair, trees and flowers; from her eyes, pools and springs and little caverns; from her mouth, rivers and large caves; from her nose, valleys and mountains; from her shoulders, mountains. And sometimes at night this goddess would weep, desiring to eat human hearts, and she would not be silent until they were delivered to her, nor would she bear fruit unless she was watered with human blood."

"The earth hates us"

Although Tlalteuctli—by this name—may have passed into history, the earth spirit who refuses to wait patiently for

The Aztec earth goddess Coatlicue ("Of Snakes Is Her Skirt");
pre-Conquest sculpture now in the Museum of
Anthropology, Mexico City.

"payment," regularly demanding it as her due, is still known widely in Mexico and Central America. Plainspoken and fiercely logical, this feminine spirit is hardly "the weeping woman" who dresses alluringly in white and travels after dark. Yet there are similarities.

In the lore of the Jicaque she appears as a vengeful mother, who says of her human children, "Today I invite them to eat, but tomorrow they are going to hate me." The cracks in the earth's surface, it is said, are her thirsty mouths; and whenever these are seen, during a dry spell, one must walk carefully.

The meaning, according to a well-informed Jicaque source, is that "the earth is asking for human death." She is "resentful against mortals because we are always puncturing her when we plant crops, when we build fences, and because we beat her when we walk." If a farmer asks permission before breaking the ground, he may even be rebuffed. "Never mind," the earth is imagined as saying. "When your death arrives, you will pay me for everything."

A Jicaque child who asks an elder, "Why do young and old and babies die?" is given the answer, "It is because the earth wants to eat them. She desires them very much."

As set forth in a well-known "history" told by the Bribri, the earth's need for vengeance was established in the ancient days. At first, we are told, there was no actual soil, only rock. The earth herself was at this time a newborn infant, resting in a cradle deep in the underworld.

In order to bring soil to the surface, a bat descended repeatedly to the cradle and nibbled on the child's body. Although the infant screamed with pain, the creature succeeded in "eating" the poor child mouthful by mouthful. Taking her flesh to the surface, he voided it as excrement. Thus the bare rock became covered with workable land.

Even so, the earth's ordeal was not finished. In the words of a Bribri narrator, "when the earth came into this world, she suffered much from the hands of human beings." Therefore, "the earth hates us humans, and because of it Sibú [the supreme deity] established that all human corpses would be buried inside her. But the ancestors believed that this was more than burial. Rather it was the earth taking vengeance on humanity."

The more usual position, however, is that the earth, having struck a compromise with humans in the ancient days, holds her (or his) anger in check. According to a story told by the Cora, the earth, regarded as female, cried out in agony when the digging stick first punctured her flesh, then agreed to be used in this manner when it was explained to her that all humans and animals would become her nourishment after death. As expressed in a myth from the Mazatec, "The earth agreed that people would mistreat her, but they would have to return to her in the form of payment."

Phrased somewhat differently in testimony recorded from the Achi Maya of Guatemala, the story is that earth, once again regarded as female, originally cried, "It hurts me!" when people tried to cultivate her. To protect her interest, a "contract" was made with the earth. By this agreement she feeds us while we are alive; when we die, we become "the earth's meat."

As conceived by the Mayo of northwestern Mexico (unrelated to the Maya of southern Mexico and Guatemala), the agreement allows humans not only to plant the earth, but to excavate it for potting clay. With reference to the eternal contract, one hears the expression, "The earth will devour you."

P A R A B L E / The hungry old man

Our mother commanded her sons, "Get over there and do the sowing!"

So they went, and they got there. They were sowing.

And then there was crying, a man was crying. He said, "Why do you hurt me?" Then they listened, and the old man said to them, "My grandchildren, why do you hurt me? Can't you ask her to give me a little something to nourish myself with?"

Then they said to their mother, "How can this be? There's an old man crying. There's a person here. We're supposed to tell you to give him something. He's hungry."

Then she made up some cornmeal soup and commanded them, "This you must give him, and tell him, 'This and no more!' He can expect nothing further from us. He must live on this. He must give you permission to use him."

—Told by Leocadio Enriquez,
Cora (Mexico)

Though typical of Mexico and Central America, the idea of the ill-humored earth extends both northward into Arizona and New Mexico and southward into the central Andes. Among the Quechua of southern Peru the earth's anger is said to put humans at risk for short periods during August and December. In the words of one Quechua traditionalist, "the earth comes to life the first six days of August. Then at Christmas the earth comes to life again. . . . The earth suffers if she is worked on these days. She becomes angry, she cries out with pain if the people touch her on these days." Others say that when the earth comes "alive" in August, she must be appeased with offerings of coca. If this is not done, the people fall prey to diseases.

Among the Navajo of Arizona and New Mexico the earth is said to have exhibited ill humor in the ancient time when the wind first breathed life into her. In those days, as now, she was a recumbent figure, lying on her stomach, facing east with "her feet being placed over there where the sun goes down." Predicting a future of defilement, she invoked the familiar contract: "When she spoke, [the people] were embarrassed. 'From now on,' " she said, " 'you will urinate on me and defecate on me and do whatever to me and throw bad things on me. And when you die you will go back in the Earth. You will not go elsewhere.' "

Like the human beings who are bound to live and die upon it, the land itself does not go "elsewhere" either. Further myths reveal that the earth and her human charges are mutual captives. Yet the earth has a distinct advantage.

Offended spirits

It would appear that the earth is with us, physically, even if it does not approve of our lives. It may make a gesture as if to reject us, but it cannot actually depart. "The earth was offended," reads a passage from an origin myth of the Jicaque. "She turned her face to one side."

In a myth of the Navajo she seems to act more decisively. "There will be people," she says, contemplating the origin of humans, "so I cannot remain here and have myself tramped upon." But the speaker in this case—who indeed stands beyond the view of ordinary mortals—is Changing Woman, spirit of the earth. This is not quite the same as the earth herself (at least not here).

If the earth is unable to pick up and leave, its demand for "payment" would seem to be the only way of protecting its well-being. Yet there is another tactic, more subtle but just as effective, which is brought to bear by the removal of selected aspects of earth's power.

While earth itself cannot withdraw, plants, animals, and minerals can. This is in fact a fairly common idea in North America north of Mexico, where it largely replaces the notion of the "contract" by which the earth "eats" the dead.

In some cases the earth may personally intervene, acting on behalf of the separate parts of nature. In a report on the herb-gathering strategies of the Ojibwa of Parry Island, the anthropologist Diamond Jenness has explained that "Nokomis, 'grandmother earth,' is the source of all the power that exists in trees and shrubs. . . . If a medicine man should fail to offer tobacco in payment for his plants, Nokomis would be offended and his remedies would lose their potency."

But the more usual idea, commonly expressed in mythology, is that earth's charges, acting on their own, simply choose to withdraw. Crops, food animals, and even mineral deposits may shrink from sight, typically in response to human recklessness.

In an old myth of the Micmac of eastern Canada, which accounts for the disappearance of the moose from Prince Edward Island, it is told that many years ago moose were already diminishing because of the island's small size and its increasing human population. Despite this, and against the advice of the older people, hunters staged a great roundup and killed nearly all the moose that were left. In the aftermath, those few that had not been killed, offended by the people's wastefulness, departed from the island, never to return.

The Haida of British Columbia used to tell a similar story, in which a young man, while out hunting, finds two young women bathing. The women are geese who have temporarily removed their skins. Threatening to keep the two goose skins, the man forces the younger of the women to become his bride and leads her to his village. Later, when the people are hungry, the helpful bride hears a flock of geese overhead and runs with her husband into the woods, where they discover a pile of food. A few days afterward more food is delivered by the geese, and again the people eat. When the villagers begin to complain that the geese are stingy and do not bring enough, the goose woman becomes angry and flies off, never to return.

P A R A B L E / The salmon woman

[Raven] went to the graveyard and asked the dead people, "Are there any twins here?" And he heard a voice from one of the graves saying, "I was once a salmon."★

He opened the grave, and inside it he found the corpse of a woman. He washed it with water-of-life, and the woman stood up and rubbed her eyes as if she had been sleeping.

[Raven] brought her to his house. He said, "There are no salmon here. Can you provide some?"

At her request she was given a mat and gull feathers. Then she swam around in the river. Wherever she disturbed the water, salmon appeared. The woman was called Chief Headfirst Woman.

Then [Raven] caught many salmon in his net and laid them on the drying rack inside the house. He carried in firewood and heaped it beneath the salmon to make a good fire. But he bumped against the drying rack, and salmon got caught in his hair. Enraged, he threw down the firewood and cried, "Why must you tug at my hair?" And Chief Headfirst Woman asked, "What did you say?"

[Raven] quickly replied, "Oh, nothing important." But she knew perfectly well he had insulted the salmon, and once again she became a dry corpse.

—Anonymous, Oowekeeno
(British Columbia)

★Human twins are regarded as salmon.

But not all of the myths end unhappily. In a story formerly told by the Delaware, the corn mother is offended when she learns that there are young boys who doubt she is a living spirit. As a consequence, "the heart of Corn turned into living beings [evidently insects], and all began disappearing in flight with wings." Aware that an offense had been committed, two boys traveled to the sky world, where the corn mother had withdrawn, and persuaded her to return to earth in exchange for an offering of burnt mussel shells.

Stories of the offended corn woman are also told by the Huichol, the Cora, and other tribes of western Mexico. In these myths the fictional people make the mistake of working the poor woman too hard when she appears among them as the wife of a farmer. In agony she flees. Yet she leaves behind her the important lesson that corn must be handled with respect.

With reference to this famous story, and speaking of the corn in particular, a Huichol commentator has observed, "We must treat it well, as a sacred thing. So that it does not leave us."

Perhaps even better known to the outside world is the offended corn woman of Zuni lore. She and her sisters, usually referred to in English as "corn maidens," are said to have been mistreated in the ancient days, either by men who made improper advances or by the people in general, who wasted the corn, playing games with it and using it to make fancy foods that were not needed.

Irritated, the Zuni corn maidens fled southward. They finally returned, however, after people made amends by observing a strict fast, adhering to the instructions: "Do not stir, do not urinate, do not drink water, do not eat, do not smoke, do not sleep, do not speak to each other. Sit with your arms crossed on your breast." Finally, with that, the absent spirits softened their position, saying, "Let us go to give our people corn."

Another well-known Zuni myth tells how Salt Woman became offended when people polluted her salt beds with trash and debris. Angry, she disappeared. The people redeemed themselves by "praying for forgiveness for being so careless." As a result, the Zuni eventually found new salt beds—though these were not so close to the village as the ones that had been lost to pollution.

Still another Zuni story is told of Turquoise Man, whose beds were being mined carelessly. Saying, "My flesh is valuable but they waste it," he, too, disappeared. In this case, unfortunately, the loss was permanent. The Zuni from that time on did not have their own source of high-quality turquoise, and the people were forced to say, "We do not know where he went."

Evidently there is a limit to what can be accomplished through remorse or prayer or the reaffirmation of good intentions. But however it is expressed, respect for the parts of nature on which humans rely is necessary if there is to be any possibility of sustaining yields and of renewing resources that have become endangered—or, as the myths tell, offended and withdrawn.

14

Earth's Past
and Future

No one can tell how long
daylight may last.
—*Zuni saying*

In the old days, when talking to children, a Lakota elder
would place a hand on the ground and explain: "We sit in the
lap of our Mother. . . . We shall soon pass, but the place where
we now rest will last forever."

The same reassurance, though with slightly less certainty, is
expressed in a traditional prayer of the Shawnee, spoken
directly to the earth: "The Creator created you to be still and
hold us on your lap for eternity. You must grow out well and
settle down with a green head."

Equally comforting, but without making an incautious
claim, Navajo traditionalists have sometimes said that earth's
outer surface is *bike hozhon*, "beauty," as revealed in plants,

water, and mountains, while its inner form is *saa nagai*, "long life."

Such observations reflect the apparent truth that the earth is always with us; and in the ordinary course of events this cannot be questioned. The earth as we know it has no power to withdraw.

But the art of prophecy—for which Native America is justly renowned—paints a somewhat different picture. Without fear of contradiction, and often in the form of a warning whose value is instantly recognized, the prophet envisions a time when the earth will end.

Indeed, it may vanish entirely. In a prophecy of the Tahltan of British Columbia it is said that the "Earth-mother [who lives under the earth and holds it up] is becoming older and weaker all the time, and by and by she will not be able to hold up the earth any longer. Then it will fall into the water which is below the earth, and disappear."

Occasionally the prophecies are hopeful, as in the case of the Peruvian Campa, who say that when the present world is destroyed a new one will take its place. At that time the sky will again be close to the earth, just as it was in the ancient days, and the earth, which has long been silent, will "speak" once more.

In general, however, the prophet's vision dwells on the end without imagining that the new earth, should there be one, will bring an improvement. This style of prophecy holds even in Mexico, where it is widely theorized that the earth has been destroyed and rebuilt one or more times in the past. The coming destruction is viewed with dread, and it is often thought to be close at hand. In the mid-twentieth century the Totonac of Puebla State were predicting that the next "cleaning of time" would be the year 2000. The same date has been used by the Tzotzil of Chiapas State, who have said that the earth itself will turn over.

In Mexico, as elsewhere, fire and flood are commonly mentioned as agents of the earth's undoing. But the threat of "turning," or "turning over"—implying an earthquake or worse—is equally prominent.

The Cayapa of Ecuador used to have a tradition that the earth would eventually overturn, burying the human race. According to the old-time Maricopa of Arizona, any disturbance of the earth was caused by the "turning over" of an underworld deity; and in the view of the Cupeño of southern California this deity would someday "turn over" and the world in its entirety would be destroyed.

With reference to the mythic prototype of the dread event, a riddle of the Brazilian Cashinahua asks: "What turned over?" Answer: "the earth."

An alternate view is that the earth will deteriorate gradually, often with omens signaling the end. "When the time is coming," reads a prophecy recorded for the Pima, "young men will grow old in a short time, and a young woman will grow old in a very short time. When the time is near, they will plant corn and sometimes it will fail, and with the corn will come up all kinds of weeds."

A comparable text from the Wichita of the southern Great Plains predicts that the end of the world will be near when planted corn comes up "something else."

Well acquainted with prophecy, the Iroquois of New York likewise have foreseen a time when the earth will lose its fruitfulness and the Creator—in the words of one of the prophets—"will bring to an end the duties with which we are severally charged." Continuing, the prophetic text spells out the dangers: "Then shall the waters which are held in their several places become polluted; finally all other things shall likewise become old and decayed upon the earth; and all things that grow out of the ground, too, shall grow old."

Relating this process to the beginning of earth's history, when the people had just emerged and the land was still soft and wet, the twentieth-century Zuni have fashioned a view of the future—or even the present—which includes the observation that the earth today has become old and dry. The result will be famine, which some say has already arrived, though for the time being it has been made invisible by the food displayed in the supermarket.

An infection of the land

The Zuni allusion to the supermarket points discreetly to one of the recurring themes in Native American prophecy. The presence of European newcomers, it is often observed, has changed the earth, and it is this change that will bring about the end.

As with the late-twentieth-century Zuni, a Pima prophet of the 1920s foresaw that the end would come by stealth. "Here stays the earth," reads his testimony, "and you [the Pima] drop seeds into it, and it will be the proper thing to do. Here stays the earth, and water is in the earth's veins, bones are in the earth's mountains. Gold, iron, and silver are the earth's bones. Therefore the Earth is living; it is not just earth. It stays here living. And you will not be the ones to kill the staying earth. I will leave it to [the non-Pimans] and they will do it. And these will kill the staying earth, even if you don't know anything [about it] and you will just be feeling fine. And you will see it when it happens."

The obscure references to greed, mining, and money in the Piman testimony become clearer in statements made by California Wintun prophets of the same period. In the words of the seer Tilly Griffen, as recorded by the ethnographer Cora Du Bois, "They dug money out of our land and took it far away and piled it up. . . . Gold rattles, and silver rattles with a different sound. . . . We Indians never hurt the ground to get it out because we never knew we would have to eat on it [i.e., spend it for food]. We had our own food. We got our own acorns, our own deer, our own fish, our own seeds. We didn't have gold and silver to buy food with. We knew nothing of blasting rocks and crushing them all up."

Another of the Wintun shaman-prophets, Kate Luckie, observed: "The white people dig deep long tunnels. They make roads. They dig as much as they wish. They don't care how much the ground cries out. How can the spirit of the earth like the white man? That is why God will upset the world—because it is sore all over. Everywhere the white man has touched it, it is sore. It looks sick. . . . But eventually the water will come."

Emma Wallace, yet another of the Wintun shamans (also called "natural doctors"), explained to Cora Du Bois that the floodwaters would rise in the north and "clean the whole world."

Earlier, in the 1800s, following the gold rush, the Wintun had envisioned not water but a great tremor as the agent of destruction. In response to the surge in population, the earth would stretch, it was said, flattening the mountains until they became a plain, like the land of the dead.

Preparing for the end, the Wintun and other northern California groups began to assemble in special houses. As recalled much later by a Pomo man, "The world was to end and all were to build an earth house to die in. . . . The new houses were different. They were deeper and bigger. They were called *le tca* [death house]."

Resignation, with suicidal overtones, echoes through much of the post-contact prophetic lore. For the old-time Shawnee, who, like other tribes of the eastern United States, kept an eternal flame, it is recorded that this came to be thought of as a means of lighting a world fire when the Europeans achieved dominance.

The Delaware, or Lenape, who were closely associated with the Shawnee during their forced migration westward, had prophets among both the northern Lenape, or Munsee, and the southern Lenape, or Unami. With reference to the world fire (which, according to the Shawnee prophecy, the people themselves would kindle), one of the Munsee prophets is said to have advised his followers, "You my people will be driven back westward until your backs are against the place where the fire has gone through. The other Lenape [also] shall be driven back until the incoming waves of the great western saltwater will make death-laughter in the grinning jaws of your standing skeletons."

In South America, tribal suicide as a fact, not a prediction, was reported for the Bororo of Brazil in the 1970s, where in one community the women as a group (using unidentified drugs) stopped bearing children. Among the Kaiowá, another

of the Brazilian tribes, literal suicide by individuals was reported in the early 1990s as a response to population pressure
from outsiders.

Deliberate, uncharacteristic stripping of the environment is
yet another form of self-destructive response. In late-twentieth-century Ecuador, Shuar hunters in some areas are reported to have engaged in a wasteful slaughter of monkeys,
birds, and peccaries, saying, "Things are changing," "We
must prove that we are capable," "Soon the cattle ranches
will be here."

Such wholesale harvests recall the overhunting of the beaver in eastern North America during the eighteenth century.
Why native people, supposedly respectful of natural resources, should have waged a campaign of extermination
against the beaver is a question that has been much debated.
A widely held theory is that Indian hunters were simply
seduced by the profits to be made in the fur trade with
Europeans. An alternate explanation, offered by the historian
Calvin Martin, is that hunters were rebelling against the animal masters.

Since native people themselves were being exterminated
by epidemics (introduced from Europe), and since the masters
were thought to control disease, the warfare against the beaver may—in part at least—have been a campaign of retribu-
tion.

Yet for many cultures keenly aware of change, and even
among those gripped by the need for prophecy, the future is
not without hope. Among Pimans, who have heard dire
warnings from their prophets, it has also been said that after
the railroad came through their country, the deity I'itoi,

"elder brother," was seen in the guise of a little old man, driving all the game to safety.

Ancient destructions

It should be remembered that theories of world collapse were not devised simply to accuse Europeans. The idea of universal destruction is a recurring feature in the mythic history of the earth, and the culprit, if there is one, is not a single ethnic group but humanity as a whole.

As revealed in a passage from Shawnee lore, the world flood of ancient times was brought about by the Creator herself. She had found it necessary to take action, so it is said, in order to get rid of the people she had made during the first creation. They were too large, too strong, and too destructive.

Earth Doctor, the Piman Creator, is also said to have destroyed the first world—not by flood but by pulling down the sky. The reason was that the first people had become too populous, overspreading the earth until food had become scarce and there was no longer enough water to supply their needs.

As with the Pima, overpopulation is cited as the cause of ancient cataclysms in the lore of the Gran Chaco region of Paraguay and Argentina. According to the Toba, one of the Argentine groups, the earth was "devastated" by a great darkness. As told by one of the Toba narrators, this came about "probably because when the earth is full of people it has to change: the population has to be thinned out to save the world."

In a version recorded for the Argentine Chorote, population again provides the motive. But in this case "the earth
sank, and some water began to seep out like in a dry riverbed,
and then came more and more . . . , killing all the people. No
one was left."

In some of the more exquisitely subtle variants of this
far-flung lore, simply to be human is to offer a cause for
revulsion on the part of the earth. According to an old text
taken from the Kalapuya of Oregon, the people of the first
creation lived peacefully without sickness or death—until five
men went out to hunt. When it was announced that they had
killed five deer, the earth "turned over" and all the people of
the first age became stars.

The hidden nature of culture

In the doomsday lore of Native America it is not always the
people themselves who suffer destruction but the work that
people do: clearing land, building fires, cooking meat, using
tools. These are the things, or the activities—in short, human
culture—that will be undone when the world ends.

For example, in a story widely told in Mexico the farmer
survives the world flood. But his work is proscribed. As the
end draws near, he finds that the trees he cuts in order to clear
land for planting are spontaneously healed each morning. In
a modern variant from central Mexico a spirit finally material-
izes and delivers the command "Don't work anymore."

According to a similar story told by the Mixe of Oaxaca
State, the farmer, still alive and still human after the flood, is
given the warning "Don't make fire." This time the man

disobeys, and as punishment the spirit changes him into a monkey.

In other stories the world's end is foretold when game animals refuse to be cooked or when domestic animals suddenly become wild. Thus a Mixe tale recalls a time shortly before the flood when food animals came mysteriously into town and allowed themselves to be boiled in pots; before they could be eaten, however, they sprang to life. In a Mixtec account the people's dogs ran off to the woods and became coyotes.

Disturbing occurrences of the same sort are envisioned by a twentieth-century prophet among the Machiguenga of Peru, who warns that when the world ends, "Monkeys will say, 'Now I do to you what you used to do to me, boiling me in water and making me suffer.' " Also: "The dogs will hate us, remembering that we beat them . . . and the various things—the mats, the arrows, the chairs, and so forth—will rise up and start speaking to us."

The revolt of the "things," or utensils, is a familiar motif, recorded mainly along the western mountain chains from Canada to Argentina. Sometimes the utensils "start speaking," as in the Machiguenga prophecy. Similarly, in a mythological account from the Tzotzil of Mexico, "pots spoke" when the first age of the world came to an end.

But the pots, baskets, and other artifacts are capable of more than raising their voices. In the Quiché Maya Popol Vuh, or "book of counsel," it is written that "everything spoke" at the close of the third creation: jars, griddles, plates, pots, dogs, mortars. Moreover, joined by the dogs presumably, the murderous utensils "crushed [the people's] faces."

In an old Quechua text from Peru they "ate" their human masters. Likewise, according to the Barasana of northwest Amazonia, they changed into anacondas, caymans, and piranhas, and "began to eat the people." Looking to the future rather than the past, the Zuni of New Mexico, by the same token, say that "our possessions will turn into beasts and devour us whole."

In myths of the Thompson of British Columbia the various tools (bows, arrows, baskets, combs) are said to have attacked humans in the ancient days, until the god-hero Coyote ordered them to desist "forever." Similarly, the lore of the Totonac stipulates that the utensils are quiet today. But when the world ends, they will stir once again and "eat" the human population.

PARABLE / The revolt of the utensils

In the old days clay pots and other objects were like people. They could talk, visit, dance, and make chicha.

One day a man left his house, and the pots decided they would go to the garden and the stream to get the maize and the water to make maize chicha. Off they went to the garden, the stream. They got the maize and the water. Then they made the chicha.

They felt happy. "Now we will make music and have dancing," they said, and when they had prepared the chicha, they made the music and had the dancing. They were in good spirits, they were enjoying each other's company. When they had played for a long while, they realized that the man of the house would soon return.

They began to put everything back. They cleaned up, and the place was just as it had been.

The man came back. He looked around. "Everything is in order," he said—and all the pots doubled up with laughter.

—Anonymous, Tacana
(Bolivia)

According to old lore of the Chiriguano of Paraguay, the revolt of the utensils will occur during an eclipse of the sun; and in some cultures (as among the Maya of Yucatán) the event is spoken of as a possibility during any eclipse. In a word, the artifacts of culture are time bombs, to be regarded warily.

Prolonging the world

Just as there are omens of doom, however, there are agents of continuation. Deities, animal helpers, and various celestial supports are postulated as ongoing causes that prevent the demise of the earth.

A set of four cords is mentioned in a Cherokee tradition, each attached to the sky and to one of the earth's four cardinal points. The cords keep the earth from sinking into the waters below—though one day, when the world is "old and worn out," the cords will break.

A comparable Ojibwa idea is that the Milky Way is an enormous bucket handle that holds the earth in place. Some-

An eclipse of the moon,
drawn by a Chiriguano man,
Bolivia, 1929. Below is the "blue tiger"
about to attack the moon (center),
with the sun (top) looking on.
After Métraux 1931.

day, however, it will break, and the world will come to an end.

Or, according to an old text from the Guaraní of southern Brazil, the earth is propped from underneath. The culture hero Nanderyquey, so it used to be said, "worries about the earth and holds the earth-support. If he lets go, the earth will fall."

Time rather than physical structure is the subject of postponement lore that involves the art of weaving. For the Colombian Kogi the agent of postponement, or continuation, is the sun itself, who is said to weave two pieces of cloth each year, finishing them at the spring and fall equinoxes. By contrast, in Delaware, Iroquois, and Shawnee traditions, continuation depends not on the weaving itself but on its periodic unraveling.

In Shawnee belief the agent is a dog belonging to the supreme deity, Our Grandmother, who sits weaving a net or basket. Each night the dog unravels the work of the previous day. Should the basket ever be finished, the world will end.

Iroquois have said that it is the Moon who does the weaving and that her work is regularly unraveled by her dog (some say her cat). In a Delaware tradition an "old woman" is the weaver, whose work is chewed up at night by mice. In each case the helpful animal, or animals, forestall the end of time.

Such ideas are theories, subject to variation. For instance, an alternate Delaware tradition has it that the earth is carried perpetually toward the sunset on the back of an outsized tortoise—perpetually, that is, until the animal has "completed his road," at which time the earth "will come to end."

A somewhat similar theory held by the Lakota and the

Pawnee—at least formerly—is that an outsized buffalo stands in the far west, keeping back the floodwaters that would otherwise engulf the earth. Every year the animal loses one hair. Should it ever become bald, the world will end.

In many cultures, humans themselves participate in the work of continuation, either through simple acts that give evidence of caring or through imposing ceremonies that may involve an entire community.

Among the Navajo, sand paintings representing the earth (used in acts of healing), are banded with protective lines, or "rings," of color. As explained by one of the better-known traditionalists, this precaution was taught in the ancient days by deities who revealed the use of the paintings: "For a border they placed a black ring, a blue ring, a yellow ring, and a white ring, which is the earth's edge. These rings are for the earth's protection; no power shall harm her."

On a grander scale the old-time Big House ceremony of the Delaware, involving the entire community, was said to serve a protective, or perpetuating, function. In the words of one of the participants, the post in the center of the house "is what protects the people on the earth. So as long as that stands up the earth will stand. It is that pole that holds the earth down. So when that Delaware meetinghouse, whenever that is quit and the house destroyed, the world will come to an end."

By the same token, the old *kuksu* dances of northern California were supposed to prevent a disintegration of the physical world; the great *wiigita* ceremony of the Papago, even today, is said to "keep the world in order" and prevent natural calamities, especially floods; and in Venezuela, among the

Panare, the correct performance of ceremonies is said to ensure the continuation of day and night and the annual round
of the seasons.

The underlying sentiment, perhaps—and even the ultimate
rationale for all such theory and its associated practices—is the
one openly expressed by the old-time Fox ritualist, who used
to address the assembled participants in clan festivals, urging
them to continue the custom: "Until-this-earth-ceases-to-
be-an-earth is as far as it will take care of you, if you always
think seriously of it—and if you keep on holding [these]
festivals."

Not without justification, one may infer that the Papago,
the Panare, and other native ceremonialists concerned with
world order, protection, and continuation are "thinking seriously" of the earth.

15

Acts of Re-creation

Today there's sun,
there's light.
—Aztec saying

The earth may be "offended" by people's carelessness, and in the view of doom-saying prophets its very existence may be threatened. Yet the deterioration of the land and of the life it supports—as a basic concept—is not necessarily related to human interference. Rather, the concept may be drawn from the observation of biological cycles, which, on their own, enact a worrisome drama of growth and decay. In simple terms, the earth loses its youth.

Fortunately, or so it would seem, the reverse is also true. Navajo say that the familiar Changing Woman, also known as White Shell Woman, is "transformed time and again." In the opinion of the late, well-known ceremonialist Slim Curly, "White Shell Woman is in reality the earth which changes in summer and becomes young again, then relaxes or dies off in winter, but remains the same woman."

Again speaking of White Shell Woman, the Navajo narrator Sandoval, a contemporary of Slim Curly, has explained that in the ancient days "our grandmother lay curled up, nearly killed by old age." But she went into her east room and reemerged "somewhat stronger." Then she went into her south room and "came back walking." From her west room she "came out a young woman"; and from her north room, "a girl so handsome we were abashed."

Teachings along the same lines come from the Tucanoan cultures of northwest Amazonia, where the corresponding deity is Romi Kumú, "woman shaman," also known as Sitá-Romi-Kumú, "earth woman shaman." According to a Makuna source, she is "old and wrinkled" during the rainy season. But "during the dry season she is young and beautiful." Among the Barasana, who know her both as "woman shaman" and as "all people's grandmother," she is "old and ugly" in the evening, "but in the morning when she has bathed she is young and beautiful; she changes her skin."

Much the same has been said of the spirit known to tribes of the North American Great Plains as Old Woman or Old-Woman-Who-Never-Dies. Linked to plant growth, she renews her youth by bathing. In Iroquois mythology, once again to the same effect, the dead "mother's" body is "remade" by her son, the deity Teharonhiawagon, who then gives her authority over "things that habitually grow on the earth."

Often the power of rejuvenation is attributed not to the earth itself but to rain or, especially, thunder—as suggested by the Navajo formula "Thunder will first sound. Vegetation will come to life." In Zuni lore, thunder awakens the hibernating bear; or, as the saying goes, "First thunder in the east, the bear has stretched his right arm and comes forth." For the Huastec of Mexico the *maam*, or rain spirit, is said to become an old man as the year progresses, changing into a newborn child after the winter solstice. For the Pawnee, Thunder passes over the land at the close of winter, reawakens the earth, then returns to his lodge in the sky world and kindles new fire.

None of this, however, is meant to suggest that humans are excused from responsibility. The pleasant idea that nature can take care of itself is not acceptable and may even be dangerous. The human community, periodically, has the duty to help nature in its awakening, to remake the earth, and even to kindle new fire.

Wakening

Direct action to reverse the world's decline, or to bring back its lost powers, is typical of societies that practice at least some farming. The business is conducted at one of the turning points of the year, often in spring or, even earlier, at the winter solstice, when the noon sun has reached its lowest point in the sky.

The accompanying rites may be lengthy and complex, involving initiations for young people, healing of the sick, entertainment, and socializing. But the quickening function is seldom obscured.

One of the simplest, most elegant acts is the retelling of the creation myth by old-time Papago narrators at the midpoint of winter, "when the sun stands still." This was done in former times to ensure that the seasons would follow one another in proper order. The same idea motivates the elaborate Hopi *soyal* ceremony, also held at the winter solstice, in which a dancer who represents the hesitant sun is forced by a group of singers to turn back toward summer.

In addition, the *soyal* is said to "open" the way for the return of the kachinas, or ancestor spirits that bring rain and corn. According to Hopi theory, the kachinas withdraw at the summer solstice and are absent as the year declines.

In the corresponding Navajo ritual the *yei*, or deities, are "wakened" by a chanter who shakes each of the *yei* masks in turn, while singing, "He stirs, he stirs, he stirs, he stirs. Among the lands of the dawning, he stirs, he stirs. . . ."

The Navajo ritual saves for last the climactic "wakening" of Changing Woman herself, as the chanter sings, "She stirs, she stirs, she stirs, she stirs. Now Estsánatlehi [Changing Woman], she stirs, she stirs. Now her plants of all kinds, she stirs, she stirs. . . ."

PARABLE / The flowering of the trumpet-vine tree

The primal wind in which our Father lived returns with the yearly return of the primal time-space, with the yearly recurrence of the time-space that was.

As soon as the season that was has ended, the trumpet-vine tree bears flowers. The winds move on to the following time-space. New winds and a new space in time come into being.

Comes the resurrection of space and time.

—Anonymous, Mbyá Guaraní
(Paraguay)

Especially well documented is the so-called Thunder Ceremony of the Pawnee, held not at the solstice but at the close of winter. (The telling moment is when the first full roll of thunder is heard following the appearance of two small stars in the northeastern sky.) The techniques of the ritual were described in the early twentieth century by the anthropologists G. A. Dorsey and Ralph Linton and again, more than a generation later, by the anthropologist Gene Weltfish in her classic work *The Lost Universe*. Weltfish presents a concise, dramatic account of the procedure, noting that its purpose was to "bring the world back to life."

The basic description, however, is the one prepared by the author-ethnographer James Murie, himself a Pawnee, working independently under a United States government grant during the period 1914–1921. In Murie's words, the Thunder Ceremony was performed as an "aid" to "revivify the earth."

Progressing through three essential stages, the ritual recounts the myth of world creation in a lengthy chant, summons thunder by means of song and a smoke offering, then "sings" the thunder across the earth. The third of these three stages is the "real" creation, because even though the world has already been given form, as told in the myth, it remains lifeless until stirred by thunder.

Outside the ritual, the myth is recited as a story, or narrative. But within the ceremony, it is chanted in a highly condensed form, indirectly recalling the ancient council of the gods, in which they decided to create the earth, followed by the actions of the supreme deity, Tirawahat, who actually performed the work.

The chant begins with the words "Above, this is what they said. The earth, he took it out. . . ." The same phrases are immediately repeated, substituting for "earth" the words "timber," "waters," "seeds," "fog," "dew," "rain," "rainstorm," "wind," and "night." Further verses give additional details.

With the creation in place, the ritualists now summon thunder, performing a song cycle whose key words are "above," "thunder," "lightning," "clouds," and "winds." Each of the songs is accompanied by an offering of tobacco or meat thrown on the fire.

Having reached the moment of quickening, the ceremony turns to a cycle of 119 songs in which the deity Tirawahat, represented by the "voices" of the thunder, descends to the earth to give it life. The first few songs are built on the phrases "his thoughts moved," "his thoughts flew," "he arose," and other phrases recounting the god's decision to stir the world.

Next "he took a breath," "he made lightning here and there."

Then "the voices drop to the earth."

As the "voices" roll across the land, "the lightning enters a tableland" . . . "the storm wades through the river" . . . "the thunders start again to dry land."

Finally "the storm, noises, lightning, and thunders climb the hills on the north" and "the storm, noises, lightning, and the thunder are taken up into the clouds."

It is at this point, according to native testimony, that the thunder spirit returns to his sky lodge and kindles the new fire.

New fire

The expected rite in imitation of the spirit's final act is not said to have been part of the Pawnee Thunder Ceremony. Evidently no special fire was kindled on earth by human hands. The act in this case was left to the deity to perform on his own in the sky world.

But the old-time Pawnee did nevertheless have a new-fire rite, reported to have been performed whenever a successful war party returned to camp. On this occasion all the people of the community let their fires die out and cleared their fireplaces of ashes. Afterward the leading priest handed the fire sticks to the warrior who was to kindle the fire, saying, "You are to create new life."

When the flames had blazed up, the priest sang a song that included the words "thunder power is what it is." Then, after people had taken coals to rekindle their hearth fires, a meat offering was burned in order to "shake the earth."

In general, though, the kindling of new fire in the Americas is—or was—a seasonal event, timed to coincide with a turning point in the yearly round. For the Cherokee it came with the annual spring festival, following several days of ceremonial preparation. As in the Pawnee case, all hearth fires were extinguished, then relit from the new flame.

Among the Inuit of Baffin Island, as recorded in the 1860s by the Arctic explorer Charles Francis Hall, the new-fire ceremony marked the winter solstice. At this time (in Hall's words), "two men start out, one of them being dressed to represent a woman, and go to every house in the village, blowing out the light in each. The lights are afterwards rekindled from a fresh fire. When Taqulitu [Hall's well-known companion in his journeys] was asked the meaning of this, she replied, 'New sun—new light,' implying a belief that the sun was at that time renewed for the year."

South of the equator, where the shortest days of the year fall in June, the Incas of Cuzco celebrated a winter solstice festival known as *inti raymi*, "sun feast," which included a three-day period during which all fires were extinguished and only raw foods were eaten. Following this period of abstinence, new fire was kindled with a convex mirror, which focused the sun's rays on a wad of cotton. The flame that resulted was used to relight all other fires and was carefully kept burning throughout the following twelve months.

Among the Aztecs the corresponding rite was held not every year but at the close of each great cycle of fifty-two years. In preparation, fires throughout the city and the countryside were doused with water; and the new flame, from which every hearth would be relit, was kindled with a fire drill at midnight on the last day of the cycle. Should the flame fail to catch, so it was said, the sun would be destroyed and there would be perpetual night.

New-fire rites have also been reported from societies that used the occasion to emphasize purity and cleansing (Iroquois, Delaware, Hopi) or to discard and renew all utensils (Creek, Natchez, Yucatec Maya).

As with the Aztec, various cultures have viewed the rites as not merely desirable but necessary in order to renew the earth, the sun, or time itself. Among the Lacandon Maya, as recently as the turn of the twentieth century, new fire was kindled to the accompaniment of prayers, requesting the "alternation of sun and shade, for many days, for many years," or, hopefully, stating the request as a fact: "Many days are coming, many years are coming." Similarly, in nineteenth- and twentieth-century northwest California the new fire was made by a priest who asked that "world luck will hold fast."

World renewal

Among the northwest California groups, especially the Karok, the Yurok, and the Hupa, the making of new fire was one of several rites in a complex ceremony held either in spring or in early autumn to mark the running of the first salmon or the ripening of the acorn crop. In the Karok language the enactment of the rites was known as "making New Year," and the ceremony itself, in all its parts, was called *isivsanen upikiavish*, "world renewal."

According to myth, the ceremony had been established in the days of Creation by a prehuman race of immortals. In retracing their steps over the earth, the principal ritualist, or "spirit man," as he was called by the Yurok, strengthened the world for another year.

The prescribed route through the countryside included significant pools, rocks, slopes, ledges, and peaks, each of which required attention. Describing the procedure in detail, the late Karok ritualist Francis Davis spoke of pulling himself out of a river pool and walking along a bedrock flat. "*Ixkareya*

A scene from the Aztec new-fire ceremony,
showing household objects broken and thrown away; painted
by a sixteenth-century Aztec artist, from Libro Septimo
of Bernardino de Ṣahagún, *Códice florentino*.

animas [i.e., one of the immortals] walked over this in mythical times," he explained. "As I walk over it, I tramp it down."

Proceeding to the next station, Davis would lift a certain stone; then "with my hands I rotate it slightly to make it sit more solidly, so that the world will be solid too."

Later, while climbing a slope: "I pick up a piece of fallen fir limb. No other will do. This I use for my cane. I pray after picking up the branch, 'This world is cracked, but when I pick up and drag the stick, all the cracks will fill up and the earth will become solid again.' "

As the ritualist walked along the high ridge: "There is a big stone near a sugar-pine tree. I pick up the stone and set it down solidly and pray as I work it into position: 'The earth, which has been tipped, will be straight again.' "

Returning to the valley, the solitary ritualist was met by two assistants, who ferried him back across the river to the village, where further duties remained to be completed.

In addition to the cross-country journey, the rites included performances by dancers whose stamping was said to help firm the "newly created" earth. (The dancing offered an opportunity to display finery, which for many participants was perhaps the leading motivation.) There was the refurbishing of a special sand heap and the rebuilding of sacred structures. For the Karok it was necessary to repair the "original sacred sweathouse," which stood for the life of the world; in the Karok language the house was named *kimaekiram iship*, meaning "the world is made by it."

With apparent reference to the death and revival of the earth, the Yurok, too, rebuilt their sacred sweathouse, and in so doing they treated the timbers as though these were a corpse (painting them with soot and bidding them farewell). At the same time, moreover, a particular stone called "brace of the world," usually kept buried, was unearthed and set up inside the building.

Accompanying the ritual acts at every stage—rebuilding, journeying, dancing, fire making—were prayers to sweep off "sickness" and summon food animals. Thus directing their thoughts toward making the earth cleaner and more productive, the "spirit men" went about their business during the long days of the ceremony, so that the "luck" of the world, in the Karok phrase, "would not fade away."

· · ·

Contemplating such intricate rituals and their associated myths, the outsider must ask whether native people would wish to share this kind of wisdom and, if so, whether it would be meaningfully received. Can world renewal, to take just one, difficult example, be shared? On the surface, the answer is an obvious no.

But if it cannot be claimed that the techniques of world renewal are applicable in modern society, inasmuch as they are ill fitted to modern taste, it may be observed, nevertheless, that if the underlying purpose is to dramatize a concern for the earth, the ceremony succeeds on a level that can be recognized across cultures without demanding literal imitation.

Native people themselves have participated in the process of adaptation, permitting traditional ideas and techniques to be appreciated in a modern setting. Refitting the concept of the earth journey, a group of Cree and Inuit people staged a trek from Hudson Bay to New York City in the spring of 1990 as part of the modern celebration known as Earth Day. Traveling by dogsled over the first stretch of the thousand-mile route, the participants ended their ordeal some seven weeks later with a canoe trip down the Hudson River. The purpose was to dramatize the people's struggle against the much debated James Bay II hydroelectric project, which threatened to flood their hunting lands in northeastern Canada. Non-native people welcomed and sheltered the travelers along their way.

Similarly, Iroquois and other native people, in order to dramatize environmental concerns, began staging a so-called Longest Run during the Olympic year, beginning in 1984. At first held only in North America, the run was extended to Japan four years later, in 1988. As in the Canada–New York trek, non-native people assisted the journeyers along their route.

Indeed, the desire to help the world at large, while not a priority for every native culture, is sufficiently widespread to deserve notice. Even the Taos of New Mexico, famously the most reticent of Native American societies, have expressed concern for the larger community—as revealed by a spokesman on the occasion of the signing over of Blue Lake to the people of Taos by the government of the United States. "When we pray," said the Taos spokesman, "it is for the betterment of the whole world. No distinctions are made."

Recognizing that human thought is linked across cultures, a Delaware ritualist has expressed the view that Delaware people were originally in possession of "the one great prayer-creed," a kind of "staff," from which all Indian prayer-creeds branched off; and from these, in turn, "came all other prayer-creeds of the world."

The idea of tribal knowledge as a gift, or donation, was phrased eloquently by Sandoval, the Navajo narrator, who prefaced one of his major testimonials with the statement: "For long years I have kept this beauty within me, it has been my life. It is sacred. I give it now that coming generations may know the truth about my people. I give it as the dew falls. I give it as sacred pollen, that there may increase a better understanding among human beings."

With similar thoughts, the Arikara priest Four Rings, in bequeathing his knowledge to the outside world, expressed the wish that non-Indian Americans might come to an understanding of these "holy teachings," and also that the teachings might be preserved for future generations.

In separate ways each of these expressions of concern echoes the old Tewa song that confidently observes: "Even to the Utes, Apaches, Navajos, Kiowas, Comanches, Cheyennes, even to all of them. To the Mexican people, even to them it reaches. To the *americano t'owa* [i.e., the American people], even to them the sound of our Mother's breathing reaches."

Sources are given by author's name with the publication date and, where needed, a volume number, followed by a comma and the page number. (If only one work by the author has been cited, the publication date is omitted.) Hence "Grinnell 1972 1, 149" refers to volume 1, page 149, of George B. Grinnell's *The Cheyenne Indians*, edition of 1972 (as listed in the References, which follow these Notes).

Epigraphs and parables

Epigraphs. *Front:* Otero, 235. *Ch. 1:* Morison, 285. *Ch. 2:* Edmonson and Bricker, 57. *Ch. 3:* Lumholtz 1, 516. *Ch. 4:* Otero, 234. *Ch. 5:* Lumholtz 1, 516. *Ch. 6:* Hilbert, x. *Ch. 7:* Otero, 234. *Ch. 8:* Bierhorst 1985a, 49; Rhodes, 18. *Ch. 9:* Otero, 234. *Ch. 10:* Fowler and Fowler, 85. *Ch. 11:* Garcilaso 1963, 243. *Ch. 12:* Rhodes, 18. *Ch. 13:* Standing Bear, 160; Powell, 56. *Ch. 14:* Cushing 1920, 147. *Ch. 15:* trans. from the Nahuatl in Sahagún 1970, 81.

Parables. *The owls (ch. 1):* adapted from Rasmussen 1929, 269. *The transformer (ch. 2):* Ballard, 75. *How humans (ch. 3):* trans. from the German in Boas 1895, 319. *The anaconda (ch. 4):* trans. (and abridged) from the German in Hissink and Hahn, 211–12. *The boy (ch. 4):* Montour. *The emergence (ch. 5):* Standing Bear, 44–45. *Chiminigagua (ch. 6):* trans. from the Spanish in Simón, 279. *The man who became (ch. 7):* trans. from the Spanish in Barrueco, 30–31. *The garden (ch. 8):* abridged from Nimuendajú 1952, 117. *The foolish (ch. 9):* Opler, 84. *The origin (ch. 10):* trans. from the Spanish in Pellizzaro, 86–92. *The eight jars (ch. 11):* trans. from the Spanish in "Ochos relatos," 14, and "Historias aportadas," 7. *The sun (ch. 12):* Harrington n.d., OC-163, folder 9. *The hungry (ch. 13):* trans. from the Cora and German in Preuss, 148. *The salmon (ch. 13):* trans. from the German in Boas 1895, 209–10. *The revolt (ch. 14):* trans. from the German in Hissink and Hahn, 364. *The flowering (ch. 15):* trans. from the Spanish in Cadogán, 15.

Text

Introduction. *Counting stars:* Cushing 1920, 469; Garcilaso 1963, 243; Standing Bear, 157. *Still learning:* Lame Deer, 252. *Tell a little less:* Radin 1970, 121. *On young people:* Matthews 1902, 153 (Navajo); Speck 1944–45 (Munsee); Lee, 411 (Wintun); Alcorn 1989, 66 (Kuna); Schutz, 204 (Shawnee); Wright, 12 (Toba); Voegelin 1935, 223 (California); Haile, 90 (Navajo).

Up from the unthinkable. *On sacrifice:* Gómara, 6; Acosta, 376. *Benjamin Lincoln:* Lincoln, 139. *Jefferson:* Richardson, 352. *Iroquois:* Myrtle, 261. *Thoreau:* Thoreau, 372. *Muir:* Callicott, 137–38. *Paz:* Paz, 21. *Leopold:* Leopold, 202–3. *Martin and Callicott:* Martin, 187–88; Callicott, 200–1, 219.

Questions. *Formulas:* Wright, 7; Voegelin 1935, 219; Skinner 1925, 103. *Inca conservation:* Heizer, 5; Garcilaso 1966, 325; Polo de Ondegardo, 165.

Proverbs and parables. *On proverbs:* Gossen 1973, 209–10 (Tzotzil); A. Molina 2, 50v (*"machiyotlatolli"*); Cushing 1883b (Zuni); Lumholtz 1, 516 (Cora); Fletcher and La Flesche, 604 (Omaha); Standing Bear, 160 (Lakota); Edmonson and Bricker, 57 (Maya). *Singing of birds:* Heckewelder, 138; Vanderwerth, 16; Croghan, 161; Wallace 1949, 129 and 281. *"Nothing lasts forever":* Densmore 1918, 231. *On parables:* Dauenhauer and Dauenhauer, 76, 171–73, 332 (Tlingit); Chapin 1985, 50–51 (Kuna). *"Yet it seems a mystery to us":* G. Dorsey 1904b, 25. *Claus Chee Sonny:* Luckert 1978, 204.

1 / Inner Forms. *On persons:* Hallowell, 143, 159; Jenness, 79; Guss, 31–32; Standing Bear, 194.

Souls and hidden bodies. *On concealed forms:* de Laguna, 823; E. Nelson, 453; Rosengren, 32. *Souls of trees:* Speck 1977, 34, 56, 251; Merrill, 92. *Souls of humans:* Sturtevant 10, 573 (Navajo); Boas 1966, 139 (Kwakiutl); Savala, 22–23, 43 (Yaqui); Crocker 1985a, 15, 35, and Crocker 1985b, 277–78 (Bororo); Furst and Nahmad, 75. *Sky, earth, and mountains:* Haile, 69. *Wind People:* Reichard, 497.

Immortality. *In Navajo and Iroquois lore:* Haile, 67; Hewitt 1928, 498; Curtin and Hewitt, 368. *Bear's head:* Rasmussen 1908, 111–12; de Laguna, 881. *Brains:* Bianchi, 21. *Reverence for bones:* Bianchi, 20–21; Hill, 128;

de Civrieux, 112 (Yekuana); Boas 1917, 173 (Thompson); R. Nelson, 25; G. Foster, 181; de Laguna, 766 (Tlinglit).

Tonalism. *Salmon:* Boas 1930, 205. *Owl:* Boas 1966, 139; Boas 1930, 208; Goldenweiser, 235. *Bear:* Grinnell 1961, 126. *Sandpiper:* Parsons 1936, 80. *Tree:* Greenberg, 100–1. *Twelve companion animals:* Wauchope 8, 679. *Jaguar:* G. Foster, 188.

The animal master. *Animal homes in hills or mountains:* Wauchope 7, 177–78; McIlwraith 1, 71; Reichel-Dolmatoff 1976b, 161, 165. *Homes beyond or beneath water:* Boas 1930, 185; Barnouw, 160; Murie 1, 160; Grinnell 1961, 358. *Gardens and fires:* de Civrieux 1974, 11; Tanner, 150–51. *Social organization:* Mooney 1900, 436 (Cherokee); Curtin and Hewitt, 704 (Iroquois); Chernela 1987, 51 (Tucano). *Animal masters as shamans:* de Civrieux 1974, 9–10. *Master is white:* Barnouw, 160; Sahagún 1963, 15 (Aztec); Perrin, 62–72 (Guajiro); Speck 1977, 85 (Inuit); Bean, 167 (Cahuilla). *Plant master:* Girard, 255. *Myths of the Canelos:* Hartmann and Oberem, 680–85. *Buffalo women:* Curtin and Hewitt, 98–102. *Bones given to Tatewarí:* Myerhoff, 175. *Shuar hunter:* Bianchi, 17.

2 / Former Lives. *Inuit narrator:* Rasmussen 1931, 208. *Hopi storyteller:* Wallis, 39. *Descent from animal:* Speck 1909, 70; McKennan 162–63; Radin 1957, 205; Whiffen, 244; Im Thurn, 184. *Osage and Kogi beliefs:* J. Dorsey, 396; Reichel-Dolmatoff 1975, 55.

When animals were people. *Mythological turning points:* Simpson, 273; Densmore 1956, 196–97; Brody, 41; Bierhorst 1988, 167 and 250 (Fuegian); Haile, 77; Taggart, 89. *Jicaque, Blackfeet, and Koyukon theories:* Chapman 59 and 145; McClintock, 476; R. Nelson, 24.

When people were animals. *Popol Vuh:* Tedlock, 78. *Kroeber:* Kroeber 1907b, 246. *Inca feast attire:* C. Molina, 27 and 45; Garcilaso 1961, 217. *Kwakiutl and Bella Coola lore:* Boas 1930, 188, and Boas 1966, 304–5; McIlwraith 1, 36–37. *Slobodin:* Sturtevant 6, 526.

Evolution. *Myths of animal-like ancestors:* Wilbert and Simoneau 1983, 74; Tedlock and Tedlock, 268–69 (Zuni); Caspar, 210; Steward 1946–59 3, 359 (Paressí); Cadogan 1962, 46 (Guayaki). *Sandoval:* O'Bryan, 2. *Ohiyesa:* Eastman, 143.

The transformer. *Yavapai and Aztec myths:* Gifford, 246; Ruiz, 70–72. *Animal people kept their coats:* O'Bryan, 34. *Coyote:* Barrett 1933, 106–7. *Duhvít:* Sturzenegger, 28–29, 30. *Sheep:* Teit 1917, 430. *Deer:*

Ballard, 75. *Swan:* Sturtevant 6, 354–55. *Santee hero:* Eastman, 130. *Nora Dean:* Rementer 1990; Dean 1977.

3 / The Organic Alternative. *Ottawa story:* Perrot, 37. *Animals from humans:* Portal, 41 (Chinantec); Horcasitas, 184 (eastern Mexico); Boas 1916, 76 (British Columbia).

Flesh into crops. *Corn boy:* Radin 1945, 323 (Winnebago); G. Foster, 180, 191–92 (Popoluca); Alcorn 1984, 204–5 (Nahua), 354 (Huastec). *Homshuk still alive:* Sammons, 370. *Hopi corn boy:* Wallis, 10, 13. *Tupinamba hero:* Métraux 1928, 232. *Crop mother:* Roth, 133–35 (Guyana); Chapman, 72 (Central America); Mooney 1900, 244 (Cherokee); Swanton 1929, 11, 14 (Creek), 230 (Natchez). *Narcotic plants:* Reichel-Dolmatoff 1971, 37. *Plants from feces, semen, and fingernails:* Hugh-Jones, 298; Speck 1909, 18; Gossen 1974, 335. *Acorn tree from hand:* Bean 111. *Popol Vuh:* Tedlock, 163–64. *Navajo myth:* Matthews 1897, 69.

From seeds and trees. *Myths of human origin:* Villas Boas and Villas Boas, 57–58; Curtis 14, 169–70 (Yuki); Angulo, 245; Curtis 15, 149–50 (Washo); Lowie 1939, 333 (Washo variant). *Tree emergence:* Curtis 14, 173; Leland, 18–19; Steward 1946–59 1, 367; Huxley, 170–71. *Pod of beach pea:* E. Nelson, 452–53. *Arawak lore:* Brett, 7–8; Im Thurn, 376–77. *Munsee story:* Danckaerts, 78. *Tree of breasts:* Armellada and Bentivenga, 236; Codex Vaticanus, lamina IV; Laughlin, 29.

Personal anguish. *Corn woman:* Bierhorst 1990, 90–98 and 215–16. *Ojibwa lore:* Jenness, 20. *Aztec lore:* Serna, 231–32. *Zapotec myth:* Parsons 1936, 230. *On tree cutting:* Swanton 1908, 454; McClintock, 301; Michelson 1912, folder 4, pp. 7 and 11; Murie 2, 265; Wauchope 7, 91. *On bark gathering:* Boas 1930, 218; R. Nelson, 53. *Blood from trees:* Wilbert 1974, 75; Williams García, 67; Gatschet, 281; Lowie 1918, 45–46; Schultze-Jena, 27; Wilbert and Simoneau 1985, 77. *Palm-tree woman:* Bean and Saubel, 15–16. *Ixil myth:* Colby and Colby, 184. *Mopan story:* Thompson 1930, 145.

4 / Within the Family. *Inuit song:* Victor, 24. *Kogi lineage:* Reichel-Dolmatoff 1975, 58. *Aguaruna hunters:* M. Brown, 76. *Use of paint and perfume:* Reichel-Dolmatoff 1971, 220; Chapin 1983, 246–47. *On pets*

and domesticated animals: Sekaquaptewa, 42, and Simmons, 62 (Hopi);
R. Nelson, 23–24; Greenberg, 94; Dean 1978, 3, and Tantaquidgeon,
36 (Delaware); Speck 1940, 55; Bean, 64; Bianchi, 30.

Adoption. *Gros Ventre myth:* Kroeber 1907, 94–97. *Bear power:* Waugh
1912–18, no. 48; Harrington n.d., OC-160, folder 1 (Delaware);
Grinnell 1961, 127–28; Boas 1930, 193–94. *Mouse mother:* Wilbert and
Simoneau 1984, 39. *Jaguar:* Wilbert 1978, 160–63.

Marriage. *Useless marriages:* Phinney, 17–18; Paredes, 65–67; Stradelli, 681
and 683. *Anaconda bride:* Bierhorst 1988, 72–74, 217–18, 246, 253–54.
Peccary bride: Bianchi, 28. *Deer bride:* Boas 1917, 40–43. *Deer husband:*
Goddard 1918, 49–62; Luckert 1975, 70–79; Goodwin, 88–93.

Human sentiment. *Iroquois variant of Bear Boy:* Curtin and Hewitt, 365–69.
Peccary man: Wilbert 1974, 116. *Marmot woman:* Boas 1896, 263–64.
Bear Boy instantly killed: E. Smith, 85. *Fuegian myths:* Wilbert 1975,
111–13, 129–31; Wilbert 1977, 51–57.

Humanity's place. *Siblings and grandchildren:* Chernela 1982, 17; Standing
Bear, 22. *Sense of proportion:* Sturtevant 8, 649 (Heizer); Bean, 170;
McIlwraith 1, 35; Weiss 1975, 426; Grinnell 1961, 17; Cushing 1883a,
9; Radin 1970, 122.

5 / The Earth as Mother. *Earth as a man:* Wilbert 1975, 115; Preuss, 148.
Quechua earth lord: Nuñez del Prado, 246; Lara 1971, 188; Urioste 2,
177. *Aztec earth lord as mother:* Sahagún 1969, 26. *Earth's rotation:*
Núñez del Prado, 239; J. Smith et al., 51; Skinner 1924–27, 177; de
Angulo, 237; Radin 1945, 253–54. *Called "mother":* M. Foster, 292–
94; Chafe, 91; Bierhorst 1992b, 150; Cobo, 34; Nuttall, folio 1.

Creativity. *Weigle:* Weigle 1991, 212. *Earth as everywoman:* Bloomfield, 137;
Guallart, 24; Hoebel, 96; Radin 1970, 122. *Allen:* Allen, 122. *Assiniboin woman:* Steiner, 218. *Spirit within the earth:* Sturtevant 10, 444
(Jicarilla); Reichel-Dolmatoff 1951, 13–14; Núñez del Prado, 243,
246; Wyman, 133, 347n. *Earth spirit as planner:* Tyler, 90–91; Chapin
1983, 62; Reichel-Dolmatoff 1951, 10; McNeley, 15.

"This earth is alive." *Life from earth's body:* Radin 1945, 27; Boas 1917, 80;
Hewitt 1928, 498. *Earth's dress:* Klah, 63; Chapin 1983, 62; Bunzel,
483–84. *Earth's hair:* "Histoyre," 29; Tyler, 99; Boas 1917, 80; Gow
and Condori, 11; Radin 1970, 123. *Body parts:* Wyman, 128–29.

The nurturing breast. *Earth suckles humans:* Gow and Condori, 10–11;

Bierhorst 1992b, 149–50. *Winnebago lore:* Radin, 1945. *Milk as corn:* Curtin and Hewitt, 412; Standing Bear, 43; Stevenson, 39. *Corn mounds:* A. Parker 1923, 64; Murie 1, 84. *Earth formed from milk:* Biocca 1, 271. *"River of milk":* Reichel-Dolmatoff 1976b, 172. *Tahltan lore:* Teit 1919, 227.

Emergence. *Humans arise spontaneously from earth:* Spinden 1908, 13–14; Lumholtz 1, 297; Guiteras-Holmes, 156, 157; Wilbert and Simoneau 1982, 129; Rasmussen 1929, 254. *Caught like fish:* Nimuendaju 1952, 129; Murphy and Quain, 74; Steward 1946–59 3, 294; Fock, 172; Farabee, 143–45. *Emerge from lake or ocean:* Caspar, 208–9; Henry, 127; Simón, 278; Warren, 43–44; Tyler, 105, 109. *From seeds or fertilization:* Dixon, 33, 34; Eastman, 123; Walde-Waldegg, 41. *Place of emergence as geographical feature:* Myrtle, 107; Bushnell, 530; Orbigny, 214. *Place of emergence defines homeland:* Halbert, 267, 270; Boyd, 51; A. Parker 1916, 50; MacMurray, 248; Standing Bear, 43. *Committee of Indian Peoples:* Riester, 74. *Blue Lake:* Leach and Fried, 1007; "Indians Hail Return of Sacred Lake," *The New York Times,* Dec. 7, 1970.

6 / The Responsive Universe. *In native languages:* Bierhorst 1985b, 338; Lara 1969, 185, and Lara 1971; Lowie 1935, 334; Densmore 1918, 131, 215, 222, and Walker 1983, 27, 275. *In sand paintings:* Reichard, 464, and Newcomb and Reichard, 37; Kroeber 1925, 662–63. *As plate and bowl:* Goetz, Morley, and Recinos, 78. *Navajo years and months:* W. Dyk, 42–43; Klah, 59; O'Bryan, 16–18. *Among Maya:* Thompson 1966, 163. *Time personified:* Wilbert and Simoneau 1986 1, 34–35; Wilbert and Simoneau 1984, 24–25; Alcorn 1984, 57, 99.

Listening. *Prayers:* Skinner 1924–27, 75; Ray, 21; Rowe, 92–93. *Mazatec little people:* Incháustegui, 113. *"Hear me":* Kroeber and Gifford, 14; Densmore 1918, 131. *Name-giving rituals:* Jenness, 93; Spier and Sapir, 258–59; Kroeber 1902, 313. *For newborn:* Fletcher and La Flesche 1, 115–16. *Arikara myth:* Gilmore, 114. *Inuit funeral:* Rasmussen 1908, 114. *Fox mourning:* Jones 1907, 357; Michelson 1921, 29.

The greater home. *Great houses:* Morgan, 40–42, 51; McIlwraith 1, 34; McAllester and McAllester, 92; "Historias recopiladas," 23; Septimo and Joly, 19; Stone, 55 (stars are knots); "Historias recogidas," 29 (Pleiades are roof-pole tips); Weltfish, 78–79 (Pawnee).

The smaller world. *Cuzco:* Garcilaso 1966, 522. *Pawnee encampment:* Weltfish, 200. *Houses:* Weltfish, 78; Reichel-Dolmatoff 1978, 16, 18; Reichel-Dolmatoff 1971, 109; Dumont, 68; Guss, 21–26; Gilmore, 104; Neihardt, 198–200, and De Mallie, 151, 290–91.

World essence. *'Iva'a:* Bean, 160–61, 170, 180. *Navala:* Sturtevant 9: 577. *Nek purpalet:* Chapin 1983, 75, 77. *"Our spirit":* Kroeber 1925, 662–63. *Wind or breath:* McNeley, xviii, 1–2, 9–10; Weiss 1972, 162; Sturzenegger, 28–29, 32; Lame Deer, 252; Walker 1980, 82. *Unifying force:* Standing Bear, 14, 193; Walde-Waldegg, 40–41. *Life Giver:* Bierhorst 1985a, 165, 201. *World kinship:* Deloria 365, 394; Grinnell 1895, 213; Fletcher and La Flesche 2, 357. *Pawnee story:* Grinnell 1961, 149–50. *Yokuts prayer:* Kroeber 1925, 511.

7 | The Consumer as Ritualist. *Hunters' and gatherers' prayers:* de Laguna 1, 49; Boas 1930, 203; Grinnell 1972 2, 288. *Yekuana statements:* Guss, 36, 94. *Paiute story:* Steward 1933, 310.

Increasing the cost. *Wild rice:* Heizer, 5. *Rituals of reseeding:* A. Parker 1913, 55–56; Mooney 1891, 339. *Laborious procedures:* Tantaquidgeon, 10; Simmons, 41; Jenness, 30. *Seemingly meaningless gestures:* R. Nelson, 53; Speck 1945. *Bones rituals:* Speck 1977, 113; Jenness, 24; Luckert 1975, 31; Simmons, 54. *Maidu ritual:* Faye, 40. *Yurok ritual:* Kroeber 1925, 68.

Economizing. *Cahuilla rule:* Bean and Saubel, 16. *Gatherers' rituals:* Mooney 1891, 339; Weslager, 57, 120; Luckert 1975, 55–57; Murie 1, 168–69. *Workaday rules:* Bean and Saubel, 16; Jenness, 76. *Bark stripping:* Weslager, 59; Mooney 1891, 336. *Harvesting of animals:* Heizer, 7; Feit, 72. *War against Illinois:* Lahontan 1, 82. *Respect for females:* Bianchi, 17; Luckert 1975, 31; Speck and Hadlock, 364.

Fallowing. *Gathering discontinued:* Bean and Saubel, 207. *Rotation:* Heizer, 5 (Cree); Jenness, 22 (Ojibwa); Balée, 3 (Ka'apor); Reichel-Dolmatoff 1976a, 313 (Tucanoan). *Respect for dead or unborn:* Holt, 316; Curtis 10, 43. *Randomizing the harvest:* Reichel-Dolmatoff 1976a, 316; Spencer, 241; Speck 1977, 58, 193–94, 243. *Scapulimancy:* Speck 1977, 153–55; Moore; Tanner, 120–24; Martin, 122.

Punishment for waste. *Parental admonitions:* Simmons, 55; George, 393–94. *On eating cranes:* Dean 1978, 2–3; Zeisberger, 65. *Death penalty:* Garcilaso 1966, 246; Morley and Brainerd, 423. *Supernatural punishments:* Jenness, 80–81; Speck 1977, 118–19; Perrin, 58–59. *Shuar parables:*

Bianchi, 17n; Barrueco, 30–31. *Huastec boys:* Alcorn 1984, 127. *Ojibwa admonitions:* Jenness, 20, 61. *Ants:* Boremanse, 267. *Worms:* Gilmore, 116.

8 / The Value of Wilderness. *Chippewa preserve:* "Landmarks," 32. *Concepts of wilderness:* H. Hale, 117, 129, 203; Merrill, 72 (Tarahumara); Bierhorst 1974, 189, 197–98 (Maya); Bierhorst 1985b, 45, and Sahagún 1963, 105 (Aztec). *White and Cronon:* Sturtevant 4, 417. *Standing Bear:* Standing Bear, 38.

Purity and power. *Cree:* Tanner, 90, 116. *Naskapi:* Speck 1977, 78. *Maya:* Redfield and Villa Rojas, 139. *Yaqui:* Savala, xvii, 39; Spicer, 63–67; F. Molina, 193; Giddings, 25, 27; Wilder, 177–93. *Aztec:* Sahagún 1963, 105–6. *Wilderness as a place of dangerous beings:* Redfield and Villa Rojas, 121–22; Behrens, 85; Guss, 26. *Tuscarora:* Wallace 1952, 24–28. *Kogi:* Reichel-Dolmatoff 1978, 23–25. *Penobscot:* Speck 1935, 32. *Shasta:* Holt, 326, 331. *Jicaque:* Chapman, 150. *Cahuilla:* Bean, 75. *Tukuna:* Nimuendajú 1952, 117. *Ka'apor:* Balée and Gély, 147–53. *Giant serpent:* Conzemius, 169. *Woman-panther:* Powers 1877, 59–60. *Kuna:* Chapin 1985, 48–49; Chapin 1991, 42. *Yekuana:* Guss, 127–28, 130.

No-man's-land. *Aztec danger zone:* Sahagún 1963, 106; Bierhorst 1992b, 128. *Mohawk and Mahican:* Sturtevant 15, 198. *California:* James and Graziani. *Ixtlahuacan:* Bierhorst 1985b, 179. *Kuna park:* Chapin 1985; Chapin 1991.

Natural gardens. *Yododai:* Guss, 128. *White Bead Woman:* O'Bryan, 113–14. *Plants "sown" by animals:* Luckert 1975, 54; Balée and Gély, 137–38; Weiss 1975, 352. *Forests of Brazil:* 54; Balée, 14; Anderson and Posey, 169; E. Parker 1992. *In North America:* Day, 339–40; Heizer, 12; Denton, 70. *Lacandon:* Rich, 13. *Iroquois gardens:* A. Parker 1910, 27, 38–39; Waugh 1916, 20; Converse, 186. *Animals:* Balée and Gély, 138; Alcorn 1989, 73; Pittier de Fábrega, 6–7; "Historias aportadas," 10. *Fish "crop":* Chernela 1987; Chernela 1982; Clay, 17–18.

9 / Control over Life. *Among Zuni:* Bunzel, 718; Cushing 1986, 33. *Lakota statement:* Walker 1917, 161. *Yucatec woman:* Redfield, 126. *Buffalo master:* Walker 1917, 161. *Cane master:* Guss, 131. *Marvin Harris:* Harris

1991, 57. *Jivaroan tale:* Chumap Lucía and García-Rendueles 1, 370–75. *Tewa mother:* Parsons 1924, 148.

The hardships of fertility. *Hare's grandmother:* Radin 1972, 79–80. *Sinkyone:* Kroeber 1925, 149. *Tlingit:* Sturtevant 7, 217. *Pregnancy:* Guss, 131; Momaday, 82; Simmons, 25; Parsons 1921, 99; Parsons 1919, 37–38; Thwaites 15, 1959, 181. *Contamination from afterbirth:* Bean, 154.

"I want only one baby." *Amulets:* Ewers, 216–17. *To ensure single birth:* Goldman, 166; Simmons, 25, 35. *Mixed feelings about twins:* Steward 1946–59 3, 419. *Kwakiutl twins:* Boas 1930, 202; Boas 1966, 360, 366. *Restrictions to prevent twins:* Goldman, 167; Parsons 1924, 148; Sturtevant 11, 403.

Honor and continence. *Winnebago tale:* Radin 1972, 5. *Aztecs and Toltecs:* Bierhorst 1992b, 34, 38, 108, 113, 128. *Ceremonial continence:* Murie 1, 173; Thompson 1930, 44; Greenberg, 160–68; M. Brown, 95; Powers 1975, 14; Myerhoff, 174; Reichel-Dolmatoff 1976a, 312–13. *Female chastity:* de Laguna 1, 296; Boas 1966, 56; Sahagún 1969, 102; Garcilaso 1966, 195–99. *Male chastity:* Yegerlehner, 293; Dumont, 115. *Marital restraint:* Jenness, 96; Voegelin et al., 39; Magalhães, 162–74; Lévi-Strauss 1948, 64; Parsons 1924, 148; Donck, 200–1; Lévi-Strauss 1948, 64–65; Standing Bear, 118; Hoebel, 84; Grinnell 1972 1, 149.

Medicines. *Aztec and Shawnee remedies:* Hernández 1, 107–8; Voegelin et al., 39. *Hopi medicines:* Voth 1905, 52. *Campa woman:* Maxwell, 8. *Piripiri:* Maxwell, 7. *Stoneseed:* Train et al., 68; Moerman; Cranston, 578; Ford, 766. *Tarahumara mother:* Lumholtz 1, 273. *Chatino data:* Greenberg, 160–68. *Starchy diets:* Harris, 23–25.

10 / The Argument for Death. *Deer:* Hill, 128–29. *Eagle:* Kroeber 1925, 529. *Squirrel:* Boas 1930, 201. *To drive off the human dead:* Dean 1978, 7; Bierhorst 1983, 152; Michelson 1925, 507; Ortiz, 54; Henry, 183; Goldman, 260; Bunzel, 510. *On the return of souls:* Redfield and Villa Rojas, 199; Rasmussen 1930, 79; Lévi-Strauss 1948, 100; Merrill, 113–14; Curtis 10, 37; Sahagún 1952, 47; de Laguna, 766. *Omaha elder:* Fletcher and La Flesche 2, 588. *Modoc woman:* Ray, 29. *Pima narrator:* J. Smith et al., 118.

In the beginning. *Origin of human death:* Niño, 300; Benedict 1926, 1; Kroeber 1919, 346; Voegelin 1935, 209; G. Dorsey 1905b, 15–16; Cooper, 437; Boas 1917, 1; Ray, 26; Kilpatrick and Kilpatrick 1967,

389; Saxton and Saxton, 6–7; Bushnell, 527; Mooney 1900, 252; Kroeber 1931, 12–13; Marriott, 39–43; Radin 1972, 90; Benedict 1981, 5.

For the lives of the elders. *Sparing the parent:* Sahagún 1969, 157; Walde-Waldegg, 42–43; Crocker 1985b, 54. *Sparing the sibling:* Russell, 186. *Penalties:* Devereux, 206, 211–12; Guerra, 73; Hoebel, 53. *On quickening:* Furst and Nahmad, 16–20 (Huichol); Greenberg, 91 (Chatino); Huxley, 186 (Ka'apor). *Protecting the newborn:* Goldman, 167–68; Steward 1946–59 3, 717; Weiss 1975, 428, 430n; Ray, 20, 24; Harrington 1910, 55. *Abortifacients:* Moerman. *Aztec emmenagogues:* Hernández 1, 138, 293, 348–49, 387.

For the lives of the young. *Chiricahua story:* Hoijer, 33. *Delaware story:* Harrington n.d., OC-163, folder 9, no. 11. *Cahuilla tale:* Bean and Saubel, 145. *Montagnais story:* Savard, 49. *Redfield:* Redfield and Villa Rojas, 200. *Wintun:* Powers 1975, 148. *Mískito:* Conzemius, 153. *Koyukon:* R. Nelson, 46. *Tlingit:* de Laguna 3, 1313–14. *Fox:* Michelson 1921, 55–57.

11 / Reduction of Ancestors. *Iroquois society:* Fenton, 116. *Changing Woman:* Matthews 1897, 148. *Chatino:* Greenberg, 84. *Zuni:* Bunzel, 514. *Aztec:* Bierhorst 1985b, 387. *Cuzco as navel:* Garcilaso 1966, 48. *Tewa:* Ortiz, 21. *Lakota bundle:* Curtis 3, 59. *Mixcoatl:* Bierhorst 1992b, 106. *Root of Cuzco:* Cobo, 58–59. *"Lie in darkness":* Bierhorst 1992b, 73, 78.

The emergence halted. *Emergence stories:* Bushnell, 527; Cushing 1896, 382, 388; Steward 1946–59 3, 550; Wilbert and Simoneau 1982, 59; Mooney 1898, 152–53; Brett, 55–60, and Im Thurn, 377 (Warrau); Melody, 163 (Lakota); Hodge 1, 797 (Mandan); Petrullo, 239; Wagley 1940, 254.

Clans and living space. *Navajo clans:* Sturtevant 10, 524; Matthews 1897, 137. *Pima:* Sturtevant 10, 186; Russell, 226, 230. *Guajiro:* Wilbert and Simoneau 1986 1, 115–16. *Ojibwa:* Warren, 43–44. *Inca:* Sarmiento, 213–16. *Yuracaré:* Steward 1946–59 3, 503. *Aztec:* Bierhorst 1992b, 149–50; Phillips, 623. *Iroquois:* Curtin and Hewitt, 654–56. *Bororo:* Wilbert and Simoneau 1983, 75–76. *Cahuilla:* Curtis 15, 109; Bean, 167; Kroeber 1925, 707. *Ojibwa:* Erikson and Vecsey, 155, 156.

Patterns on the earth. *Crow:* Lowie 1935, 12. *Omaha:* Fletcher and La

Flesche 1, 99; Hodge 1, 197. *Peru:* Cobo, 190. *Yurok:* Kroeber 1925, 8. *Cahuilla:* Curtis 15, 121. *Aztec:* Wauchope 10, 363; Bierhorst 1992b, 76. *Cuzco:* Garcilaso 1966, 44, 93–94. *Zia:* Sturtevant 9, 410–12. *Circles and ovals:* Standing Bear, 121; Grinnell 1962, 225; Lévi-Strauss 1967, 138 (Bororo) and 146 (Canela); Lowie 1963, 93–94 (Cheyenne). *Fletcher:* Hodge 1, 198. *Tapirape:* Wagley 1969, 273–74, 276; Steward 1946–59 3, 169, 171–72.

12 / The Human Payment. *Aztec "payment":* Bierhorst 1992a, Glossary (ixtlahua). *Alsop:* Alsop, 78. *Bella Coola:* Goeken, 184. *Use of monkeys for food:* Steward 1946–59 6, 366.

By command of the sun. *In Huichol myth:* Zingg, 170–80. *Cashinahua riddle:* Abreu, 521, no. 5914. *Sharanahua:* Siskind, 154. *Yupa:* Wilbert 1974, 85. *Tahltan:* Teit 1919, 228. *Shipaya:* Nimuendajú 1919–20, 1010. *Kaska:* Teit 1917, 441. *Chumash:* Blackburn, 36, 93. *Isleta:* Densmore 1957, 62.

Bringing and taking. *Sun takes payment:* Klah, 68; O'Bryan, 18, 31; Wallis, 8–9. *Light and Death:* Rasmussen 1908, 101. *Lakota observation:* Standing Bear, 49. *Tewa prayer:* Spinden 1933, 106. *Hopi midwife:* Voth 1905, 53. *Sun as father:* Reichard, 474; Sahagún 1950–69 6, 164. *Desana:* Reichel-Dolmatoff 1971, 50. *Campa:* Weiss 1972, 169. *Native America in general:* Lévi-Strauss 1985, 14; Trigger, 559. *Isleta:* Densmore 1957, 60.

Paying the earth. *Chorti ritual:* Fought, 479. *Crops from child's body:* Williams García, 87; Mishkin, 225–26; Chapman, 73; Steward 1946–59 3, 360. *Mixe myth:* Carrasco, 168. *Old woman:* Kilpatrick and Kilpatrick 1967, 391; Swanton 1929, 16–17, 230. *Nahua version:* Sandstrom n.d., 1–2; cf. Sandstrom 1991, 187, 245–46. *Huichol tale:* Myerhoff, 213–14. *In Peru:* Nuñez del Prado, 246–47.

Bargaining with the animal master. *Zuni hunter:* Cushing 1920, 419, 640. *Popoluca:* G. Foster, 181. *Bribri:* "Historias aportadas," 10; cf. Pittier de Fábrega, 6–7. *Jicaque:* Chapman, 152. *Anaconda becomes enraged:* Goldman, 169; Reichel-Dolmatoff 1976b, 168–69. *Animals cause disease:* Spier 1928, 287; Mooney 1900, 252; Speck 1909, 134; Luckert 1975, 153. *Zoque:* A. Paredes, 5–7. *Guajiro:* Perrin, 40. *Tucano:* Chernela 1987, 51. *Desana "exchange":* Reichel-Dolmatoff 1985, 123. *Cree story:* Tanner, 154. *Aguaruna prayer:* M. Brown, 77–79.

13 / The Angry Earth. *We "eat" the land:* Crumrine, 1143. *Ojibwa myth:* Jenness, 27–28. *"Don't urinate":* Wallis, 15. *"Mistreats" the earth:* Portal, 45. *"Kills" the earth:* Pereira, 46.

The weeping woman. *Penobscot:* Speck 1935, 16. *Okanagon:* Boas 1917, 112. *Chumash:* Blackburn, 93–94. *Hopi:* Voth 1902–1903, 352–53. *La Llorona of Mexico:* Horcasitas and Butterworth. *Glides over the earth:* Horcasitas 1984, 117–18. *In Tarascan lore:* Acevedo Barba et al., 50. *In the United States:* Weigle 1982, 258. *Bribri:* "Historias recogidas," 30. *Drowned her children:* Horcasitas and Butterworth, 214. *Ate her own child:* Parsons 1936, 231. *In Aztec lore:* Sahagún 1970, 11, and Sahagún 1969 I, 46–47; Durán I, 125; "Histoyre," 28–29.

"The earth hates us." *Jicaque earth spirit:* Chapman, 128–30. *Bribri:* Pereira, 46. *Cora:* Preuss, 148. *Mazatec:* Portal, 45. *Achi:* Shaw, 51. *Mayo:* Crumrine, 1143. *Quechua:* Gow and Condori, 10–11; Mishkin, 236. *Navajo:* McNeley, 15.

Offended spirits. *"She turned her face":* Chapman, 129. *In Navajo myth:* Reichard, 407. *Ojibwa:* Jenness, 38. *Micmac:* Speck 1921, 114–15. *Haida:* Curtis 11, 168. *Delaware corn mother:* Harrington n.d., OC-161, folder 1. *In Mexico:* Bierhorst 1990, 90–99, 215–16; Myerhoff, 212–13. *Zuni corn maidens:* Benedict 1935 I, 20–43. *Salt and turquoise:* Zuni people, 205–6; Benedict 1935 I, 43–49.

14 / Earth's Past and Future. *Lakota elder:* Standing Bear, 194. *Shawnee prayer:* Voegelin 1936, 14. *"Long life" and "beauty":* Reichard, 48, and cf. Wyman, 28–30. *Prophecies:* Teit 1919, 227; Weiss 1972, 170; Wauchope 8, 671–72; Laughlin, 77; Barrett 1925, 376; Spier 1933, 350, 414; Joughlin and Valenzuela, 19; Abreu, 521, no. 5897 (Cashinahua); J. Smith et al., 62; G. Dorsey 1904a, 294; Curtin and Hewitt, 620; Tedlock and Tedlock, 270, and Sturtevant 9, 508.

An infection of the land. *Pima prophecy:* Herzog; Bahr et al., 46–47. *Wintun:* Du Bois 1935, 76, and cf. Sturtevant 8, 332; Barrett 1919, 463. *Pomo:* Du Bois 1939, 90. *Shawnee:* Howard, 181. *Delaware:* Peters. *Bororo:* Crocker 1985b, 47–48, 329–32; "For Brazil's Tribes, a New Will to Live," *The New York Times,* Aug. 2, 1974. *Kaiowá:* "For Brazil's Indians, a Final Way Out," *The New York Times,* June 1, 1991. *Shuar:* Bianchi, 19. *The beaver and the fur trade:* Martin; and cf. Krech. *I'itoi drives game to safety:* Underhill 1946, 12.

Ancient destructions. *Shawnee:* Howard, 184. *Piman:* Russell, 206–8. *Gran Chaco:* Wilbert and Simoneau 1982, 96; Wilbert and Simoneau 1985, 38–39. *Kalapuya:* Frachtenberg, 381.

The hidden nature of culture. *Flood myth in Mexico:* Bierhorst 1990, 80–82, 215; A. Paredes, 3 (modern variant); Lehmann, 753–54 ("Don't make fire"); Miller, 100 (animals came into town). *Mixtec:* A. Dyk, 3. *Revolt of utensils:* Davis and Snell, 73–74; Gossen 1974, 148; Tedlock 1985, 84–85; Urioste 1, 19; Hugh-Jones, 263; Tedlock and Tedlock, 270; Teit 1898, 22; Wauchope 8, 671; Métraux 1931, 157–58; Redfield, 117, 206–7.

Prolonging the world. *Cherokee:* Mooney 1900, 239. *Ojibwa:* Jenness, 90. *Guaraní:* Nimuendajú 1914, 399. *Time and the weaver:* Reichel-Dolmatoff 1978, 19; Voegelin 1936, 21; Schutz, 64; Curtin and Hewitt, 615, 625; E. Smith, 39; D. Hale, 6–7. *Tortoise carries earth:* Speck 1931, 109. *Buffalo in the west:* J. Brown, 9n; G. Dorsey 1906, 134. *Navajo sand paintings:* O'Bryan, 23, and cf. Wyman, 90–91. *Delaware:* Michelson 1912, folder 10. *Kuksu:* Kroeber 1925, 383. *Wiigita:* Underhill 1946, 135; Galinier, 528–29. *Panare ceremonies:* Dumont, 84. *Fox ritualist:* Michelson 1921, 45.

15 / Acts of Re-creation. *White Shell Woman:* Wyman, 28–29; Goddard 1933, 175. *Romi Kumú:* Trupp, 72–73; Hugh-Jones, 264. *Old Woman:* Beckwith, 133; Bowers, 338. *Mother's body remade:* Hewitt 1928, 542. *Thunder or rain:* Goddard 1933, 167; Cushing 1883b, 126; Alcorn 1984, 58–59; Linton.

Wakening. *Papago retelling:* Underhill 1946, 8, Underhill 1938, 12; Underhill 1965, 30–31. *Hopi soyal:* Sturtevant 9, 574; Leach and Fried, 566, 1058. *Navajo ritual:* Matthews 1902, 110–11. *Pawnee Thunder Ceremony:* Linton; Weltfish, 97–106; Murie 1, 43–62.

New fire. *Pawnee:* Murie 1, 136–54. *Cherokee:* Mooney 1900, 502. *Inuit:* Boas 1964, 199. *Inca:* Garcilaso 1966, 357, 362. *Aztec:* Sahagún 1950–69 4, 143–44; Sahagún 1950–69 7, 25–26; Durán 2, 453. *Iroquois:* Hewitt 1889. *Delaware:* Speck 1931, 47, 51. *Hopi:* Fewkes, 81, 101–2. *Creek:* Hodge 1, 176–77. *Natchez:* Gilbert, 50. *Yucatec:* Landa, 152–53. *Lacandon:* Tozzer, 133–34, 144, 183–84. *"World luck will hold fast":* Kroeber and Gifford, 15.

World renewal. *Northwest California ceremonies:* Kroeber and Gifford, 1–15,

102–16; Kroeber 1925, 102, 105; Sturtevant 8, 664. *Cree and Inuit trek:* "Troubled Waters: From Hudson's Bay to the Hudson River, Saving a Way of Life," *Woodstock Times* (Woodstock, N.Y.), April 19, 1990. *Longest Run:* Printup. *Taos spokesman:* "Indians Hail Return of Sacred Lake," *The New York Times,* Dec. 7, 1970. *Delaware ritualist:* Speck 1931, 87. *Navajo narrator:* O'Bryan, 101. *Arikara priest:* Gilmore, 119. *Tewa song:* Spinden 1933, 119.

References

Date given is of the edition used; date of the first edition, if different, appears in parentheses immediately following the title. Abbreviations are as follows:

APS-AIMC = American Philosophical Society (Philadelphia), American Indian Manuscript Collections
ARBAE = Annual Reports of the Bureau of American Ethnology
BBAE = Bulletins of the Bureau of American Ethnology
JAF = *Journal of American Folklore*
TOIC = *Tradición Indígena Oral Costarricense,* Universidad de Costa Rica, Departamento de Antropología
UCPAAE = University of California Publications in American Archaeology and Ethnology

Abreu, João Capistrano de. *Rã-txa hu-ní-ku-ĩ: A lingua dos caxinahuás.* Rio de Janeiro: Typographia Leuzinger, 1914.
Acevedo Barba, Cruz R., et al. *Mitos de la meseta tarasca.* Mexico: UNAM, 1982.
Acosta, Joseph de. *Historia natural y moral de la indias* (1590). Mexico: Fondo de Cultura Económica, 1962.
Agnes Etherington Art Centre. *Inuit Art in the 1970s.* Kingston, Ont., 1979.
Alcorn, Janis B. *Huastec Mayan Ethnobotany.* Austin: University of Texas Press, 1984.
———."Process as Resource." In *Resource Management in Amazonia* (ed. Darrell A. Posey and W. Balée), pp. 63–77. New York: New York Botanical Garden, 1989.
Allen, Paula Gunn. *The Sacred Hoop.* Boston: Beacon, 1986.
Alsop, George. *A Character of the Province of Maryland* (1666). New York: William Gowans, 1869.
Anderson, A., and D. Posey. "Management of a Tropical Scrub Savanna by the Gorotire Kayapó Indians." In *Resource Management in Amazonia* (ed. Darrell A. Posey and W. Balée), pp. 159–73. New York: New York Botanical Garden, 1989.
Angulo, Jaime de. "Pomo Creation Myth," JAF 48 (1935): 203–62.

Armellada, Cesáreo, and C. Bentivenga N., *Literaturas indígenas venezolanas*. Caracas: Monte Avila, 1975.

Bahr, Donald M., J. Gregorio, D. Lopez, and A. Alvarez. *Piman Shamanism and Staying Sickness*. Tucson: University of Arizona Press, 1974.

Ballard, Arthur C. "Mythology of Southern Puget Sound." University of Washington Publications in Anthropology, 3:31–150. 1929.

Balée, W. "The Culture of Amazonian Forests." In *Resource Management in Amazonia* (ed. Darrell A. Posey and W. Balée), pp. 1–21. New York: New York Botanical Garden, 1989.

Balée, W., and A. Gély. "Managed Forest Succession in Amazonia." In *Resource Management in Amazonia* (ed. Darrell A. Posey and W. Balée), pp. 129–58. New York: New York Botanical Garden, 1989.

Barnouw, Victor. *Wisconsin Chippewa Myths and Tales*. Madison: University of Wisconsin Press, 1977.

Barrett, S[amuel] A. *The Cayapa Indians of Ecuador*. New York: Museum of the American Indian, 1925.

———. *Pomo Myths*. Bulletin of the Public Museum of the City of Milwaukee 15. 1933.

———. "The Wintun Hesi Ceremony," UCPAAE 14 (1919): 437–88.

Barrueco, Domingo. *Mitos y leyendas shuar*. Quito, Ecuador: Mundo Shuar, 1985.

Bean, Lowell J. *Mukat's People: The Cahuilla Indians of Southern California*. Berkeley: University of California Press, 1972.

Bean, Lowell J., and K. Saubel. *Temalpakh: Cahuilla Indian Knowledge and Usage of Plants*. Banning, Calif.: Malki Museum, 1972.

Beckwith, Martha Warren. *Mandan-Hidatsa Myths and Ceremonies*. Memoirs of the American Folklore Society 32. 1938.

Behrens, Clifford A. "The Scientific Basis for Shipibo Soil Classification and Land Use," *American Anthropologist* 91 (1989): 83–100.

Benedict, Ruth. "Serrano Tales," JAF 39 (1926): 1–17.

———. *Tales of the Cochiti Indians* (1931). Albuquerque: University of New Mexico Press, 1981.

———. *Zuni Mythology*, 2 vols. Columbia University Contributions to Anthropology 21, 1935.

Bianchi, César. *El shuar y el ambiente*. Ecuador: Mundo Shuar, 1980.

Bierhorst, John. *Cantares Mexicanos: Songs of the Aztecs*. Stanford, Calif.: Stanford University Press, 1985. Cited as Bierhorst 1985a.

———. *Codex Chimalpopoca: The Text in Nahuatl with a Glossary and*

Grammatical Notes. Tucson: University of Arizona Press, 1992. Cited as Bierhorst 1992a.

———. *Four Masterworks of American Indian Literature*. New York: Farrar, Straus and Giroux, 1974.

———. *History and Mythology of the Aztecs: The Codex Chimalpopoca*. Tucson: University of Arizona Press, 1992. Cited as Bierhorst 1992b.

———. *The Mythology of Mexico and Central America*. New York: William Morrow, 1990.

———. *The Mythology of South America*. New York: William Morrow, 1988.

———. *A Nahuatl-English Dictionary and Concordance to the Cantares Mexicanos*. Stanford, Calif.: Stanford University Press, 1985. Cited as Bierhorst 1985b.

Biocca, Ettore. *Viaggi tra gli indi*, 3 vols. Rome: Consiglio Nazionale delle Ricerche, 1965–66.

Blackburn, Thomas C. *December's Child: A Book of Chumash Oral Narratives*. Berkeley: University of California Press, 1975.

Blodgett, Jean. *The Coming and Going of the Shaman*. Winnipeg Art Gallery, 1979.

Bloomfield, Leonard. *Menominee Texts*. Publications of the American Ethnological Society 12, 1928.

Boas, Franz. *The Central Eskimo* (1888). Lincoln: University of Nebraska Press, 1964.

———. *Folk-Tales of Salishan and Sahaptin Tribes*. Memoirs of the American Folklore Society 11, 1917.

———. *Indianische Sagen von der nordpacifischen Küste Amerikas*. Berlin: A. Asher, 1895.

———. *Kwakiutl Ethnography*. Chicago: University of Chicago Press, 1966.

———. *The Religion of the Kwakiutl Indians*, pt. 2. Columbia University Contributions to Anthropology 10, 1930.

———. "Traditions of the Tsetsaut," JAF 9 (1896): 257–68.

———. "Tsimshian Mythology," ARBAE 31 (1916): 29–1037.

Boremanse, Didier. *Contes et mythologie des indiens lacandons*. Paris: L'Harmattan, 1986.

Bowers, Alfred W. *Hidatsa Social and Ceremonial Organization*. BBAE 194, 1965.

Boyd, Julian P., ed. *Indian Treaties Printed by Benjamin Franklin, 1736–1762*. Philadelphia: Historical Society of Pennsylvania, 1938.

Brett, W. H. *Legends and Myths of the Aboriginal Indians of British Guiana.* London, [1880].

Brody, J. "Creation that Endured," *Latin American Indian Literatures Journal* 3 (1987): 39–58.

Brown, Joseph Epes. *The Sacred Pipe.* Norman: University of Oklahoma Press, 1953.

Brown, Michael F. *Tsewa's Gift.* Washington: Smithsonian Institution Press, 1985.

Bunzel, Ruth. [Zuni ethnography], ARBAE 47 (1932): 467–1086.

Bushnell, D. "Myths of the Louisiana Choctaw," *American Anthropologist,* n.s. 12 (1910): 526–35.

Cadogán, León. *Ayvu rapyta.* Universidade de São Paulo, Faculdade de Filosofia, Ciências e Letras. Boletim 227, Antropologia 5. São Paulo, Brazil, 1959.

———. "Baiô Kará Wachú y otras mitos guayakíes," *América Indígena* 22 (1962): 39–82.

Callicott, J. Baird. *In Defense of the Land Ethic.* Albany: State University of New York Press, 1989.

Carrasco, Pedro. "El sol y la luna," *Tlalocan* 3 (1949–57): 168–74.

Caspar, Franz. *Tupari.* London: G. Bell, 1956.

Chafe, Wallace L. *Seneca Thanksgiving Rituals.* BBAE 183, 1961.

Chapin, Norman Macpherson [Mac]. Curing among the San Blas Kuna of Panama. Ph.D. dissertation. University of Arizona, 1983.

———. "Losing the Way of the Great Father," *New Scientist* (Aug. 10, 1991): 40–44. London, England.

———. "Udirbi." In *Native Peoples and Economic Development* (ed. Theodore Macdonald, Jr.), pp. 39–53. Cambridge, Mass.: Cultural Survival, 1985.

Chapman, Anne. *Hijos de la muerte.* Mexico: UNAM, 1982.

Chernela, Janet. "Endangered Ideologies," *Cultural Survival Quarterly* 11 (1987): 50–52.

———. "Indigenous Forest and Fish Management in the Uaupes Basin of Brazil," *Cultural Survival Quarterly* 6 (1982): 17–18.

Chumap Lucía, Aurelio, and M. García-Rendueles. *"Duik múun."* 2 vols. Lima: Centro Amazónico de Antropología y Aplicación Práctica, 1979.

Clay, Jason W. *Indigenous People and Tropical Forests.* Cambridge, Mass.: Cultural Survival, 1988.

Cobo, Bernabe. *Inca Religion and Customs* (trans. R. Hamilton). Austin: University of Texas Press, 1990.

Codex Vaticanus 3738. *In Antigüedades de México, basadas en la recopilación de Lord Kingsborough* (ed. Antonio Ortiz Mena, A. Yáñez, and J. Corona Núñez). vol. 3. Mexico: Secretaría de Hacienda y Crédito Pública, 1964.

Colby, Benjamin N., and L. Colby. *The Daykeeper: The Life and Discourse of an Ixil Diviner.* Cambridge, Mass.: Harvard University Press, 1981.

Converse, Harriet M. *Myths and Legends of the New York State Iroquois.* New York State Museum Bulletin 125, 1908.

Conzemius, Eduard. *Ethnographical Survey of the Miskito and Sumu Indians of Honduras and Nicaragua.* BBAE 106, 1932.

Cooper, John M. *The Gros Ventres of Montana.* pt. 2 (ed. Regina Flannery). Catholic University of America Anthropological Series 16, 1957.

Cranston, E. "The Effect of Lithospermum ruderale on the oestrous cycle of mice," *Journal of Pharmacology and Experminetal Therapeutics* 83 (1945): 130–42.

Crocker, J. Christopher. "My Brother the Parrot." In *Animal Myths and Metaphors in South America* (ed. Gary Urton), pp. 13–48. Salt Lake City: University of Utah Press, 1985. Cited as Crocker 1985a.

———. *Vital Souls.* Tucson: University of Arizona Press, 1985. Cited as Crocker 1985b.

Croghan, George. Croghan's Journal, 1765. In *Early Western Travels, 1748–1846* (ed. Reuben G. Thwaites). vol. 1, pp. 126–66. Cleveland: Arthur H. Clark, 1904.

Cronquist, Arthur, A. Holmgren, N. Holmgren, J. Reveal, and P. Holmgren. *Intermountain Flora: Vascular Plants of the Intermountain West, U.S.A.* vol. 4. New York: York Botanical Garden, 1984.

Crumrine, N. "A New Mayo Indian Religious Movement in Northwest Mexico," *Journal of Latin American Lore* 1 (1975): 127–45.

Curtin, Jeremiah, and J. N. B. Hewitt. "Seneca Fiction," ARBAE 32 (1918): 37–813.

Curtis, Edward S. *The North American Indian.* 20 vols. Cambridge, Mass., and Norwood, Mass., 1907–30.

Cushing, Frank H. "Outlines of Zuñi Creation Myths," ARBAE 13 (1896): 321–447.

———. *Zuñi Breadstuff* (1920). New York: AMS Press, 1975.

———. "Zuñi Fetiches," ARBAE 2 (1883): 3–45. Cited as Cushing 1883a.

————. *Zuñi Folk Tales* (1901). Tucson: University of Arizona Press, 1986.

————. [Zuni weather proverbs.] In *Weather Proverbs* (Signal Service Notes no. 9, ed. H. H. C. Dunwoody), pp. 124–27. U.S. War Dept. Washington: Government Printing Office, 1883. Cited as Cushing 1883b.

Danckaerts, Jasper. *Journal of Jasper Danckaerts*. New York: C. Scribner's Sons, 1913.

Danter, Sylvia, ed. *Dorset 82: Cape Dorset Graphics Annual*. Toronto: M. F. Feheley, 1982.

Dauenhauer, Nora M., and R. Dauenhauer. *Haa Tuwunáagu Yís*. Seattle: University of Washington Press, 1990.

Davis, Harold, and B. Snell. *Cuentos folklóricos de los machiguenga*. 2d ed. Comunidades y Culturas Peruanas 5. Instituto Lingüístico de Verano, 1976.

Day, G. "The Indian as an Ecological Factor in the Northeastern Forest," *Ecology* 34 (1953): 329–43.

Dean, Nora Thompson. "Delaware Indian Reminiscences," *Bulletin of the Archaeological Society of New Jersey* 35 (1978): 1–17.

————. Stories in Lenape and English, recorded by Nicholas Shoumatoff, 11/17/77. Cassette tape, call no. 52a, cat. no. 2-DE-18, side B. Delaware Resource Center, Trailside Museum, Ward Pound Ridge Reservation, Cross River, New York.

de Civrieux, Marc. "Datos antropológicos de los indios Kunuhana," *Antropológica* 8 (1959): 85–145. Caracas, Venezuela.

————. *Religión y magia kari'ña*. Caracas: Universidad Católica Andrés Bello, 1974.

de Laguna, Frederica. *Under Mt. St. Elias*. 3 vols. Smithsonian Contributions to Anthropology 7, 1972.

Deloria, E. "The Sun Dance of the Oglala Sioux," JAF 42 (1929): 354–413.

DeMallie, Raymond J., ed. *The Sixth Grandfather*. Lincoln: University of Nebraska Press, 1984.

Densmore, Frances. *Music of Acoma, Isleta, Cochiti and Zuñi Pueblos*. BBAE 165, 1957.

————. *Seminole Music*. BBAE 161, 1956.

————. *Teton Sioux Music*. BBAE 61, 1918.

Denton, Daniel. *A Brief Description of New-York* (1670). Westvaco Corp., 1973.

Devereux, George. *A Study of Abortion in Primitive Societies*, rev. ed. New York: International Universities Press, 1976.

Dixon, R. "System and Sequence in Maidu Mythology," JAF 16 (1903): 32–36.

Donck, Adriaen van der. *A Description of the New Netherlands* (1841). Syracuse: Syracuse University Press, 1968.

Dorsey, George A. "The Cheyenne." vol. 2 (The Sun Dance). *Field (Columbian) Museum Anthropological Series*, vol. 9, no. 2. Chicago, 1905. Cited as G. Dorsey 1905a.

———. *The Mythology of the Wichita.* Washington: Carnegie Institution of Washington, 1904. Cited as G. Dorsey 1904a.

———. *The Pawnee: Mythology.* Washington: Carnegie Institution of Washington, 1906.

———. *Traditions of the Arikara.* Washington: Carnegie Institution of Washington, 1904. Cited as G. Dorsey 1904b.

———. *Traditions of the Caddo.* Washington: Carnegie Institution of Washington, 1905. Cited as G. Dorsey 1905b.

Dorsey, J. Owen. "Osage Traditions," ARBAE 6 (1888): 373–97.

Du Bois, Cora A. "The 1870 Ghost Dance," *University of California Anthropological Records* 3 (1939): 1–151.

———. "Wintu Ethnography," UCPAAE 36 (1935): 1–148.

Dumont, Jean-Paul. *Under the Rainbow.* Austin: University of Texas Press, 1976.

Durán, Diego. *Historia de la Indias de Nueva España* (ed. Angel M. Garibay K.). 2 vols. Mexico: Porrúa, 1967.

Dyk, Anne. *Mixteca Texts.* Norman: Summer Institute of Linguistics of the University of Oklahoma, 1959.

Dyk, Walter, ed. *Son of Old Man Hat* (1938). Lincoln: University of Nebraska Press, 1967.

Eastman, Charles A. *The Soul of the Indian.* Boston: Houghton Mifflin, 1911.

Edmonson, M., and V. Bricker. "Yucatecan Mayan Literature," *Supplement to the Handbook of Middle American Indians*, 3:44–63. Austin: University of Texas Press, 1985.

Erikson, K., and C. Vecsey, "A Report to the People of Grassy Narrows." In *American Indian Environments* (ed. Christopher Vecsey and R. Venables), pp. 152–61. Syracuse, N.Y.: Syracuse University Press, 1980.

Ewers, J. "Contraceptive Charms among the Plains Indians," *Plains Anthropologist* 15 (1970): 216–18.

Farabee, W. C. *The Central Arawaks.* New York: Humanities Press, 1967.

Faye, Paul-Louis. "Notes on the Southern Maidu," UCPAAE 20 (1923): 35–53.

Feit, H. "Twilight of the Cree," *Natural History* 82 (1973) (July): 48–54, 56, 72.

Fenton, W. "An Iroquois Condolence Council for Installing Cayuga Chiefs in 1945," *Journal of the Washington Academy of Sciences* 36 (1946): 110–27.

Fewkes, J. "The New-Fire Ceremony at Walpi," *American Anthropologist*, n.s. 2 (1900): 80–138.

Fletcher, Alice, and F. La Flesche. *The Omaha Tribe* (1911). 2 vols. Lincoln: University of Nebraska Press, 1972.

Fock, Neils. *Waiwai: Religion and Society of an Amazonian Tribe.* Copenhagen: National Museum, 1963.

Ford, C. "Control of Conception in Cross Cultural Perspective," *Annals of the New York Academy of Sciences* 54 (1952): 763–68.

Foster, George M. "Sierra Popoluca Folklore and Beliefs," UCPAAE 42 (1945): 177–250.

Foster, Michael K. *From the Earth to Beyond the Sky: An Ethnographic Approach to Four Longhouse Iroquois Speech Events.* Canadian Ethnology Service Papers 20. Ottawa: National Museum of Man, 1974.

Fought, John G. *Chorti (Mayan) Texts 1.* Philadelphia: University of Pennsylvania Press, 1972.

Fowler, Don D., and C. Fowler, eds. *Anthropology of the Numa: John Wesley Powell's Manuscripts on the Numic Peoples of Western North America, 1868–1880.* Smithsonian Contributions to Anthropology 14, 1971.

Frachtenberg, L. "Kalapuya Texts," *University of Washington Publications in Anthropology* 11 (1945), 143–369.

Furst, Jill Leslie. *Codex Vindobonensis Mexicanus I: A Commentary.* Institute for Mesoamerican Studies, State University of New York at Albany, 1978.

Furst, Peter T., and S. Nahmad. *Mitos y artes huicholes.* Mexico: Secretaría de Educación Publica, 1972.

Galinier, J. "From Montezuma to San Francisco," *Journal of the Southwest* 33 (1991): 486–538.

Garcilaso de la Vega, El Inca. *The Incas: The Royal Commentaries of the Inca* (trans. A. Gheerbrant and M. Jolas) (1961). New York: Avon, 1964.

———. "Primera parte de los Comentarios reales de los incas" (1609), *Biblioteca de autores españoles,* vol. 133. Madrid: Atlas, 1963.

————. *Royal Commentaries of the Incas and General History of Peru.* pt. 1 (trans. H. V. Livermore). Austin: University of Texas Press, 1966.

Gatschet, A. S. "Some Mythic Stories of the Yuchi Indians," *American Anthropologist* 4 (1893): 279–82.

George, Chief Dan. "Brotherhood and Understanding." In *Contemporary Native American Address* (ed. John R. Maestas), pp. 393–96. Brigham Young University Publications, 1976.

Giddings, Ruth W. *Yaqui Myths and Legends.* Tucson: University of Arizona Press, 1959.

Gifford, Edward W. "The Southeastern Yavapai," UCPAAE 29 (1932): 177–252.

Gilbert, William Harlen, Jr. New fire ceremonialism in America. M. A. dissertation. University of Chicago, Dept. of Anthropology, 1930.

Gilmore, M. "The Arikara Book of Genesis," *Papers of the Michigan Academy of Sciences, Arts, and Letters* 12 (1929): 95–120.

Girard, Rafael. *Indios selváticos de Amazonía Peruana.* Mexico: Libro Mex Editores, 1958.

Goddard, Pliny E. *Myths and Tales from the San Carlos Apache.* Anthropological Papers of the American Museum of Natural History 24, 1918.

————. *Navaho Texts.* Anthropological Papers of the American Museum of Natural History 34, pt. 1, 1933.

Goeken, . . . von. "Das religiöse Leben der Bella Coola Indianer," *Original-Mittheilungen aus der Ethnologischen Abtheilung der Königlichen Museen* 1 (1885): 183–86. Berlin.

Goetz, Delia, S. Morley, and A. Recinos. *Popol Vuh.* Norman: University of Oklahoma Press, 1950.

Goldenweiser, Alexander. *History, Psychology, and Culture* (1933). Gloucester, Mass.: Peter Smith, 1968.

Goldman, Irving. *The Cubeo.* Urbana: University of Illinois Press, 1963.

Gómara, Francisco López de. *Historia de la conquista de México* (1552). Mexico: Porrúa, 1988.

Goodwin, Grenville. *Myths and Tales of the White Mountain Apache.* Memoirs of the American Folklore Society 33, 1939.

Gossen, Gary H. "Chamula Tzotzil Proverbs." In *Meaning in Mayan Languages* (ed. Munro Edmonson), pp. 205–33. The Hague: Mouton, 1973.

————. *Chamulas in the World of the Sun.* Cambridge, Mass.: Harvard University Press, 1974.

Gow, Rosalind, and B. Condori. *Kay pacha.* 2d ed. Cuzco, Peru: Centro de Estudios Rurales Andinos Bartolomé de las Casas, 1982.

Greenberg, James B. *Santiago's Sword: Chatino Peasant Religion and Economics.* Berkeley: University of California Press, 1981.

Grinnell, George B. *Blackfoot Lodge Tales* (1892). Lincoln: University of Nebraska Press, 1962.

———. *The Cheyenne Indians.* 2 vols. (1923). Lincoln: University of Nebraska Press, 1972.

———. *Pawnee Hero Stories and Folk-Tales* (1889). Lincoln: University of Nebraska Press, 1961.

———. *The Story of the Indian.* New York: D. Appleton, 1895.

Guallart Martínez, José María. *Antología de poesía lírica aguaruna.* Lima: Centro Amazónico de Antropología y Aplicación Práctica, 1974.

Guerra, Francisco. *The Pre-Columbian Mind.* London: Seminar Press, 1971.

Guiteras-Holmes, C[alixta]. *Perils of the Soul: The World View of a Tzotzil Indian.* New York: The Free Press of Glencoe/Crowell-Collier, 1961.

Guss, David. *To Weave and Sing: Art, Symbol, and Narrative in the South American Rain Forest.* Berkeley: University of California Press, 1989.

Haile, Berard. "Soul Concepts of the Navaho," *Annali Lateranensi* 7 (1943): 59–94.

Halbert, H. S. "The Choctaw Creation Legend," *Publications of the Mississippi Historical Society* 4 (1901): 267–70.

Hale, Duane K. *Turtle Tales: Oral Traditions of the Delaware Tribe of Western Oklahoma.* Anadarko, Okla.: Delaware Tribe of Western Oklahoma Press, 1984.

Hale, Horatio. *The Iroquois Book of Rites* (1883). Toronto: University of Toronto Press, 1963.

Hallowell, A. Irving. "Ojibwa Ontology, Behavior, and World View" (1960). In *Teachings from the American Earth* (ed. Dennis Tedlock and B. Tedlock), pp. 141–78. New York: Liveright, 1975.

Harrington, Mark R. Harrington Papers, n.d. Museum of the American Indian, Heye Foundation, New York.

———. "Some Customs of the Delaware Indians," *Museum Journal* 1 (1910): 52–60. University of Pennsylvania.

Harris, Marvin. *Cannibals and Kings* (1977). New York: Vintage/Random House, 1991.

Hartmann, R., and U. Oberem. "Quechua-Texte aus Ostecuador," *Anthropos* 66 (1971): 673–85.

Heckewelder, John. *History, Manners, and Customs of the Indian Nations* (1819). Philadelphia: Historical Society of Pennsylvania, 1876.

Heizer, R. F. "Primitive Man as an Ecological Factor," *Kroeber Anthropological Society Papers* 13 (1955): 1–31.

Henry, Jules. *Jungle People*. New York: Vintage/Random House, 1964.

Hernández, Francisco. *Historia natural de Nueva España*. 2 vols. Mexico: UNAM, 1959.

Herzog, George. Pima speeches. APS-AIMC, no. 2961.

Hewitt, J. N. B. "Iroquoian Cosmology," pt. 2, ARBAE 43 (1928): 37–813.

————. "New Fire among the Iroquois," *American Anthropologist* 2 (1889): 319.

Hilbert, Vi. *Haboo: Native American Stories from Puget Sound*. Seattle: University of Washington Press, 1985.

Hill, W. W. *The Agricultural and Hunting Methods of the Navaho Indians*. Yale University Publications in Anthropology 18, 1938.

Hissink, Karin, and Albert Hahn. *Die Tacana*. vol. 1. Stuttgart: W. Kohlhammer, 1961.

"Historias aportadas por las hermanas de la caridad de Santa Ana, Escuela de Amubre," TOIC, vol. 2, nos. 1–2, pp. 5–12, 1984.

"Historias recogidas en Coroma, Coen y Amubre," TOIC, vol. 2, nos. 1–2, pp. 27–33, 1984.

"Historias recopiladas en la comunidad de Katsi," TOIC, vol. 2, nos. 3–4, pp. 18–24, 1987.

"Histoyre du Mechique," *Journal de la Société des Américanistes de Paris*, n.s. 2 (1905): 1–41.

Hodge, Frederick W., ed. *Handbook of American Indians North of Mexico*. 2 vols. BBAE 30, 1907–10.

Hoebel, E. Adamson. *The Cheyennes*. New York: Holt, Rinehart and Winston, 1960.

Hoijer, Harry. *Chiricahua and Mescalero Apache Texts*. Chicago: University of Chicago Press, 1938.

Holt, C. "Shasta Ethnography," *University of California Anthropological Records* 3 (1946): 299–349.

Horcasitas, Fernando. *The Aztecs Then and Now*. 2d ed. Mexico: Minutiae Mexicana, 1984.

————. "La narrativa oral náhuatl," *Estudios de Cultura Náhuatl* 13 (1978): 177–209.

Horcasitas, Fernando, and D. Butterworth. "La llorona," *Tlalocan* 4 (1963): 204–24.

Houston, James. *Eskimo Prints*. Barre, Mass.: Barre Publishers, 1971.

Howard, James H. *Shawnee!: The Ceremonialism of a Native American Tribe and Its Cultural Background*. Athens: Ohio University Press, 1981.

Hugh-Jones, Stephen. *The Palm and the Pleiades*. Cambridge, England: Cambridge University Press, 1979.

Huxley, Francis. *Affable Savages*. New York: Viking, 1957.

Im Thurn, Everard F. *Among the Indians of Guiana* (1883). New York: Dover, 1967.

Incháustegui, Carlos. *Relatos del mundo mágico mazateco*. Mexico: INAH, 1977.

James, S., and S. Graziani. "California Indian Warfare," *Contributions of the University of California Archaeological Research Facility* 23 (Ethnographic Interpretations 13), 1975. Berkeley.

Jenness, Diamond. *The Ojibwa Indians of Parry Island*. National Museum of Canada Bulletin 78, Anthropological Series 17, 1935.

Jones, William. *Fox Texts*. Publications of the American Ethnological Society 1, 1907.

Joughlin, R., and S. Valenzuela. "Cupeño Genesis," *El Museo*, n.s. 1, no. 4, pp. 16–23, 1953.

Kilpatrick, Jack F., and A. Kilpatrick. "Eastern Cherokee Folktales," BBAE 196 (Anthropological Papers 80), 1967.

Klah, Hasteen. *Navajo Creation Myth*. Santa Fe: Museum of Navajo Ceremonial Art, 1942.

Krech, Shepard, III, ed. *Indians, Animals, and the Fur Trade: A Critique of Keepers of the Game*. Athens: University of Georgia Press, 1981.

Kroeber, Alfred L. *The Arapaho*. Bulletins of the American Museum of Natural History 18, 1902.

———. *Gros Ventre Myths and Tales*, 1907. Anthropological Papers of the American Museum of Natural History 1. Cited as Kroeber 1907a.

———. *Handbook of the Indians of California*. BBAE 78, 1925.

———. "Indian Myths of South Central California," UCPAAE, 4 (1907): 167–250. Cited as Kroeber 1907b.

———. *The Seri*. Southwest Museum Papers 6, 1931.

———. "Sinkyone Tales," JAF 32 (1919): 346–51.

———. "Two Myths of the Mission Indians of California," JAF 18 (1905): 309–21.

Kroeber, Alfred L., and E. Gifford. "World Renewal," *University of California Anthropological Records* 13 (1949): 1–156.

Kussmaul, Friedrich, ed. *Ferne Völker, frühe Zeiten: Kunstwerke aus dem Linden-Museum, Stuttgart.* Recklinghausen, Germany: Aurel Bongers, 1982.

Lahontan, Baron de. *New Voyages to North-America,* 2 vols. Chicago: A. C. McClurg, 1905.

Lame Deer, John. *Lame Deer, Seeker of Visions* (1972). New York: Washington Square Press/Pocket Books, 1976.

Landa, Diego de. *Landa's Relación de las Cosas de Yucatan* (ed. Alfred M. Tozzer). Papers of the Peabody Museum of American Archaeology and Ethnology (Harvard University) 18, 1941.

"Landmarks," *Nature Conservancy* (Jan.–Feb. 1992): 30–32.

Lara, Jesús. *Diccionario qhëshwa-castellano, castellano-qhëshwa.* La Paz, Bolivia: Editorial "Los Amigos del Libro," 1971.

———. *La literatura de los quechuas.* 2d ed. La Paz, Bolivia: Editorial Juventud, 1969.

Laughlin, Robert M. *Of Cabbages and Kings: Tales from Zinacantán.* Smithsonian Contributions to Anthropology 25, 1977.

Leach, Maria, and J. Fried, eds. *Funk and Wagnalls Standard Dictionary of Folklore, Mythology, and Legend* (1949–50). New York: Funk and Wagnalls, 1972.

Lee, D. "Some Indian Texts Dealing with the Supernatural," *The Review of Religion* 5 (1940–41): 403–11.

Lehmann, W. "Ergebnisse einer . . . Forschungsreise nach Mexiko und Guatemala," *Anthropos* 23 (1928): 749–91.

Leland, Charles G. *The Algonquin Legends of New England.* Boston: Houghton Mifflin, 1884.

Leopold, Aldo. *A Sand County Almanac* (1949). London: Oxford University Press, 1968.

Lévi-Strauss, Claude. *Structural Anthropology* (1963). New York: Anchor/Doubleday, 1967.

———. "La Vie familiale et sociale des Indiens Nambikwara," *Journal de la Société des Américanistes,* n.s. 37 (1948): 1–131.

———. *The View from Afar.* New York: Basic Books, 1985.

Lincoln, Benjamin. Journal of a Treaty held in 1793, with the Indian Tribes northwest of the Ohio by Commissioners of the United States. In *Collections of the Massachusetts Historical Society,* 3rd ser., vol. 5, pp.

109–76. Boston: John H. Eastburn, 1836.

Linton, Ralph. *The Thunder Ceremony of the Pawnee*. Anthropological Leaflet 5. Chicago: Field Museum of Natural History, 1922.

Lowie, Robert H. *The Crow Indians*. New York: Holt, Rinehart and Winston, 1935.

———. "Ethnographic Notes on the Washo," UCPAAE 36 (1939): 301–52.

———. *Indians of the Plains* (1954). New York: Natural History Press, 1963.

———. *Myths and Traditions of the Crow Indians*. Anthropological Papers of the American Museum of Natural History 25, 1918.

Luckert, Karl W. *A Navajo Bringing-Home Ceremony*. Flagstaff: Museum of Northern Arizona Press, 1978.

———. *The Navajo Hunter Tradition*. Tucson: University of Arizona Press, 1975.

Lumholtz, Carl. *Unknown Mexico*. 2 vols. (1902). New York: Dover, 1987.

McAllester, David, and S. McAllester. *Hogans*. Middletown, Conn.: Wesleyan University Press, 1980.

McClintock, Walter. *The Old North Trail* (1910). Lincoln: University of Nebraska Press, 1968.

McDowell, John Holmes. *Sayings of the Ancestors: The Spiritual Life of the Sibundoy Indians*. Lexington: University Press of Kentucky, 1989.

McIlwraith, T. F. *The Bella Coola Indians*. 2 vols. Toronto: University of Toronto Press, 1948.

McKennan, Robert A. *The Upper Tanana Indians*. Yale University Publications in Anthropology 55, 1959.

MacMurray, J. "The 'Dreamers' of the Columbia River Valley, in Washington Territory," *Transactions of the Albany Institute* 11 (1887): 241–48.

McNeley, James Kale. *Holy Wind in Navajo Philosophy*. Tucson: University of Arizona Press, 1988.

Marriott, Alice. *Saynday's People*. Lincoln: University of Nebraska Press, 1963.

Martin, Calvin. *Keepers of the Game*. Berkeley: University of California Press, 1978.

Matthews, Washington. *Navaho Legends*. Memoirs of the American Folklore Society 5, 1897.

———. *The Night Chant*. Memoirs of the American Museum of Natural History 6, 1902.

Magalhães, [J. Vieira] Couto de. *O Selvagem*. Rio de Janeiro, 1876.

Maxwell, N. "Medical Secrets of the Amazon," *Américas* (June–July 1977): 2–8.

Melody, M. "Maka's Story," JAF 90 (1977): 149–67.

Merrill, William L. *Rarámuri Souls*. Washington: Smithsonian Institution Press, 1988.

Métraux, Alfred. "Mitos y cuentos de los indios chiriguano," *Revista del Museo de la Plata* 33 (1931): 119–84. La Plata, Argentina.

———. *La religion des tupinamba*. Paris: Librairie Ernest Leroux, 1928.

Michelson, Truman. Ethnological and linguistic field notes from the Munsee in Kansas and the Delaware in Oklahoma, 1912. Ms. 2776. National Anthropological Archives, Smithsonian Institution, Washington.

———. [Fox ethnography], ARBAE 40 (1925): 23–658.

———. *The Owl Sacred Pack of the Fox Indians*. BBAE 72, 1921.

Miller, Walter S. *Cuentos mixes*. Mexico: Instituto Nacional Indigenista, 1956.

Mishkin, B. "Cosmological Ideas among the Indians of the Southern Andes," JAF 53 (1940): 225–41.

Moerman, Daniel E. *Medicinal Plants of Native America*. 2 vols. University of Michigan Museum of Anthropology Technical Reports 19, 1986.

Molina, Alonso de. *Vocabulario en lengua castellana y mexicana y mexicana y castellana* (1571), 2 vols. in one. Mexico: Porrúa, 1970.

Molina, Cristóbal de. "The Fables and Rites of the Yncas." In *Narrative of the Rites and Laws of the Yncas* (trans. Clements R. Markham), pp. 3–64. Hakluyt Society, 1873.

Molina, Felipe. "Maso Bwikam." In *The South Corner of Time* (ed. Larry Evers), pp. 193–202. Tucson: University of Arizona Press, 1980.

Momaday, N. "Native American Attitudes to the Environment." In *Seeing with a Native Eye* (ed. Walter H. Capps), pp. 79–85. New York: Harper and Row, 1976.

Montour, Josiah. Texts, 1931. APS–AIMC, no. 1173.

Mooney, James. "Calendar History of the Kiowa Indians," ARBAE 17 (1898): 129–445.

———. "Myths of the Cherokee," ARBAE 19 (1900): 3–548.

———. "The Sacred Formulas of the Cherokees," ARBAE 7 (1891): 301–97.

Moore, O. "Divination." In *Environment and Cultural Behavior* (ed. Andrew

P. Vayda), pp. 121–29. New York: Natural History Press, 1969.

Morgan, Lewis Henry. *League of the Iroquois* (1851). New York: Corinth Books, 1962.

Morison, O. "Tsimshian Proverbs," JAF 2 (1889): 285–86.

Morley, Sylvanus G., and G. Brainerd. *The Ancient Maya*. 3d ed. Stanford, Calif.: Stanford University Press, 1956.

Murie, James R. *Ceremonies of the Pawnee*. 2 vols. Smithsonian Contributions to Anthropology 27, 1981.

Murphy, Robert F., and B. Quain. *The Trumaí Indians of Central Brazil*. Seattle: University of Washington Press, 1966.

Myerhoff, Barbara G. *Peyote Hunt*. Ithaca, N.Y.: Cornell University Press, 1974.

Myers, Marybelle, ed. *Povungnituk 1980: 1980 Povungnituk Print Collection and Six New Works by Tivi Etook*. Ville St. Laurent, Québec: La Fédération des Coopératives du Nouveau-Québec, 1980.

Myrtle, Minnie. *The Iroquois*. New York: D. Appleton, 1855.

Neihardt, John G. *Black Elk Speaks* (1932). Lincoln: University of Nebraska Press, 1961.

Nelson, E. W. "The Eskimo About Bering Strait," ARBAE 18 (1899): 3–518.

Nelson, Richard K. *Make Prayers to the Raven: A Koyukon View of the Northern Forest*. Chicago: University of Chicago Press, 1983.

Newcomb, Franc J., and G. Reichard. *Sandpaintings of the Navajo Shooting Chant* (1937). New York: Dover, 1975.

Nimuendajú, Curt. "Bruchstücke aus Religion and Uberlieferung der Sipáia-Indianer," *Anthropos* 14–15 (1919–20): 1002–39.

———. *The Eastern Timbira* (UCPAAE 41), 1946.

———. "Die Sagen von der Erschaffung und Vernichtung der Welt als Grundlagen der Religion der Apapocúva-Guaraní," *Zeitschrift für Ethnologie* 46 (1914): 284–403.

———. *The Tukuna*, UCPAAE 45 (1952).

Niño, Hugo, ed. *Literatura de Colombia aborigen*. Bogotá: Instituto Columbiano de Cultura, 1978.

Núñez del Prado, J. "The Supernatural World of the Quechua." In *Native South Americans* (ed. Patricia J. Lyon). Boston: Little, Brown, 1974.

Nuttall, Zelia. *The Codex Nuttall* (1902). New York: Dover, 1975.

O'Bryan, Aileen. *The Díné*. BBAE 163, 1956.

"Ochos relatos bribris," TOIC, vol. 1, no. 4, pp. 5–26, 1983.

Opler, Morris E. *Myths and Tales of the Chiracahua Apache Indians.* Memoirs of the American Folklore Society 37, 1942.

Orbigny, Alcide d'. *Voyage dans l'Amérique méridionale.* vol. 3, pt. 1. Paris: P. Bertrand, 1844.

Ortiz, Alfonso. *The Tewa World.* Chicago: University of Chicago Press, 1969.

Otero, Gustavo Adolfo. *La piedra mágica: Vida y costumbres de los indios callahuayas de Bolivia.* Ediciones Especiales del Instituto Indigenista Interamericano 5. Mexico, 1951.

Paredes, Américo. *Folktales of Mexico.* Chicago: University of Chicago Press, 1970.

Paredes, M. Rigoberto. *El arte folklórico de Bolivia.* 2d ed. La Paz, Bolivia, [1949].

Parker, Arthur C. *The Code of Handsome Lake.* New York State Museum Bulletin 163, 1913.

———. *The Constitution of the Five Nations.* New York State Museum Bulletin 184, 1916.

———. *Iroquois Uses of Maize and Other Food Plants.* New York State Museum Bulletin 144, 1910.

———. *Seneca Myths and Folk Tales.* Buffalo, N.Y.: Buffalo Historical Society, 1923.

Parker, Eugene. "Forest Islands and Kayapó Resource Management in Amazonia: A Reappraisal of the *Apêtê*," *American Anthropologist* 94 (1992): 406–28.

Parsons, Elsie C. "Hopi Mothers and Children," *Man* 21 (1921): 98–104.

———. *Mitla: Town of the Souls.* Chicago: University of Chicago Press, 1936.

———. "Mothers and Children at Laguna," *Man* 19 (1919): 34–38.

———. "Tewa Mothers and Children," *Man* 24 (1924): 148–51.

Paz, Octavio. "The Power of Ancient Mexican Art," *New York Review of Books* (Dec. 6, 1990): 18–21.

Pellizzaro, Siro. *Ayumpúm.* Sucua, Ecuador: Mundo Shuar, 1980.

Pereira, F. "Narraciones de Francisco Pereira," TOIC, vol. 1, no. 3, pp. 11–48, 1983.

Perrin, Michel. *Le chemin des indiens morts.* Paris: Payot, 1976.

Perrot, Nicholas. "Memoir on the Manners, Customs, and Religion of the Savages of North America." In *The Indian Tribes of the Upper Mississippi Valley and Region of the Great Lakes* (ed. Emma Helen Blair), vol. 1, pp.

25–274. Cleveland: Arthur H. Clark, 1911.

Peters, Nick. Letters to Frank G. Speck. APS-AIMC, no. 898.

Petrullo, Vincenzo. "The Yaruros of the Capanaparo River, Venezuela," BBAE 123 (Anthropological Papers 11), 1939.

Phillips, H. "Notes upon the Codex Ramírez, with a Translation of the Same," *Proceedings of the American Philosophical Society* 21 (1884): 616–51.

Phinney, Archie. *Nez Percé Texts.* Columbia University Contributions to Anthropology, 1934.

Pittier de Fábrega, H. "Folk-Lore of the Bribri and Brunka Indians in Costa Rica," JAF 16 (1903): 1–9.

Polo de Ondegardo, Juan. "Report of Polo de Ondegardo." In *Narrative of the Rites and Laws of the Yncas* (trans. Clements R. Markham), pp. 151–71. Hakluyt Society, 1873.

Portal, María Ana. *Cuentos y mitos en una zona mazateca.* Serie Antropología Social. Mexico: INAH, 1986.

Powell, J. W. "Sketch of the Mythology of the North American Indians," ARBAE 1 (1881): 17–56.

Powers, Stephen. *The Northern California Indians.* Contributions of the University of California Archaeological Research Facility 25, 1975.

———. *Tribes of California.* Contributions to North American Ethnology 3. Washington: U.S. Geographical and Geological Survey of the Rocky Mountain Region, 1877.

Preuss, Konrad T. *Die Nayarit-Expedition.* vol. 1 (Die Religion der Cora-Indianer). Leipzig: B. G. Teubner, 1912.

Printup, Wade. "Run II . . . for Land and Life," *Turtle Quarterly*, vol. 3, no. 1, pp. 4–13, 1989.

Radin, Paul. *Primitive Religion* (1937). New York: Dover, 1957.

———. *The Road of Life and Death.* New York: Pantheon, 1945.

———. *The Trickster* (1956). New York: Schocken, 1972.

———. *The Winnebago Tribe* (1923). Lincoln: University of Nebraska Press, 1970.

Rasmussen, Knud. *Intellectual Culture of the Caribou Eskimos.* Copenhagen: Gyldendal, 1930.

———. *Intellectual Culture of the Iglulik Eskimos.* Copenhagen: Gyldendal, 1929.

———. *The Netsilik Eskimos.* Copenhagen: Gyldendal, 1931.

———. *The People of the Polar North.* London: K. Paul, Trench, Trübner, 1908.

Ray, Verne F. *Primitive Pragmatists: The Modoc Indians of Northern California.* Seattle: University of Washington Press, 1963.

Redfield, Robert. *A Village That Chose Progress* (1950). Chicago: University of Chicago Press, 1962.

Redfield, Robert, and A. Villa Rojas. *Chan Kom* (1934). Chicago: University of Chicago Press, 1962.

Reichard, Gladys. *Navaho Religion* (1950). New York: Pantheon, 1963.

Reichel-Dolmatoff, Gerardo. *Amazonian Cosmos.* Chicago: University of Chicago Press, 1971.

———. *Beyond the Milky Way.* Los Angeles: UCLA Latin American Center, 1978.

———. "Cosmology as Ecological Analysis," *Man* 11 (1976): 307–18. Cited as Reichel-Dolmatoff 1976a.

———. "Desana Curing Spells," *Journal of Latin American Lore* 2 (1976): 157–219. Cited as Reichel-Dolmatoff 1976b.

———. *Los kogi.* vol. 2. Bogotá: Editorial Iqueima, 1951.

———. "The Loom of Life," *Journal of Latin American Lore* 4 (1978): 5–27.

———. *The Shaman and the Jaguar.* Philadelphia: Temple University Press, 1975.

———. "Tapir Avoidance in the Colombian Northwest Amazon." In *Animal Myths and Metaphors in South America* (ed. Gary Urton). Salt Lake City: University of Utah Press, 1985.

Rementer, James. Letter to John Bierhorst, 5/11/90.

Rhodes, Willard. "Music of the American Indian: Kiowa." Booklet accompanying Library of Congress phonograph album AFS-L35. Library of Congress, Archive of Folk Song, n.d.

Rich, Bruce. "Time Running Out for Mexico's Last Tropical Forest," *Cultural Survival Quarterly* 6 (1982): 13–14.

Richardson, James D. *A Compilation of the Messages and Papers of the Presidents, 1789–1897.* vol. 1. Washington: U.S. Government Printing Office, 1898.

Riester, J. "CIDOB's Role in the Self-Determination of the Eastern Bolivian Indians." In *Native People and Economic Development* (ed. Theodore Macdonald, Jr.). Cambridge, Massachusetts: Cultural Survival, 1985.

Rosengren, Dan. *In the Eyes of the Beholder: Leadership and the Social Construction of Power and Dominance among the Matsigenka of the Peruvian Amazon.* Ethnological Studies 39. Göteborg, Sweden: Göteborgs Etnografiska Museum, 1987.

Roth, W. E. "An Inquiry into the Animism and Folk-Lore of the Guiana Indians," ARBAE 30 (1915): 103–386.

Rowe, J. "Eleven Inca Prayers from the Zithuwa Ritual," *Kroeber Anthropological Society Papers* 8–9 (1953): 83–99.

Ruiz de Alarcón, Hernando. *Treatise on the Heathen Superstitions* (trans. J. Richard Andrews and R. Hassig). Norman: University of Oklahoma Press, 1984.

Russell, Frank. *The Pima Indians* (1908). Tucson: University of Arizona Press, 1975.

Sahagún, Bernardino de. *Códice florentino.* 3 vols. Mexico: Secretaría de Gobernación, 1979.

———. *Florentine Codex.* Bks. 1–12. Salt Lake City: University of Utah Press, 1950–69.

———. *Florentine Codex.* Bk. 1, rev. ed. Salt Lake City: University of Utah Press, 1970.

———. *Historia general de las cosas de Nueva España* (ed. Angel M. Garibay K.). 4 vols. Mexico: Porrúa, 1969.

Sammons, Kay. "Translating Poetic Features in the Sierra Popoluca Story of Homshuk." In *On the Translation of Native American Literatures* (ed. Brian Swann), pp. 368–86. Washington: Smithsonian Institution Press, 1992.

Sandstrom, Alan. *Corn Is Our Blood: Culture and Ethnic Identity in a Contemporary Aztec Indian Village.* Norman: University of Oklahoma Press, 1991.

———, ed. Myths recounted by Jesús Bautista Hernández . . . Puyecaco, Ixhuatlán de Madero, Veracruz . . . January 1986. Transcribed by Daniele Bafile and translated from the Nahuatl by Roman Güemes J. Typescript, n.d., in the possession of Alan Sandstrom, Dept. of Anthropology, Indiana University–Purdue University, Fort Wayne.

Sarmiento de Gamboa, Pedro. "Historia de los incas." In *Biblioteca de autores españoles.* vol. 135. Madrid: Atlas, 1965.

Savala, Refugio. *The Autobiography of a Yaqui Poet.* Tucson: University of Arizona Press, 1980.

Savard, Rémi. *Contes indiens de la Basse Côte Nord du Saint-Laurent.* Canadian Ethnology Service Papers 51. 1979.

Saxton, Dean, and L. Saxton. *O'othham Hoho'ok A'agitha.* Tucson: University of Arizona Press, 1973.

Schultze Jena, Leonhard. *Indiana.* vol. 2 (Mythen in der Muttersprache der

Pipil von Izalco in El Salvador). Jena, Germany: Gustav Fischer, 1935.

Schutz, Noel W., Jr. The study of Shawnee myth in an ethnographic and ethnohistorical perspective. Ph.D. dissertation. Indiana University, 1975.

Sekaquaptewa, Emory. "Hopi Indian Ceremonies." In *Seeing with a Native Eye* (ed. Walter Holden Capps), pp. 35–43. New York: Harper and Row, 1976.

Septimo, Roger, and L. Joly. *Kugue kira nie ngabere / Sucesos antiguos dichos en guaymí.* David, Panama: Asociación Panameña de Antropología, 1986.

Serna, Jacinto de la. "Manual de ministros de indios" (1892). In *Tratado de las idolatrías, supersticiones, dioses, ritos, hechicerías y otras costumbres gentílicas* (ed. Franciso del Paso y Troncoso). vol. 1, pp. 40–368. Mexico: Ediciones Fuente Cultural, Librería Navarro, [1953].

Shaw, Mary. *According to Our Ancestors.* Norman: Summer Institute of Linguistics of the University of Oklahoma, 1971.

Simmons, Leo W., ed. *Sun Chief: The Autobiography of a Hopi Indian.* New Haven: Yale University Press, 1942.

Simón, Pedro. *Noticias historiales de las conquistas de tierra firme en las indias occidentales.* vol. 2 (Segunda Parte). Bogotá: Medardo Rivas, 1891.

Simpson, G. "A Carib (Kamarakoto) Myth from Venezuela," JAF 57 (1944): 263–79.

Siskind, Janet. *To Hunt in the Morning.* New York: Oxford University Press, 1975.

Skinner, Alanson. "The Mascoutens or Prairie Potawatomi Indians," *Bulletin of the Public Museum of the City of Milwaukee* 6 (1924–27): 1–411.

———. "Notes on Mahikan Ethnology," *Bulletin of the Public Museum of the City of Milwaukee* 2 (1925): 87–116.

Smith, E. "Myths of the Iroquois," ARBAE 2 (1883): 47–116.

Smith, Juan, William Allison, Julian Hayden, and Donald Bahr. The Hohokam Chronicles. Typescript, 1992, in the possession of D. Bahr, Dept. of Anthropology, Arizona State University, Tempe.

Speck, Frank G. *Beothuk and Micmac.* Museum of the American Indian, Heye Foundation. Indian Notes and Monographs, Misc. ser. 22. 1921.

———. Delaware field notes, 1945. APS-AIMC, no. 1177.

———. *Ethnology of the Yuchi Indians.* Anthropological Publications of the University Museum 1. Philadelphia, 1909.

———. Miscellaneous notes, 1944–45. APS-AIMC, no. 912.

————. *Naskapi* (1935). Norman: University of Oklahoma Press, 1977.

————. *Penobscot Man*. Philadelphia: University of Pennsylvania Press, 1940.

————. "Penobscot Tales and Religious Beliefs," JAF 48 (1935): 1–107.

————. *A Study of the Delaware Indian Big House Ceremony*. Publications of the Pennsylvania Historical Commission 2. Harrisburg, 1931.

Speck, Frank G., and W. Hadlock. "A Report on Tribal Boundaries and Hunting Areas of the Malecite Indian of New Brunswick," *American Anthropologist*, n.s. 48 (1946): 355–74.

Spencer, D. "Notes on the Maidu Indians," JAF 21 (1908): 242–45.

Spicer, Edward H. *The Yaquis*. Tucson: University of Arizona Press, 1980.

Spier, Leslie. *Havasupai Ethnography*. Anthropological Papers of the American Museum of Natural History 29, 1928.

————. *Yuman Tribes of the Gila River*. Chicago: University of Chicago Press, 1933.

Spier, Leslie, and E. Sapir. "Wishram Ethnography." University of Washington Publications in Anthropology 3, pp. 151–300, 1930.

Spinden, Herbert J. "Myths of the Nez Percé Indians," JAF 21 (1908): 13–23.

————. *Songs of the Tewa*. New York: Exposition of Indian Tribal Arts, 1933.

Standing Bear, Luther. *Land of the Spotted Eagle* (1933). Lincoln: University of Nebraska Press, 1978.

Steiner, Stan. *The New Indians* (1968). New York: Delta/Dell, n.d.

Stevenson, M. "The Sia," ARBAE 11 (1894): 3–157.

Steward, Julian H. "Ethnography of the Owens Valley Paiute," UCPAAE 33 (1933): 308–11.

————, ed. *Handbook of South American Indians*. 7 vols. (1946–59). New York: Cooper Square, 1963.

Stone, Doris. *The Talamancan Tribes of Costa Rica*. Papers of the Peabody Museum of Archaeology and Ethnology (Harvard University), vol. 43, no. 2, 1962.

Stradelli, E. "Leggenda dell' Jurupary," *Bollettino della Societá Geografica Italiana* 28 (1890): 659–89, 798–835.

Sturtevant, William C., ed. *Handbook of North American Indians*, vols. 4–11 and 15. Washington: Smithsonian Institution, 1978–90.

Sturzenegger, Odina. "El ciclo mítico de Mítsca y Duhvít," *Mitológicas 2, 1986–87*, pp. 23–33. Buenos Aires: Centro Argentino de Etnología Americana, 1989.

Swanton, John R. *Myths and Tales of the Southeastern Indians*. BBAE 88, 1929.

———. "Social Conditions, Beliefs, and Linguistic Relationships of the Tlingit Indians," ARBAE 26 (1908): 391–485.

Taggart, James M. *Nahuat Myth and Social Structure*. Austin: University of Texas Press, 1983.

Tanner, Adrian. *Bringing Home Animals: Religious Ideology and Mode of Production of the Mistassini Cree Hunters*. New York: St. Martin's Press, 1979.

Tantaquidgeon, Gladys. *A Study of Delaware Indian Medicine Practice and Folk Beliefs*. Harrisburg: Pennsylvania Historical Commission, 1942.

Tedlock, Dennis. *Popol Vuh*. New York: Simon and Schuster, 1985.

Tedlock, Dennis, and B. Tedlock. *Teachings from the American Earth*. New York: Liveright, 1975.

Teit, James. "Kaska Tales," JAF 30 (1917): 427–73.

———. "Tahltan Tales," JAF 32 (1919): 198–250.

———. *Traditions of the Thompson River Indians of British Columbia*. Memoirs of the American Folklore Society 6, 1898.

Thompson, J. E. S. *Ethnology of the Mayas of Southern and Central British Honduras*. Anthropological Series, vol. 17, no. 2. Chicago: Field Museum of Natural History, 1930.

———. *The Rise and Fall of the Maya*. 2d ed. Norman: University of Oklahoma Press, 1966.

Thoreau, Henry. *Walden* (1854). New York: Illustrated Modern Library, 1946.

Thwaites, Reuben G., ed. *The Jesuit Relations*. 73 vols. (1896–1901). New York: Pageant, 1959.

Tozzer, Alfred M. *A Comparative Study of the Mayas and the Lacandones*. New York: Macmillan, 1907.

Train, Percy, J. Henrichs, and W. Archer. *Medicinal Uses of Plants by Indian Tribes of Nevada* (1957). Lawrence, Mass.: Quarterman, n.d.

Trigger, B. "Distinguished Lecture in Archeology," *American Anthropologist* 93 (1991): 551–69.

Trupp, Fritz. *Mythen der Makuna*. Acta Ethnologica et Linguistica 40. Vienna, 1977.

Tyler, Hamilton A. *Pueblo Gods and Myths*. Norman: University of Oklahoma Press, 1964.

Underhill, Ruth. *Papago Indian Religion*. New York: Columbia University Press, 1946.

————. *Red Man's Religion.* Chicago: University of Chicago Press, 1965.

————. *Singing for Power.* Berkeley: University of California Press, 1938.

Urioste, George L. *Hijos de Pariya Qaqa: La tradición oral de Waru Chiri.* 2 vols. Syracuse, N.Y.: Maxwell School of Citizenship and Public Affairs, Syracuse University, 1983.

Villas Boas, Orlando, and C. Villas Boas. *Xingu.* New York: Farrar, Straus and Giroux, 1973.

Vanderwerth, W. C. *Indian Oratory* (1971). New York: Ballantine, 1972.

Victor, Paul-Emile. *Poèmes esquimaux,* 2d ed. Paris: Pierre Seghers, [1951].

Voegelin, Charles F. *The Shawnee Female Deity.* Yale University Publications in Anthropology 10, 1936.

————. "Tubatulabal Texts," UCPAAE 34 (1935): 191–246.

Voegelin, Charles F., et al. "Shawnee Laws," *Memoirs of the American Anthropological Association* 79 (1954): 32–46.

Voth, H. "Oraibi Natal Customs and Ceremonies," *Field (Columbian) Museum Anthropological Series* 6 (1905): 47–61.

————. "The Oraibi Summer Snake Ceremony," *Field (Columbian) Museum Anthropological Series* 3 (1902–1903): 262–358.

Wagley, C. "Cultural Influences on Population." In *Environment and Cultural Behavior* (ed. Andrew P. Vayda). New York: Natural History Press, 1969.

————. "World View of the Tapirape Indians," JAF 53 (1940): 252–60.

Walde-Waldegg, H. von. "Notes of the Indians of the Llanos of Casanare and San Martin (Colombia)," *Anthropological Quarterly* 9 (1936): 38–45.

Walker, James R. *Lakota Belief and Ritual.* Lincoln: University of Nebraska Press, 1980.

————. *Lakota Myth.* Lincoln: University of Nebraska Press, 1983.

————. *The Sun Dance and Other Ceremonies of the Oglala.* Anthropological Papers of the American Museum of Natural History 16, 1917.

Wallace, Anthony F. C. *King of the Delawares: Teedyuscung, 1700–1763.* Philadelphia: University of Pennsylvania Press, 1949.

————. *The Modal Personality Structure of the Tuscarora Indians.* BBAE 150, 1952.

Wallis, Wilson D. "Folk Tales from Shumopovi," JAF 49 (1936): 1–68.

Warren, William W. *History of the Ojibway Nation* (1885). Minneapolis: Ross and Haines, 1957.

Wauchope, Robert, ed. *Handbook of Middle American Indians*. 16 vols. Austin: University of Texas Press, 1964–76.

Waugh, F. W. *Iroquois Foods and Food Preparation*. Memoirs of the Canadian Geological Survey 6, 1916.

———. Waugh Collection of Iroquois Folktales, 1912–18. Typescript. Canadian Ethnology Service, Canadian Museum of Civilization. Hull, Québec.

Weigle, Marta. Review of *Mother Russia*, JAF 104 (1991): 211–12.

———. *Spiders and Spinsters*. Albuquerque: University of New Mexico Press, 1982.

Weiss, Gerald. "Campa Cosmology," *Ethnology* 11 (1972): 157–72.

———. *Campa Cosmology*. Anthropological Papers of the American Museum of Natural History, vol. 52, pt. 5, 1975.

Weltfish, Gene. *The Lost Universe: The Way of Life of the Pawnee* (1965). New York: Ballantine, 1971.

Weslager, C. A. *Magic Medicines of the Indians* (1973). New York: Signet/New American Library, 1974.

Wheelwright, Mary C. *Hail Chant and Water Chant*. Santa Fe: Museum of Navajo Ceremonial Art, 1946.

Whiffen, Thomas. *The North-west Amazons*. New York: Duffield, 1915.

Wilbert, Johannes. *Yupa Folktales*. Los Angeles: UCLA Latin American Center, 1974.

———, ed. *Folk Literature of the Gê Indians*. vol. 1. Los Angeles: UCLA Latin American Center, 1978.

———, ed. *Folk Literature of the Selknam Indians*. Los Angeles: UCLA Latin American Center, 1975.

———, ed. *Folk Literature of the Yamana Indians*. Los Angeles: UCLA Latin American Center, 1977.

Wilbert, Johannes, and K. Simoneau, eds. *Folk Literature of the Bororo Indians*. Los Angeles: UCLA Latin American Center, 1983.

———, eds. *Folk Literature of the Chorote Indians*. Los Angeles: UCLA Latin American Center, 1985.

———, eds. *Folk Literature of Guajiro Indians*. 2 vols. Los Angeles: UCLA Latin American Center, 1986.

———, eds. *Folk Literature of the Mataco Indians*. Los Angeles: UCLA Latin American Center, 1982.

———, eds. *Folk Literature of the Tehuelche Indians*. Los Angeles: UCLA Latin American Center, 1984.

————, eds. *Folk Literature of the Toba Indians.* vol. 1. Los Angeles: UCLA Latin American Center, 1982.

Wilder, Carleton S. "The Yaqui Deer Dance," BBAE 186 (Anthropological Papers 66), 1963.

Williams García, Roberto. *Mitos tepehuas.* Mexico: Secretaría de Educación Pública, 1972.

Wright, Pablo G. *NgataGako* (advice): a Toba oral genre. Paper presented at the 90th Meeting of the American Anthropological Association, Chicago, 1991.

Wyman, Leland D. *Blessingway.* Tucson: University of Arizona Press, 1970.

Yegerlehner, J. "The First Five Minutes of Shawnee Laws in Multiple Stage Translation," *International Journal of American Linguistics* 20 (1954): 281–94.

Zingg, Robert M. *The Huichols* (1938). Milwood, N.Y.: Kraus Reprint, 1977.

Zeisberger, David. "History of the Northern American Indians," *Ohio State Archaeological and Historical Quarterly* 19 (1910): 1–189.

Zuni people, the. *The Zunis: Self-Portrayals* (trans. Alvina Quam). Albuquerque: University of New Mexico Press, 1972.

INDEX

abortion, 184, 186–87
acorn, 58, 271
Acosta, Joseph de, 5
Aguaruna, 72, 92, 158, 226
Allen, Paula Gunn, 92–93
Alsop, George, 212
anaconda, 79, 80, 224, 257
Anambé, 167
ancestors, *see* animal ancestors
animal ancestors, 40–42,
    45–47; deer as, 47. *Cf.*
    evolution.
animal master, *see* master of
    species
Apache, 81, 82, 83, 93, 187,
    276; proverb, 164
Arapaho, 108, 161
Arawak, 62
Arikara, 17, 109, 112, 138, 276
armadillo, 35, 48, 195
Assiniboin, 93, 161
Aymara proverbs, xiii, 71, 123,
    156
Aztec, 13, 105, 117, 176, 183,
    192–93, 199; earth spirit, 90,
    91, 95, 96; emmenagogues,
    187; new fire,
    270–71; no-man's-land,
    147; payment (sacrifice), 211,
    213, 219, 220; proverbs, 140,
    263; reincarnation,

177; sensuality proscribed,
    164, 166, *cf.* 167; sacred
    bundle, 192; sun lore, 49, 53,
    217; town planning,
    203–4; tree lore, 62,
    64–65; weeping woman,
    235–36; white deer,
    33; wilderness, 141, 143,
    148; word for parable,
    14; world essence, 118

Barasana, 257, 264
bat, 238
Bauré, 162
Bean, Lowell John, 86
bear, 26–27, 33, 40, 65, 179; as
    healer, 29; prayer to, 76; as
    teacher, 75–76. *See also* Bear
    Boy.
Bear Boy, 75, 82, 83, 131
beaver, 28, 65, 130, 253
Beaver Indians, 51
Bella Coola, 31, 46, 87, 110, 212
birth control, 156–72
Black Elk, Nicholas, 113
Blackfeet, 44, 65, 161, 204
blue jay, 79
bones rituals, 27–28, 36, 127
Bora, 153
Bororo, 47, 184, 200, 204, 213,
    252